IMAGES of America

AROUND FREDERICK

On the Cover: This photograph of miners in front of the Summit Mine was taken in 1943. Summit was one of the 21 mines in the Carbon Valley region, all of which have closed. Not many photographs like this were taken, as the workday rarely allowed time for pictures. (Courtesy of the Town of Frederick.)

IMAGES
of America

AROUND FREDERICK

Sean Scott

ARCADIA
PUBLISHING

ISBN 978-1-4671-3035-6

Published by Arcadia Publishing
Charleston, South Carolina

Printed in the United States of America

Library of Congress Control Number: 2013946711

For all general information, please contact Arcadia Publishing:
Telephone 843-853-2070
Fax 843-853-0044
E-mail sales@arcadiapublishing.com
For customer service and orders:
Toll-Free 1-888-313-2665

Visit us on the Internet at www.arcadiapublishing.com

This book is dedicated to the residents of Frederick, past, present, and future.

CONTENTS

ACKNOWLEDGMENTS

Images of America: *Around Frederick* is the product of the hard work and dedication of many people. I am grateful for all of the assistance, encouragement, and suggestions I have received while writing this history. Without this help, this project could not have been accomplished. Many sources provided the photographs documenting Frederick's history.

The most complete history of Frederick and the Carbon Valley region is the result of the hard work of Eleanor H. Ayer, who wrote *Green Light on the Tipple: Pioneering the Carbon Valley*. Some of the photographs in this book first appeared in *Green Light on the Tipple*. *Celebrating 100 Years of Carbon Valley*, published by the *Longmont Times Call*, was also very helpful. Another useful source was Nancy Lynch's *Weld County Towns: The First 150 Years*.

Mike and Liberta Hattel (MLH) provided many of the old mining photographs, as well as access to mining artifacts. As longtime residents, they were invaluable in putting names to faces in many of the images in this book. Pete Pascoff (PP) donated his time and personal family photographs and documents relating to his father's work in the mines. Barb "Trudy" Baker (BTB) provided a wealth of photographs covering school functions and parades, as well as photographs detailing the 1957 Frederick flood.

Cathy Constable (CC) provided a number of photographs detailing everyday Frederick life in the 1940s, 1950, and 1960s. The Laughlin family (LF) shared family photographs that depict Frederick in its early days. The Alaux family (AF) made available family photographs that gave insight into Frederick's early days. The Workman family (WF) provided photographs of the early days of the *Farmer and Miner* newspaper, as well as copies of documents relating to Frederick politics.

Carmen DeSantis has lived in Frederick all his life and has served as an elected official for 40 years. He provided invaluable background information regarding identities and places shown in these photographs. He also offered much information concerning Frederick politics.

Meghan Martinez, the town clerk for Frederick, provided so much help that she should be listed as a coauthor. She helped scan and organize images and provided a clearinghouse for the collection of all of the information used in this book. All of this was done in addition to her substantial responsibilities owed to the town of Frederick.

Stacia Bannerman from Arcadia Publishing kept me on track and on deadline. Her patience with this computer-illiterate amateur author deserves special praise.

Rhett, my wife, supported and encouraged me throughout this project. Her suggestions and kind words made me a better author than I otherwise would have been.

Introduction

Before white settlers came to the northern plains of the Colorado Territory, it was the home of the Arapaho Indian tribe. The Arapahos lived along the Platte and Arkansas Rivers. Their territory encompassed the states of Wyoming, Nebraska, Kansas, and Colorado. Around 1830, the Arapahos split into northern and southern groups, with the northern group inhabiting the area along the Platte River. This area of the eastern plains later became the site of Frederick, as well as the towns of Firestone and Dacono.

The area, now known as Carbon Valley, has been largely ignored by historians of Colorado and the St. Vrain Valley. Because no rivers or streams of any size ran through the area, Carbon Valley was not a natural site for growth. One early settler described the area as fit only for rabbits, snakes, and coyotes. Other early inhabitants make special mention of the area's large and hungry mosquitoes.

This began to change with the discovery of coal. As is the case in so much of American history, the Indians were first. Their mining efforts were limited to what they could scrape off the surface and take away by hand. The early white settlers could do little better; at first, coal was scraped up from just beneath the surface and carried off in handcarts. In the early 1900s, underground mining began.

The Ely Mine and the McKissick Mine were the first operations to begin hauling coal out in wagons. In 1905, the first shaft was sunk in what became the Baum Mine. The Firestone, Slope, Evans, and Grant Mines opened shortly after.

Some of the mines were simple shafts from which coal was dug and hauled away by wagon. The Emerson mine, which opened in 1897 and closed in 1904, was one such mine. The Evans Jones shaft, for which there are no dates of operation, was another.

The Sterling Mine was one of the more profitable early mines. In 1919, the Grand Junction Mining & Fuel Company began a shaft just east of Dacono. By the mid-1930s, it employed 150 men at peak season. It closed in 1965.

Another profitable operation was the Grant Mine, located northwest of Firestone. It was purchased by the Rocky Mountain Fuel Company and remained in operation until 1939. The Grant Mine employed more men during its peak season than any other mine. This made it a favorite among the local miners. The Grant Mine workers also pulled more coal from the ground than from any other mine.

Area mines did not experience any large-scale cave-ins or fires. The Evans Mine did have a cave-in in 1918, but no one was killed. The miners were more concerned with rescuing the mules that pulled the coal cars than with their own safety.

Despite the lack of large-scale disasters, mining remained a dangerous occupation. Many miners were injured and, occasionally, killed. Carmen DeSantis's father was a rare miner who had a nearly injury-free career. His only injury, despite working in the mines for nearly 40 years, was caused by a drill that knocked out four of his teeth.

Early mining technology was primitive. Coal was loosened from native rock by the use of black powder charges. Once loosened, it was moved to coal cars by miners using picks and shovels. Once it was in the cars, mules were used to pull the cars to the surface. Today, an original coal car sits on the west side of the Miners' Memorial, located in Frederick's Crist Park.

The influx of miners led to other settlers who were interested in providing the mines and miners with clothing and food. Farmers began to take an interest in the prairie land, which allowed for the growth of crops. Wheat was the biggest crop. Later, truck farms were established for other crops such as alfalfa.

The Tesone family moved to Frederick in 1915. Prior to Frederick, they had lived in Louisville. The patriarch, Felix Tesone, worked as the fire boss at the Evans Mine from 1915 to 1940. He started each day at 4:00 a.m. checking the canaries caged in the mine. He also checked for cracks in the walls and timbers. No work began until he gave the all clear.

The youngest child, Peter Tesone, was two years old when the family moved to Frederick. He remembers the mine towers dotting the landscape in and around Frederick. He specifically recalls the Firestone, Slope, Evans, Russell, Grant, Baum, and Sterling Mines.

Julia Tesone, wife of Felix, provided meals for five miners, as well as her family of eight. Her lunches were carried to the miners in custom pails. The lunch pail carried a gallon of water along with lunch.

In the 1920s, Julia cooked at a boardinghouse at the Slope Mine. She prepared breakfast, lunch, and dinner for 20 men, seven days a week. She also made pasta dinners for the school and the Catholic Church.

In 1930s, the Tesone family built and operated the Evans store. The store served a greater role in the community than just selling groceries. Miners cashed their paychecks at the store, in effect using it as a bank. During hard times, many families were extended credit for purchases. During the Depression, the Tesones lost a great deal of money. The store remained in operation until it was sold in 1955.

Julia Tesone remained in Frederick until 1960. Her son Alec Tesone became principal of Frederick High School. He held this position for many years. In addition to serving as principal, he also coached basketball and football.

One of the larger grocery stores in Frederick was the Red & White grocery. Its primary competition was the Revielle grocery, which was run by Joseph Revielle until his death in 1940. His brother Julius then took over operations until the store closed in 1968. The store building still stands and is now home to a liquor store.

The sale of liquor, both legal and illegal, was a prominent part of Frederick life. The Sunshine Tavern was a longtime Frederick landmark. It underwent several name changes but remained in the same location. Other taverns ran in competition with the Sunshine.

During Prohibition, bootlegging was prevalent. The local residents generally sold only to people they knew in town. Somehow, they always seemed to know when an inspection was planned. Burying liquor in the backyard did not always mean it was safe from the inspectors, who would often dig in backyards if they suspected liquor was being hidden there.

It was common for bars to be owned by people who also worked in the mines. This came to an end when John L. Lewis, the president of the United Mine Workers, decided that no union member could own an interest in a bar. To keep their mine jobs, many owners had to sell out.

Illegal gambling is also a feature of Frederick's history. This is not to suggest that Frederick was a *Deadwood*-type frontier town. Still, if one wanted to find some action, Frederick was known as the place to go. The heart of the gambling activity was Fifth Street, where there were dice games in the pool hall beneath Revielle's. Big Jack's was also a well-known gambling hot spot. It was later taken over by a Greek man known only as "Nick" or "Pappas."

The Smalldones were Denver's best-known crime family. Due to its relative lack of law enforcement, Frederick became one of their favorite haunts. One local resident was involved in a game with the Smalldones when he decided to cash out. The Smalldones then told him he could do that, but the next time they came to Frederick, the family would bring their guns.

Carmen DeSantis recalls being caught in a gambling raid in 1940. Since he was preparing to leave for college, he was facing considerable problems. He and his father paid a visit to Greeley to talk to the police officer in charge of the case. He agreed to keep Carmen's name out of the papers. On the way out, Carmen's father grabbed the dice cup, telling the officer that it was not needed as evidence anymore. The dice cup was back in action later that night.

At first glance, Frederick would not seem a good spot to establish a town. Its present site was first mentioned as a lake three feet deep in spots. Frederick's early years were defined by mining and flooding. Yet, with all of the people moving to the Frederick area, it soon was decided to seek incorporation.

Frederick was the first tri-town community to seek incorporation. On November 19, 1907, a group of 43 petitioners filed a petition before the county court judge, John C. Nixon, requesting appointment of commissioners to start incorporation proceedings. Since no newspapers were available to post notice of the planned incorporation, public posting in the area that was to become Frederick was used instead. One of the posting places was Tom McAfee's building, which later became the McAfee Hotel and then a private residence.

The election was held on December 17, 1907. The petition was approved by a vote of 49-1. The papers establishing incorporation were signed by Judge Nixon on February 25, 1908. Frederick was on its way.

Frederick is named after Frederick Clark, one of the area's early settlers, who owned much of the land on which the town was constructed. Before that, the area was known for as McKissick, for one of the early mines.

The populations of Frederick and the nearby towns of Firestone and Dacono were largely made up of immigrants. The early population reads like a who's who of northern and southern Europe. The largest ethnic groups were Greek, Bulgarian, French, and Italian. During its mining heyday, the population of Frederick was reported to be 90 percent Italian.

In addition to food stores and taverns, residents needed community and government services. This meant that schools had to be established, as did a post office and a telephone exchange.

The first Frederick High School was built in 1916. Since then, due to population growth, other high schools have taken its place. The newest Frederick High School opened in 2012 just to the west of Frederick, near the old Baum Mine.

The post office opened in August 1907. The first postmaster was Roy Dunton. The first tavern, set up in a tent, opened at the same time. The old city hall was built in 1907 and still stands in Crist Park, on Fifth Street.

Water was a constant source of problems, and the primary sources were well water and, later, water drawn from the local mine shafts. Up until the 1930s, Frederick depended on Firestone for its water supply.

By the early 1950s, the water supply issue was in need of a more permanent solution. The best solution to many seemed to be purchasing Firestone Lake, situated to the northwest of Frederick.

At first, the cost of the purchase and its method of financing posed many problems. The first bond proposal was insufficient, and the total cost of $107,000 seemed more than some residents were willing to pay. Mayor I.W. Thompson resisted the bond issue, which led to calls for his impeachment and the dismissal of his son Ira Thompson as town clerk.

Town residents decided to fix existing pumping equipment rather than purchase a guaranteed water supply, a stopgap measure that lasted until 1957.

In May 1957, Frederick experienced a substantial flood. This flash flood caused damage estimated at $300,000. Worse, the town's water supply was contaminated. Houses had begun to cave in when Frederick mayor A.J. Hicks started discussions with Colorado governor Stephen McNichols to get help. Despite pleas for help, the state refused to declare Frederick a disaster area.

Discussions then began again concerning the purchase of Firestone Lake, and after much negotiation, Frederick did purchase it, ensuring a secure water supply for Frederick. Today, Firestone Lake has been renamed Milavec Reservoir. On its eastern boundary is a park, and on its southern, a wetlands area. Bella Rosa Golf Course is located on the lake's northern boundary.

Mining continued to flourish in the 1930s and 1940s but began to decline thereafter. One by one, the mines closed, with the Imperial mine the last to close its doors, in 1972. By that time, natural gas and oil drilling had proven to be more profitable. Today, Frederick's landscape is dotted with oil and gas pumping stations. Little physical evidence of the mining industry that established Frederick remains.

Frederick's population remained small until growth returned to the area in the 1980s and 1990s. Interstate 25, which runs two miles to the west of Frederick, has helped spark growth in housing and business. Today, more and more businesses are being developed along the Interstate 25 corridor.

Frederick's population is quickly approaching 10,000 residents. There is every reason to expect this number to continue to grow, as Frederick becomes part of the greater northern Denver area. In addition, to the north, Fort Collins and Loveland are pushing south towards Frederick. In the very near future, it is not hard to envision a residential and business corridor running from the southern Denver area almost to the Wyoming border.

Frederick's history is not dramatic or earth shattering. Its founding and growth are not unlike countless other towns. Still, Frederick remains important to its residents, both past and present. When Frederick natives are asked what Frederick is like, they say that it is a nice place to call home.

Frederick started as an isolated outpost in the plains of northeastern Colorado. Today, it has taken its place as part of the fabric that makes up the greater northern Front Range.

One

A Town on the Plains

At first glance, the Carbon Valley region is not a natural location for settlement. There are no rivers or streams nearby, and the mountains are anywhere from 60 to 100 miles to the west. Eastern Colorado is often referred to as high desert plains, making the summers extremely hot and the winters often heavy with snow. Due to the lack of rainfall, the opportunity to grow crops is limited.

Frederick benefited from two factors: coal and the Union Pacific Railroad. Once coal was discovered in sufficient quantities to be commercially viable, a railway was necessary to bring the coal to market.

The Union Pacific owned a tremendous amount of land. As it laid its tracks, it granted alternating 160-acre tracts to potential homesteaders and those interested in establishing towns. It is no exaggeration to say that the railroad made or broke potential towns.

Since Frederick and the surrounding area were rich with coal deposits, the railroad had a reason to lay track. At first, there was no thought of establishing any sort of townships. It was enough that miners could work in the area and have a way to transport their coal to Denver.

The desire to establish towns only came as the population grew and others, besides miners, settled in the region. Of the three towns in the Carbon Valley region—Frederick, Firestone, and Dacono—Frederick was the first to incorporate. Mining was still the chief occupation at the time; however, farmers, lured by cheap land and the railroad, had begun to gather in the area as well.

It soon became clear that Frederick was not a transitory community, as the miners and the farmers showed no desire to move. When shops and other businesses servicing the needs of miners began coming in larger numbers, it was time to incorporate Frederick as a town.

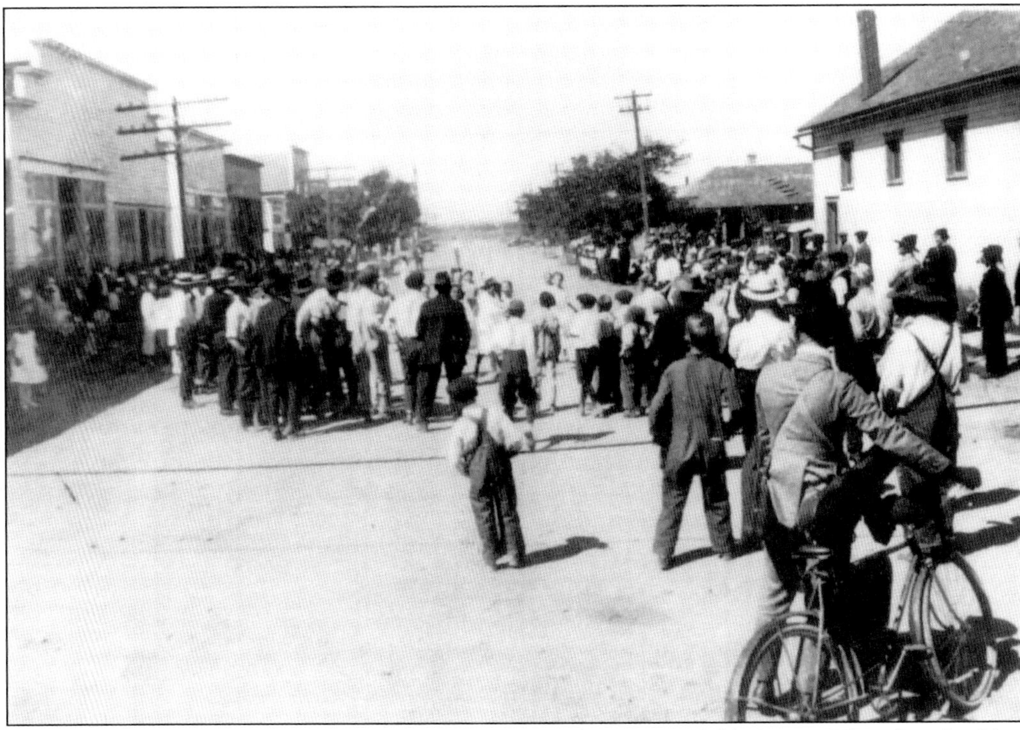

This is an early view of Frederick looking west down what is now Fifth Street. The white building in the right foreground is the Sunshine Tavern. The second building on the left was home to the Red & White grocery store and the *Farmer and Miner* newspaper. This photograph was taken around 1920. (Courtesy of the Town of Frederick.)

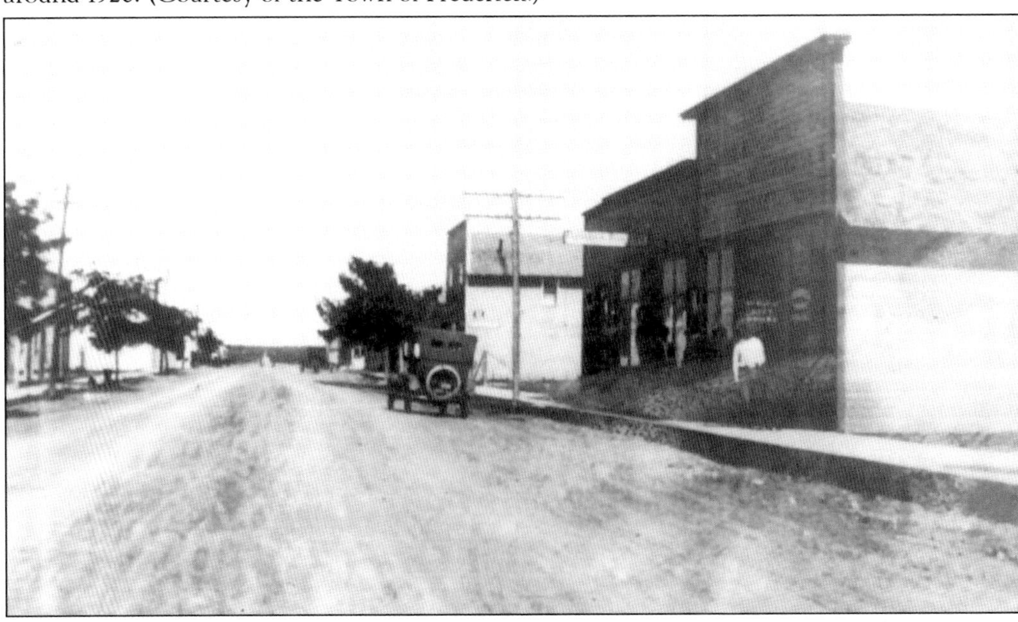

In this view of Fifth Street, the lettering on the buildings cannot be made out, but it appears that the second building on the right, with the extended sign, is a bakery. (Courtesy of the Town of Frederick.)

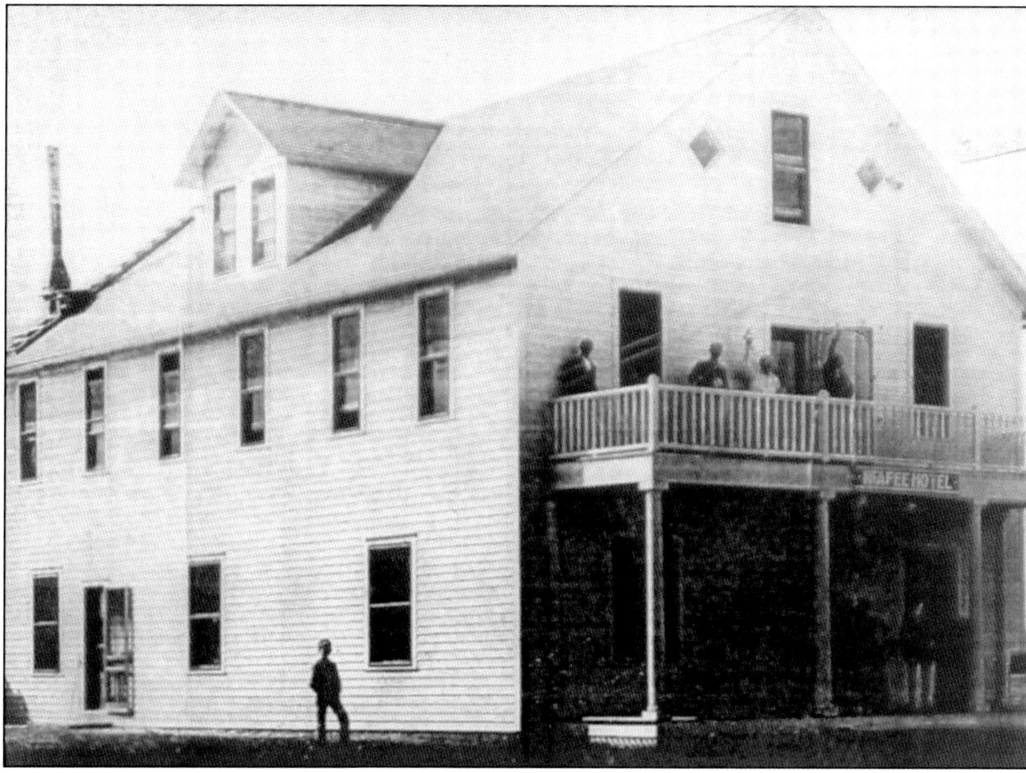

This photograph shows the McAfee Hotel, which served as a boardinghouse for miners and visitors to the town. This building still stands in Frederick and is essentially unchanged. (Courtesy of the Town of Frederick.)

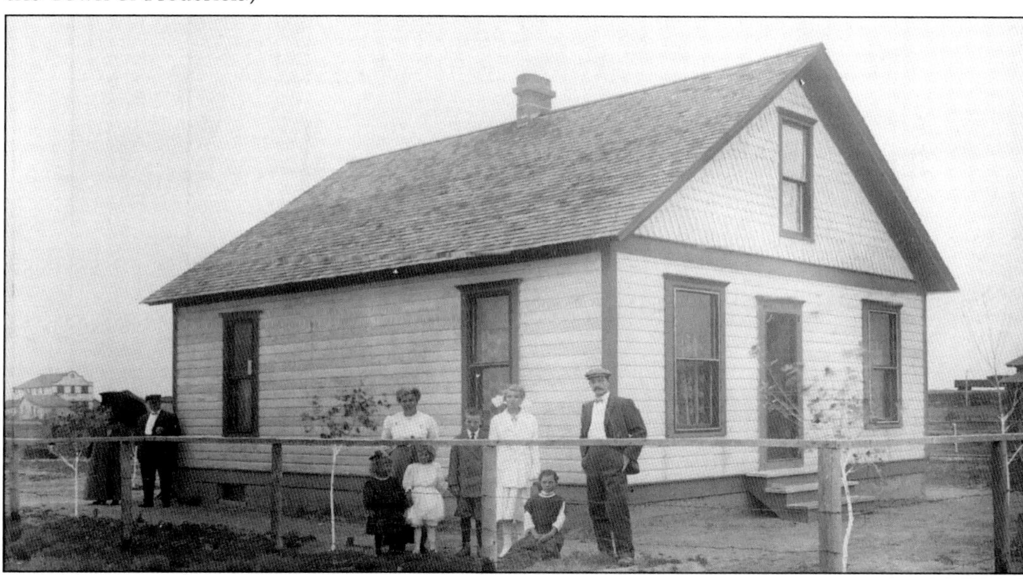

This is the Stede family home in Frederick. The large building in the left background was owned by Pop Laughlin. At various times, it housed a movie theater and a skating rink. The smaller building to the left and in front of it is the city hall. Note the almost complete absence of trees, as Frederick was built on the eastern plains. (Courtesy of MF.)

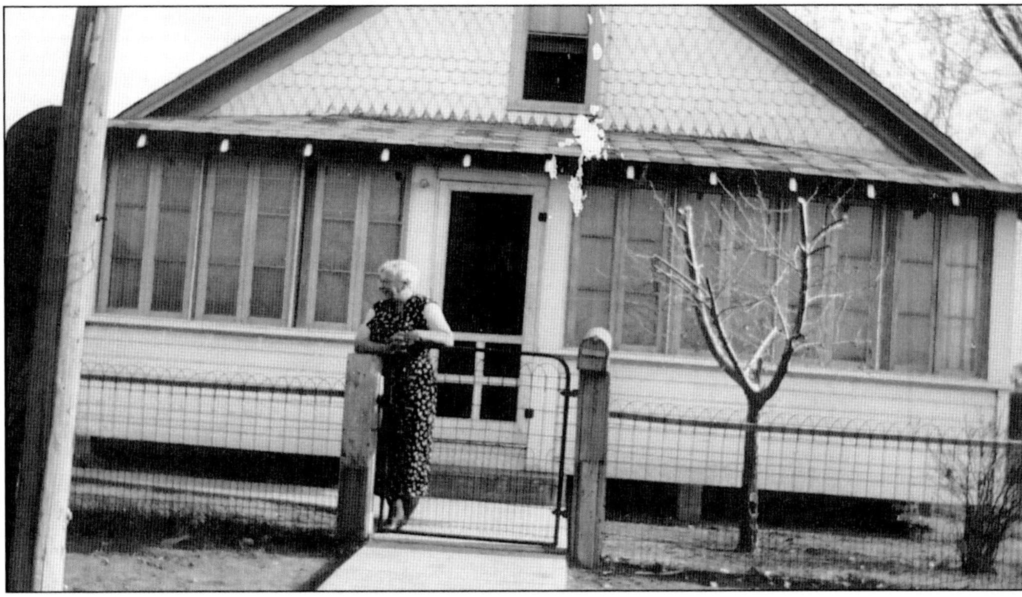

This later view of the Stedes' family residence shows Grandmother Stede leaning on the gate. (Courtesy of MF.)

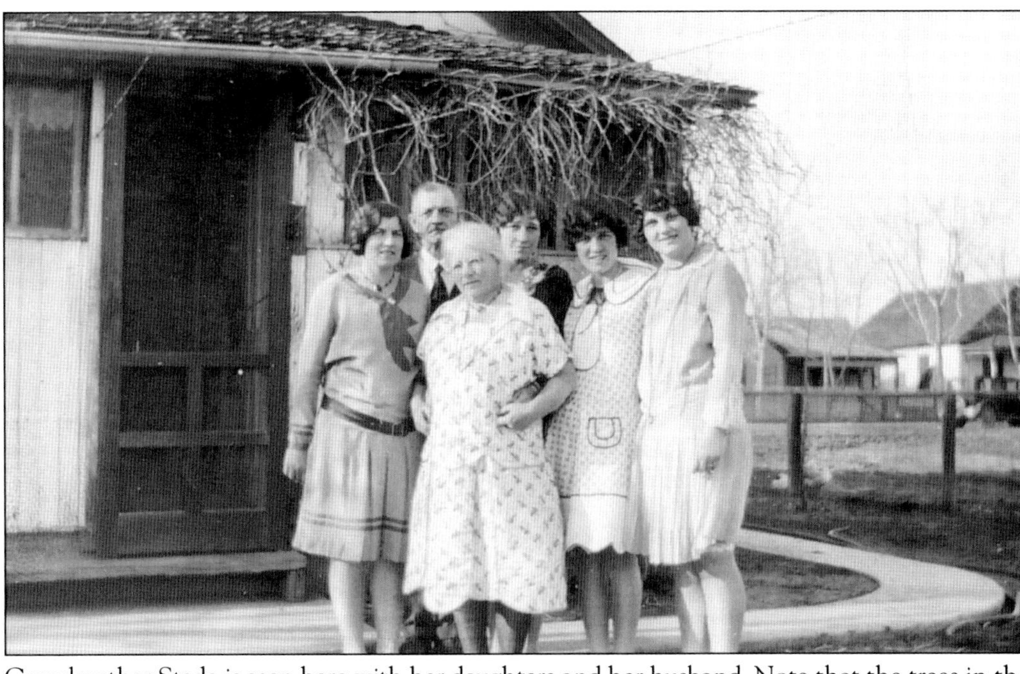

Grandmother Stede is seen here with her daughters and her husband. Note that the trees in the background have grown. (Courtesy of MF.)

This is Jenny Stede's high school diploma from Frederick High School, granted in May 1925. The superintendent at the time was Paul Nicholson, whose signature appears in the lower right corner. (Courtesy of MF.)

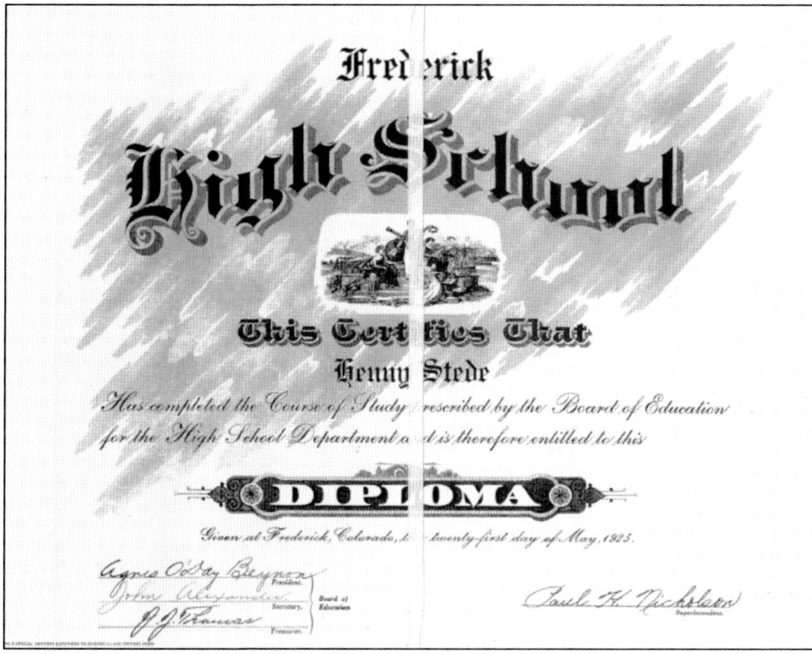
Frederick High School

This Certifies That

Jenny Stede

Has completed the Course of Study prescribed by the Board of Education for the High School Department and is therefore entitled to this

DIPLOMA

Given at Frederick, Colorado, the twenty-first day of May, 1925.

President. Secretary. Treasurer. Board of Education

Superintendent.

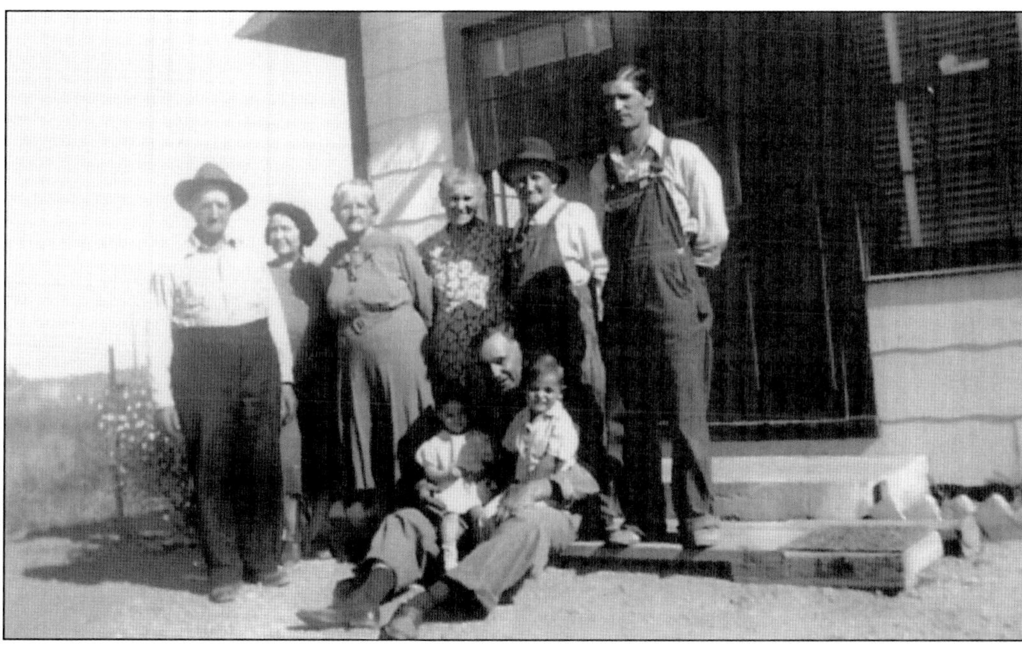

This photograph was taken of the Alaux homestead, located across from the Washington Mine, in 1943. From left to right are (first row) Alna Alaux, Frank LaRoche, and four-year-old Vernon Alaux; (second row) Herb Richel, Alice Richel LaRoche, Richel Sarah Deliere, LaRoche Alaux, Charles Alaux Jr., and Edward Alaux. (Courtesy of AF.)

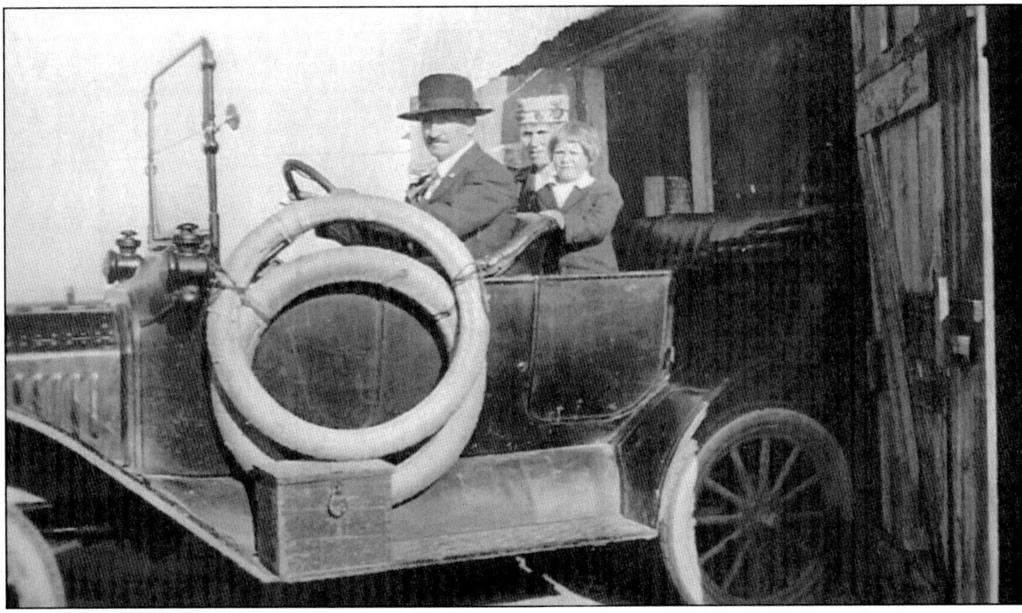

This early photograph of the Alaux family was taken on the Alaux homestead. Sitting in the driver seat is Charlie Alaux, who was born in 1868. His wife, Sarah Alaux, is sitting behind him with their son Edward. The automobile is a Ford Model T. (Courtesy of AF.)

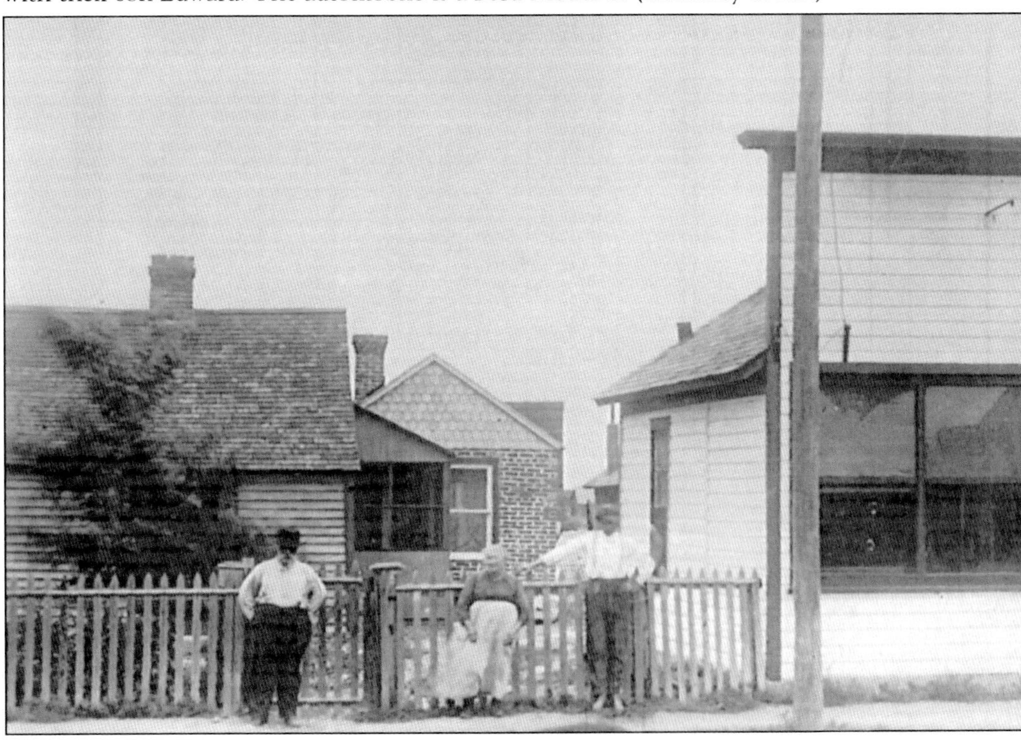

Seen here from left to right are Charles Alaux Sr., Hortense Alaux, and Charles Alaux, the nephew of Charles Alaux Sr. Note the building on the right, an early commercial establishment with a false front. In early Colorado architecture, false fronts were often added to buildings to make them seem larger and to provide uniform height. (Courtesy of AF.)

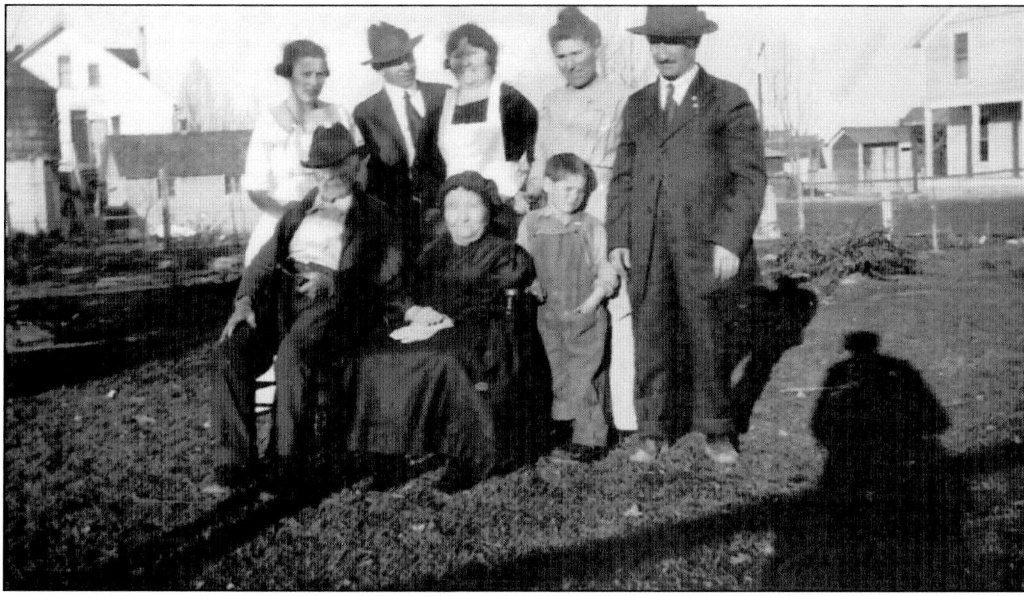

The extended Alaux family is seen here in 1916. They are, from left to right, (seated) Charles Alaux Sr., Hortense Alaux, and Edward Alaux; (standing) Alma LaRoche, Charles Koctner, Rose (Alaux) Koctner, Sarah Alaux, and Charles Alaux Jr. (Courtesy of AF.)

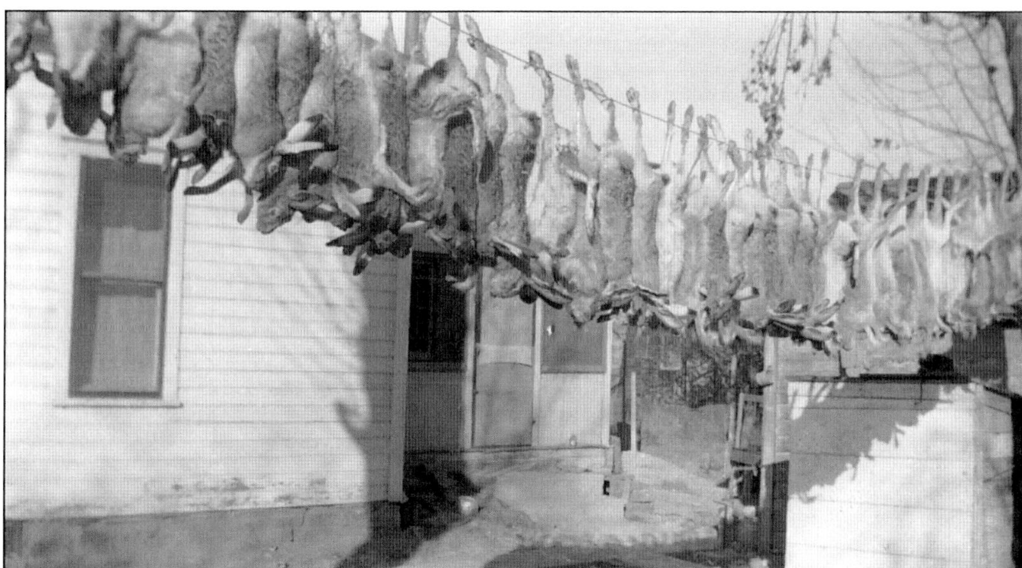

Rabbits were both a source of food and a plague in Frederick. To keep them from destroying crops, they were killed in rabbit roundups, during which the animals were driven into an enclosure where local townspeople and farmers clubbed them to death. During the Depression, this was necessary to keep the rabbits from destroying crops. This photograph, taken at Millie Burks's house, shows the fruits of a roundup. (Courtesy of MF.)

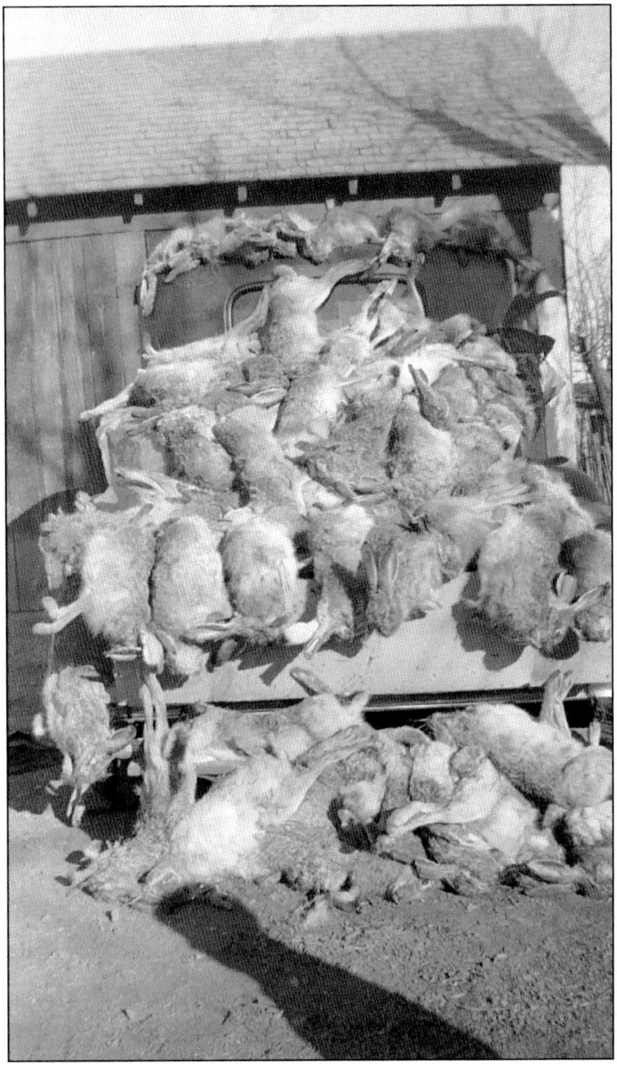

More rabbits are seen here after a rabbit roundup. Rabbits were also sometimes killed for food. Carmen DeSantis remembers hunting in a field at 3:00 a.m. once and coming across a family pulling a wagon with rabbits laid in the wagon, alternated with a layer of snow. It was clear that the rabbits were intended for the stewpot. (Courtesy of MF.)

This photograph shows Antelope carcasses piled high in a field outside of Frederick. The antelopes were not pests like the rabbits but were killed for food. This photograph shows the take from numerous hunts. (Courtesy of MF.)

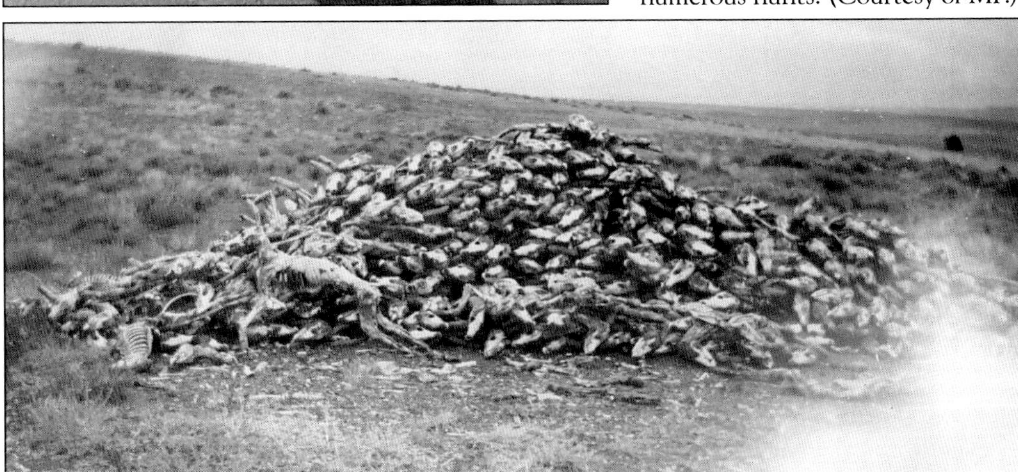

Grandpa Laughlin is seen here playing with one of his grandchildren in front of his home. (Courtesy of MF.)

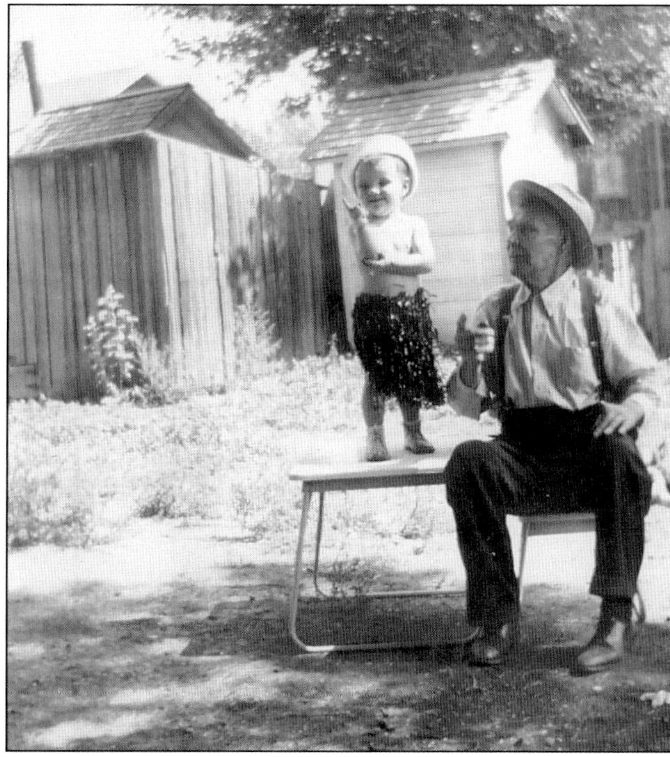

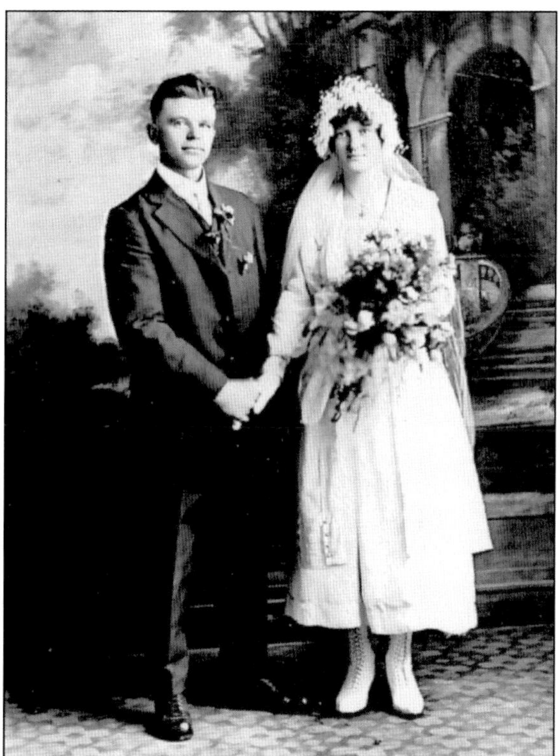

This photograph shows John and Ann Tursick on their wedding day. The picture was taken in 1928. (Courtesy of PP.)

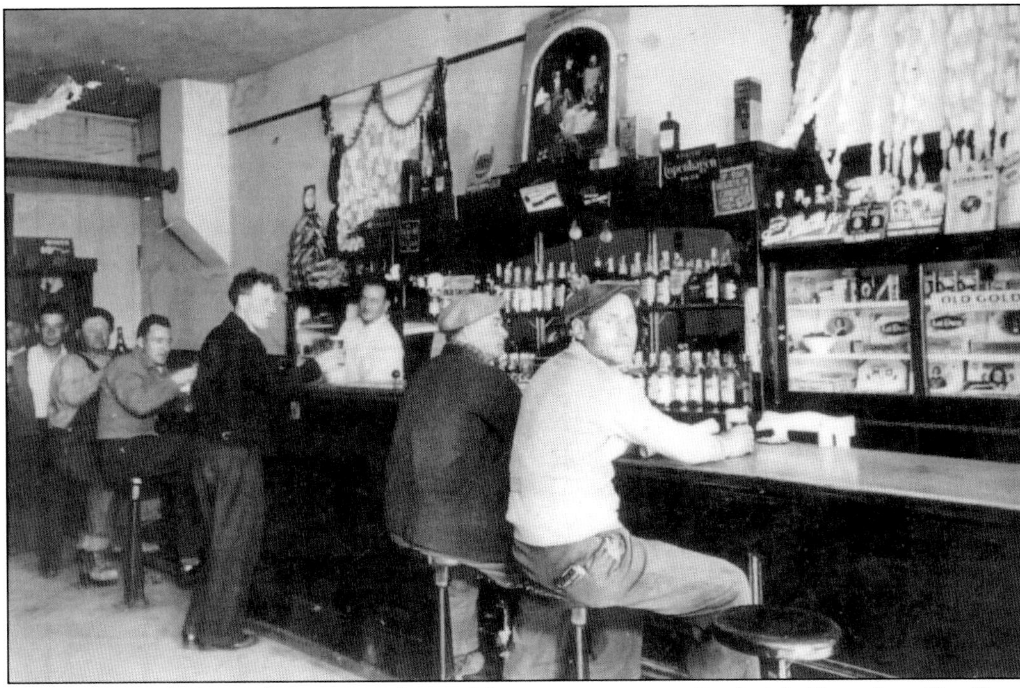

This photograph shows the interior of one of the many taverns in Frederick. Note the tall ceilings. While there is some dispute, it is believed that this photograph was taken inside Dailey's Tavern, which is now Pete's Place. The photograph was clearly taken after Prohibition ended and probably dates from the late 1920s. (Courtesy of the Town of Frederick.)

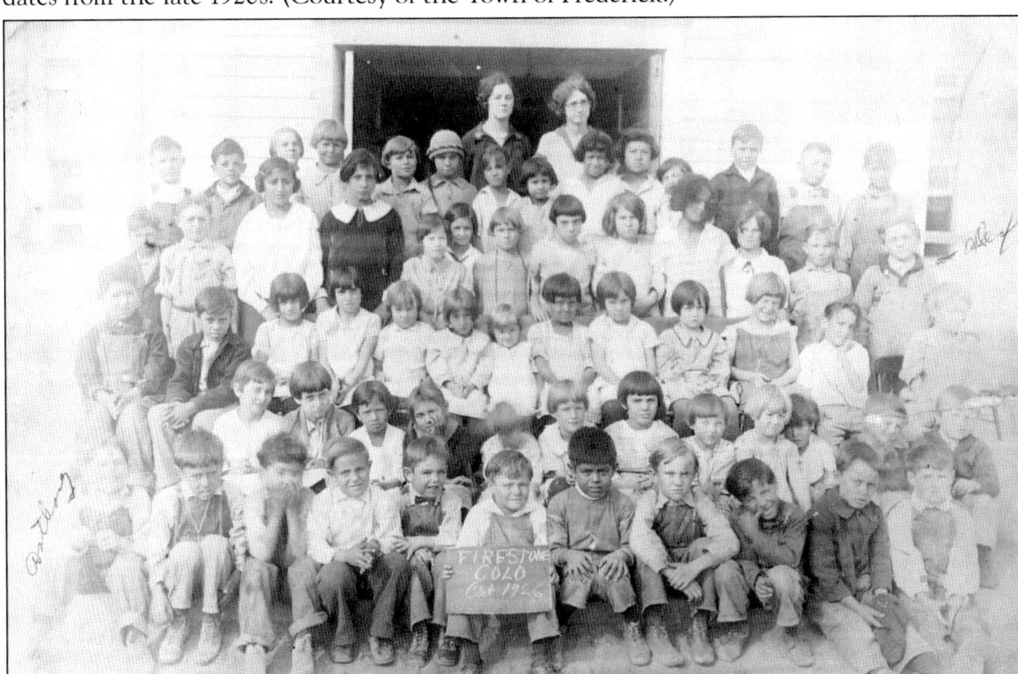

The students of Firestone Elementary School are seen here in 1926. Firestone is north of Frederick. (Courtesy of the Town of Frederick.)

Shortly after incorporation, Frederick took the steps necessary to install a water system. The system had to be financed through the sale of bonds, so the issue was put to the voters. This is a notice of the special meeting of the trustees that took place before a vote could be held. (Courtesy of the Town of Frederick.)

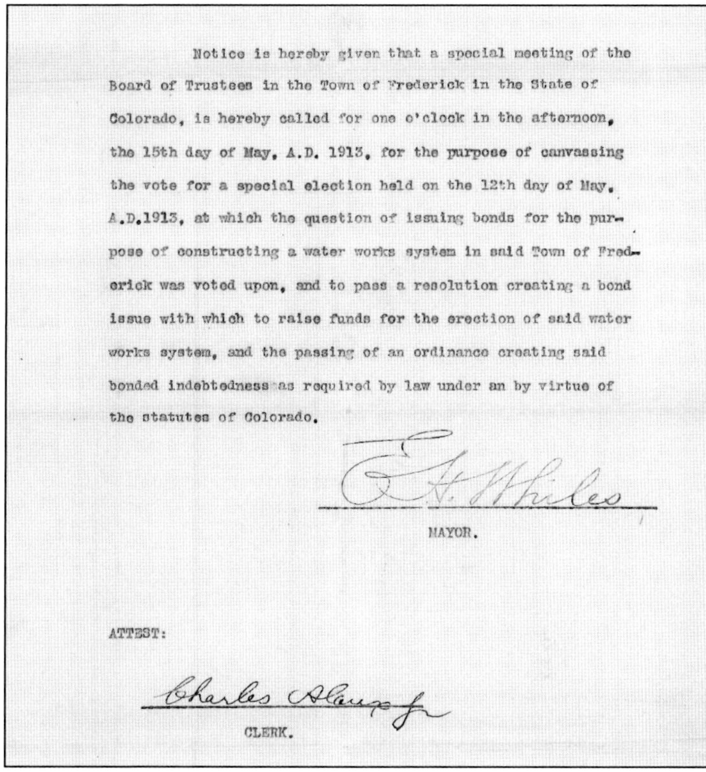

Notice is hereby given that a special meeting of the Board of Trustees in the Town of Frederick in the State of Colorado, is hereby called for one o'clock in the afternoon, the 15th day of May, A.D. 1913, for the purpose of canvassing the vote for a special election held on the 12th day of May, A.D.1913, at which the question of issuing bonds for the purpose of constructing a water works system in said Town of Frederick was voted upon, and to pass a resolution creating a bond issue with which to raise funds for the erection of said water works system, and the passing of an ordinance creating said bonded indebtedness as required by law under an by virtue of the statutes of Colorado.

E. A. Whiles

MAYOR.

ATTEST:

Charles Alaupe Jr

CLERK.

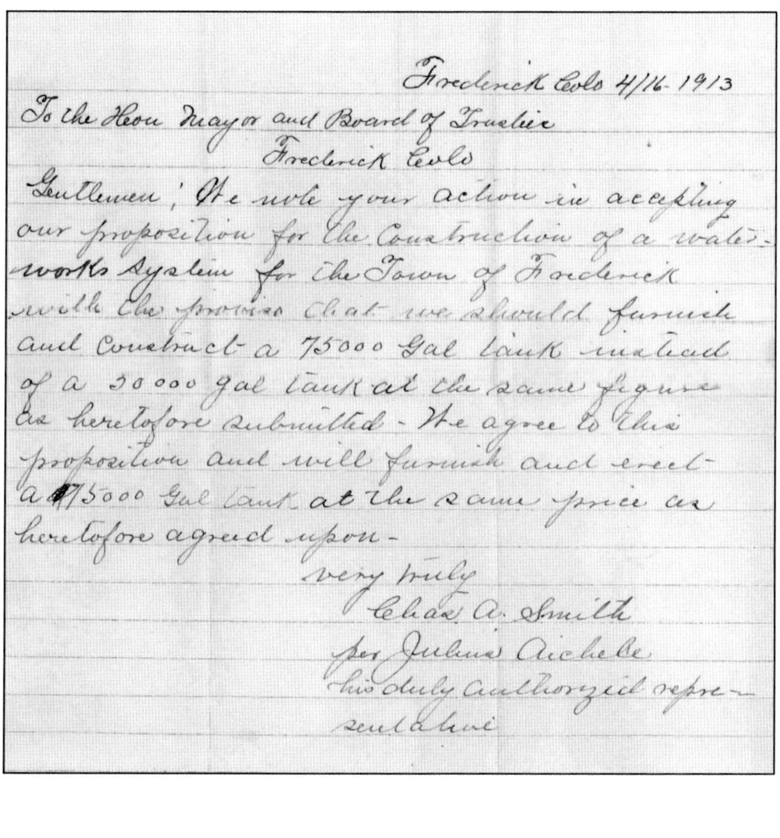

Frederick Colo 4/16-1913

To the Hon Mayor and Board of Trustees
Frederick Colo

Gentlemen; We note your action in accepting our proposition for the Construction of a water-works System for the Town of Frederick with the proviso that we should furnish and Construct a 75000 Gal tank instead of a 50000 gal tank at the same figure as heretofore submitted - We agree to this proposition and will furnish and erect a 75000 Gal tank at the same price as heretofore agreed upon -

very truly
Chas A. Smith
per Julius Aichele
his duly authorized representative

This letter, dated April 16, 1913, is from the contractor to the board of trustees, acknowledging acceptance of their proposal to build a water system. The proposal called for the construction of three tanks: one of 75,000 gallons, the other of 50,000 gallons, and the last of 5,000 gallons. (Courtesy of the Town of Frederick.)

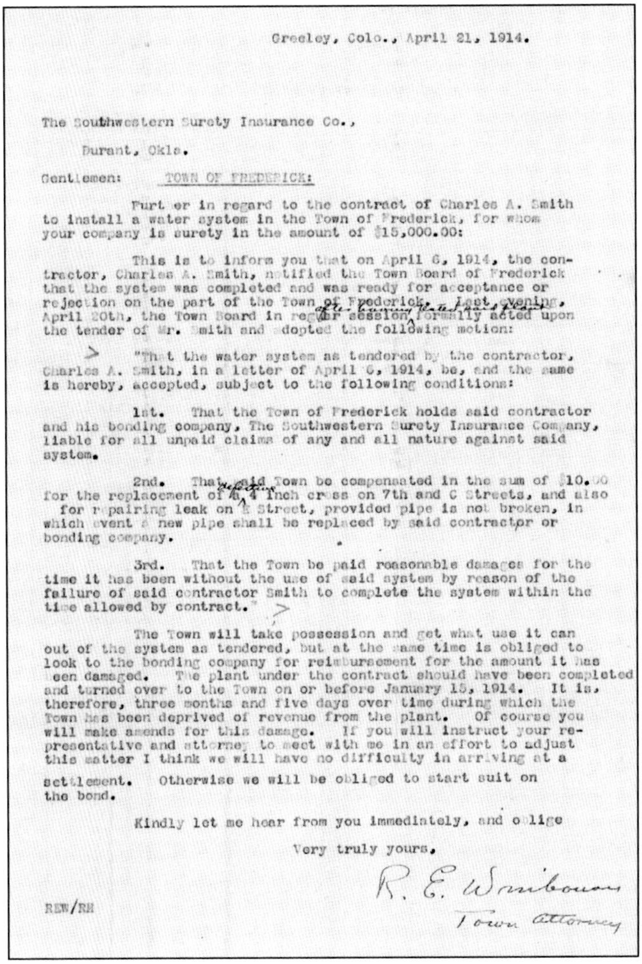

Greeley, Colo., April 21, 1914.

The Southwestern Surety Insurance Co.,

Durant, Okla.

Gentlemen: TOWN OF FREDERICK:

Further in regard to the contract of Charles A. Smith to install a water system in the Town of Frederick, for whom your company is surety in the amount of $15,000.00:

This is to inform you that on April 6, 1914, the contractor, Charles A. Smith, notified the Town Board of Frederick that the system was completed and was ready for acceptance or rejection on the part of the Town of Frederick. Last evening, April 20th, the Town Board in regular session formally acted upon the tender of Mr. Smith and adopted the following motion:

"That the water system as tendered by the contractor, Charles A. Smith, in a letter of April 6, 1914, be, and the same is hereby, accepted, subject to the following conditions:

1st. That the Town of Frederick holds said contractor and his bonding company, The Southwestern Surety Insurance Company, liable for all unpaid claims of any and all nature against said system.

2nd. That said Town be compensated in the sum of $10.00 for the replacement of a 4 inch cross on 7th and C Streets, and also for repairing leak on E Street, provided pipe is not broken, in which event a new pipe shall be replaced by said contractor or bonding company.

3rd. That the Town be paid reasonable damages for the time it has been without the use of said system by reason of the failure of said contractor Smith to complete the system within the time allowed by contract."

The Town will take possession and get what use it can out of the system as tendered, but at the same time is obliged to look to the bonding company for reimbursement for the amount it has been damaged. The plant under the contract should have been completed and turned over to the Town on or before January 15, 1914. It is, therefore, three months and five days over time during which the Town has been deprived of revenue from the plant. Of course you will make amends for this damage. If you will instruct your representative and attorney to meet with me in an effort to adjust this matter I think we will have no difficulty in arriving at a settlement. Otherwise we will be obliged to start suit on the bond.

Kindly let me hear from you immediately, and oblige

Very truly yours,

R. E. W[illegible]

Town Attorney

REW/RH

This letter from the Southwestern Surety Insurance Company to the board of trustees informs the board that the water system is complete. The letter also addresses the issue of damages to town property caused by the contractor. The third paragraph of the letter seems to indicate that the water system was not presented as complete. However, the insurance company has put the town on notice that, regardless, it will expect full payment. (Courtesy of the Town of Frederick.)

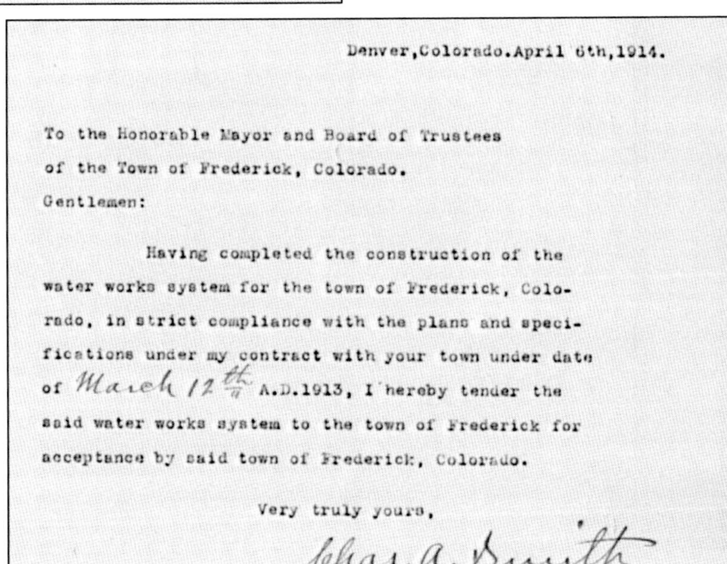

Denver, Colorado. April 6th, 1914.

To the Honorable Mayor and Board of Trustees of the Town of Frederick, Colorado.

Gentlemen:

Having completed the construction of the water works system for the town of Frederick, Colorado, in strict compliance with the plans and specifications under my contract with your town under date of March 12th A.D.1913, I hereby tender the said water works system to the town of Frederick for acceptance by said town of Frederick, Colorado.

Very truly yours,

Chas. A. Smith

On April 6, 1914, the contractor tendered the waterworks system to the town. (Courtesy of the Town of Frederick.)

This receipt shows that Bert Mills paid $1 to the town as a dog tax. This was one of the many ways in which townspeople had to pay for services. (Courtesy of the Town of Frederick.)

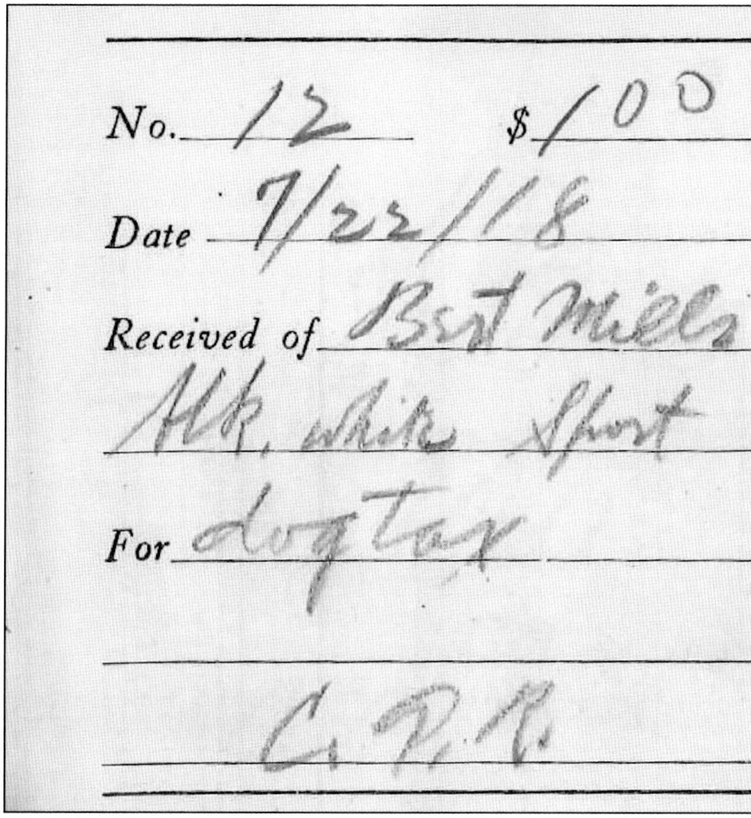

No. 12 $1.00

Date 7/22/18

Received of Bert Mills

Blk. white Sport

For dog tax

C.R.R.

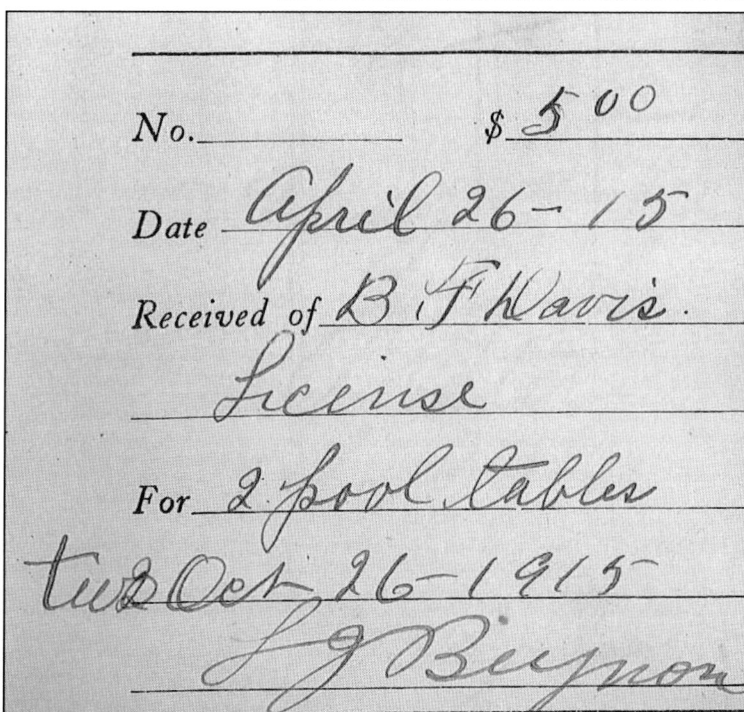

No. $5.00

Date April 26-15

Received of B F Davis.

License

For 2 pool tables

two Oct 26-1915

L J Bignon

Like many small towns in eastern Colorado, collecting revenue was a constant battle in the early years. Taxes on liquor establishments and places where gambling could be found were popular sources of revenue. In this instance, B.F. Davis had to pay $5 for two pool tables, an early example of attempts to govern gambling in the town. (Courtesy of the Town of Frederick.)

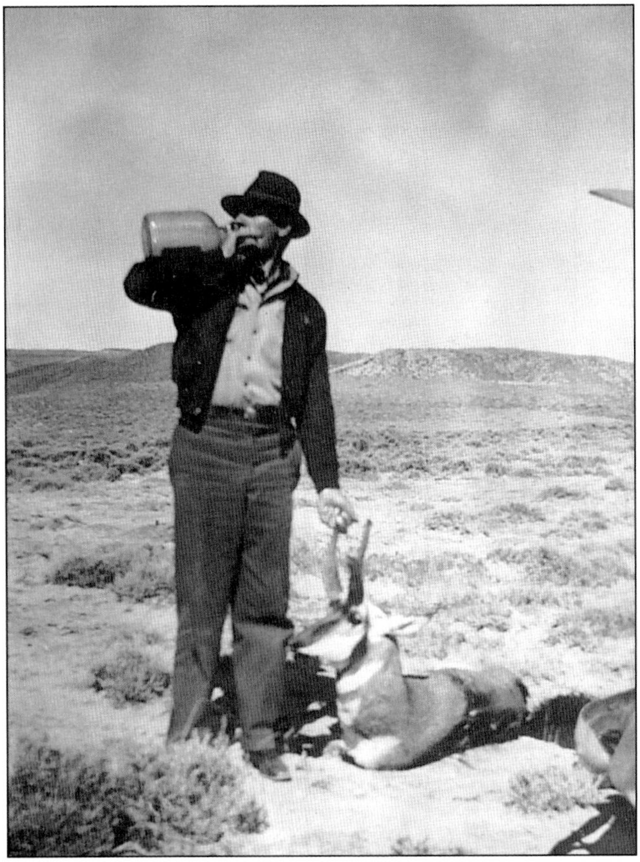

An unidentified hunter stands with his kill. Judging from his clothing, it appears to be in the early 1930s. It is unknown what the man is drinking from the jug, but it is fair to assume that it is not water. (Courtesy of the Town of Frederick.)

This is an early photograph of the Frederick High School boys' and girls' basketball teams. Sitting on the right in the front is Paul Nicholson, the school superintendent. (Courtesy of the Town of Frederick.)

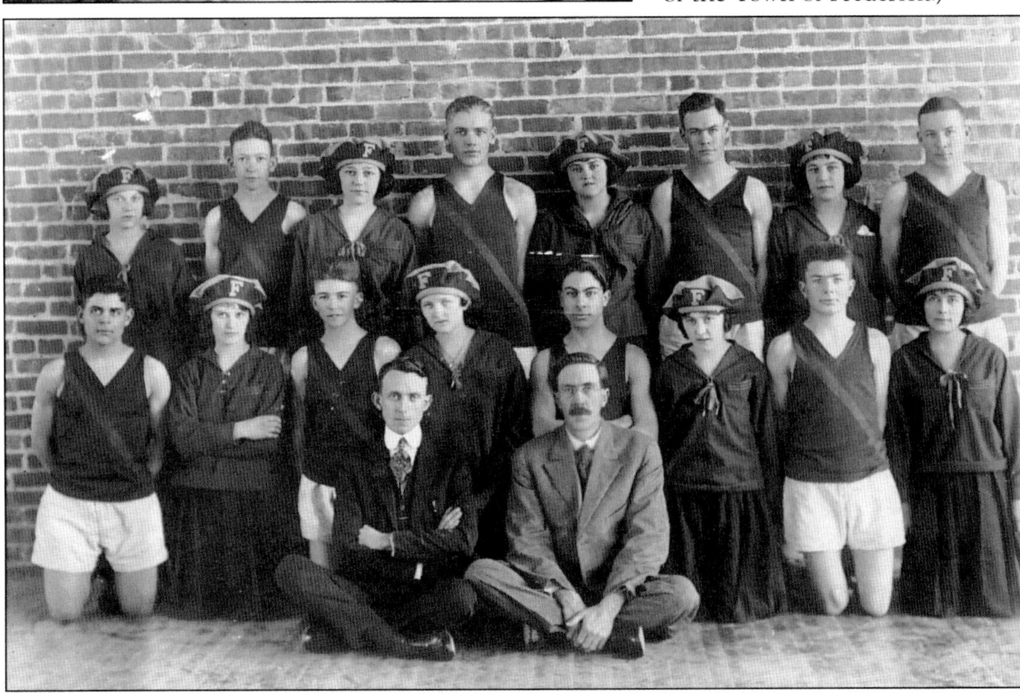

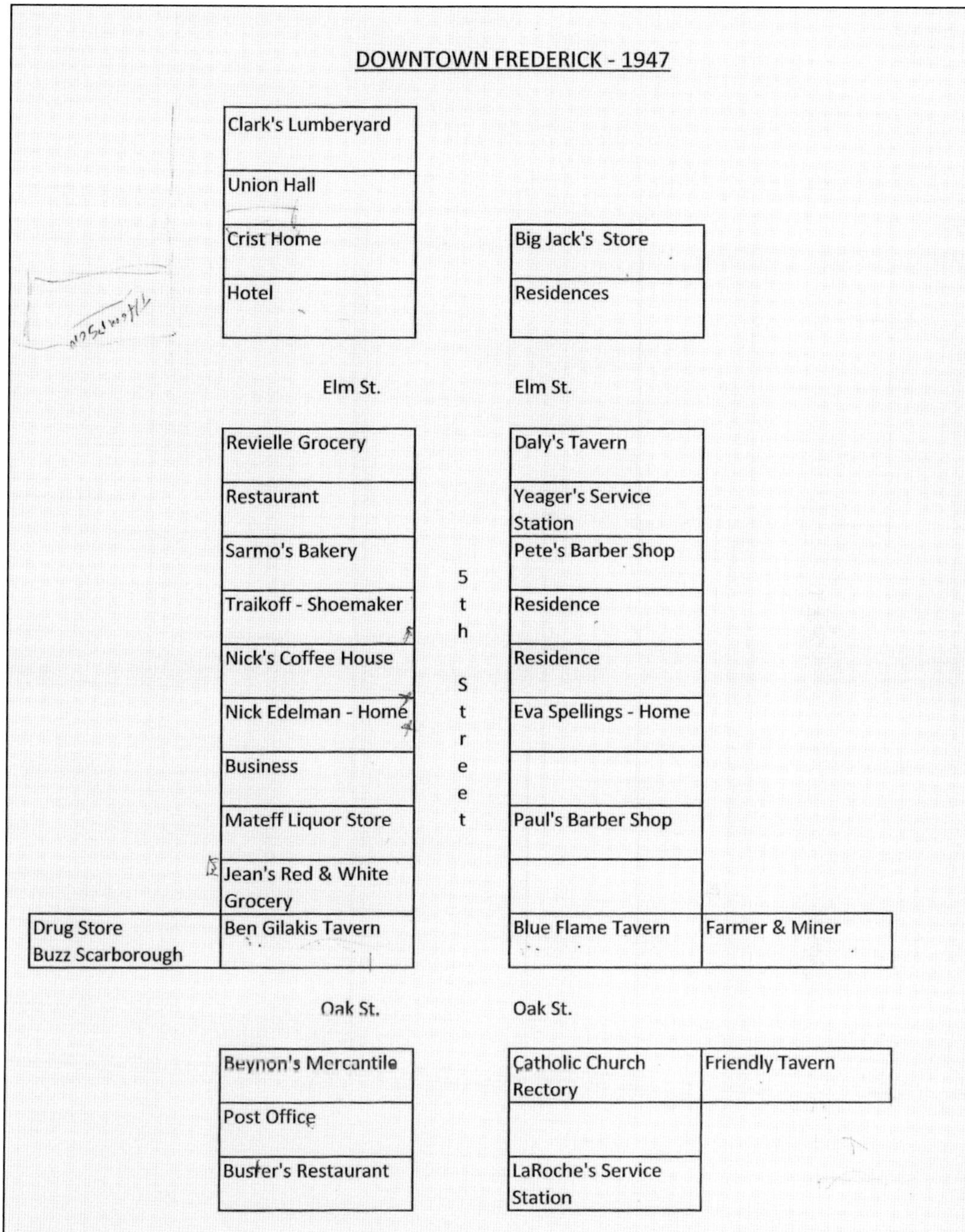

This sketch shows downtown Frederick in 1947. The business district was located on both sides of Fifth Street. Note that there were four taverns and a liquor store within a block and a half. Residences were sprinkled in between the shops, including two groceries: Jean's Red & White and Revielle's. (Courtesy of PP.)

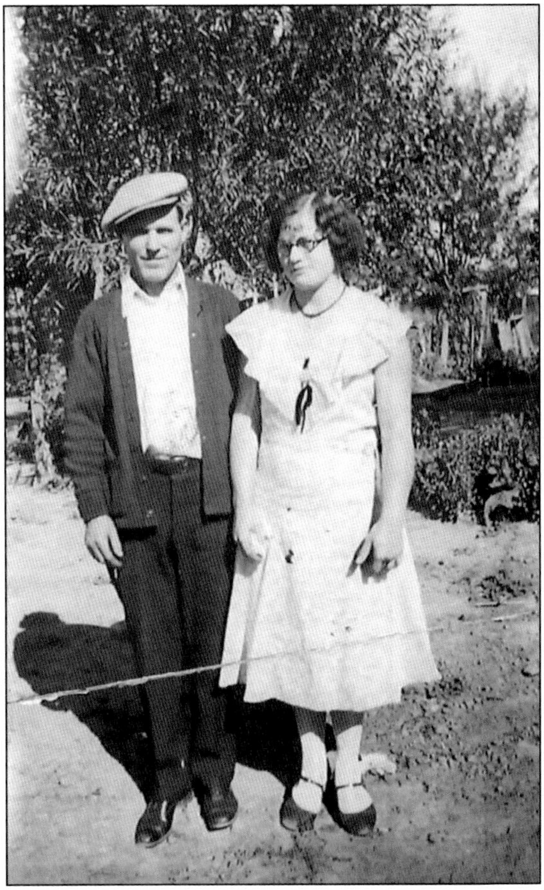

Pete Pascoff and his wife, Mary, are seen here in 1931 in Frederick. Pete Pascoff worked at the mines, and his pay stubs are featured in this book. (Courtesy of PP.)

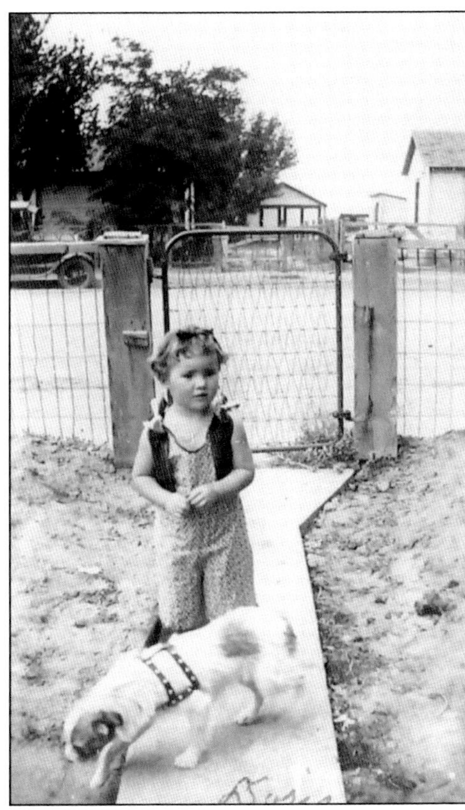

Doris Pascoff, the sister of Pete Pascoff Jr., is seen here in Frederick in 1937. She is still a resident of Frederick today. Note the dog with his harness. (Courtesy of PP.)

Two

The Miners

Coal seams existed in the area before Frederick was established. Coal mining was prevalent early on in Erie and Lafayette, and miners also migrated to Frederick from the Trinidad-Walsenburg area.

At first, coal was mined from the surface. Later, shafts were driven and coal was blasted from underground. Once the mines began to grow, the difficulty and danger of the work began to increase.

Mining was hard, dirty physical labor. Once coal was loosened by blasting, picks and shovels were used to load coal into coal cars. In the early years, the only way to get the coal cars to the surface was to use mules. Each mine had its contingent of mules, which needed to be cared for.

As the shafts grew in length, they had to be tempered to avoid cave-ins. Once those portions of the mines were closed, the timber was removed. At that point, shafts would cave in on their own. Next to blasting, this was the most dangerous aspect of mining.

Fires and poisonous gases were also everyday hazards. Miners were not paid extra wages for the more dangerous work. In fact, miners had a constant struggle to be paid for the work they actually did.

Miners moved from mine to mine, depending on closures. Pay rates were consistent between mines, so there was no reason to move for pay. During the Depression, it was common to be paid $1 a day.

Many miners remember the generosity of the Tesone family. It was common for miners to buy groceries on credit and pay for them later.

While the Frederick area did not see violence of the type experienced in Ludlow or in Erie, there were still work-stoppage issues. The biggest difficulty occurred in 1927, when work stoppages occurred at mines in the Frederick area as well as in other areas of eastern Colorado. The strike pitted the International Workers of the World (IWW) against the mine owners. While no miners were killed as a result of labor strife, a militia did patrol the streets.

Mining remained a strong industry in the area through the 1940s and into the early 1950s. After that, the mines began to close. By 1972, the last mine in the region had closed. Oil and gas exploration took the place of mining. Today, the Carbon Valley landscape is dotted with oil and gas pumping stations, and exploration is growing.

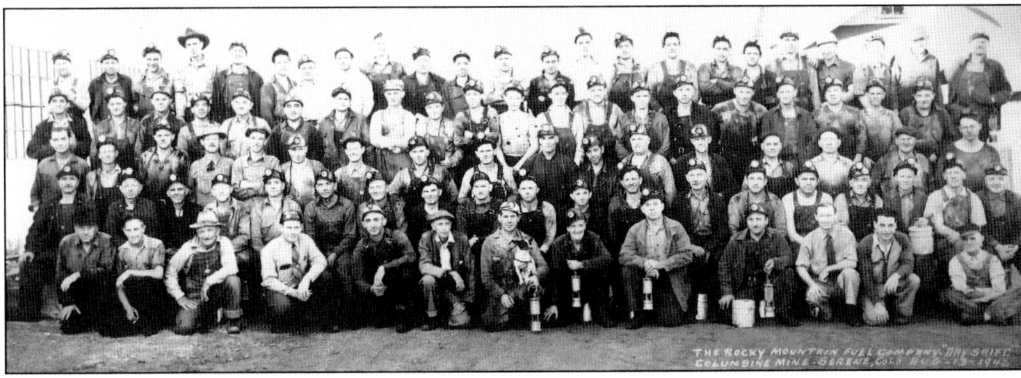

This photograph was taken on August 13, 1942. It shows the day shift at the Rocky Mountain Fuel Company's Columbine Mine. Miner Melvin Dewey Wright remembers getting his job by showing up every day until being noticed by the hiring boss. The two men in the first row wearing ties are supervisors. Note the miner in the first row holding the dog. Judging from the number of miners in the photograph, the Columbine Mine was a profitable venture. (Courtesy of the Town of Frederick.)

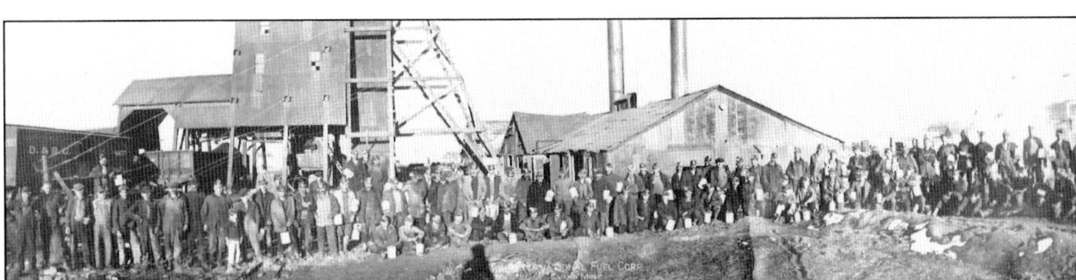

These miners assembled for a group photograph at the Evans Mine, which was owned by the International Fuel Corporation. This mine was located in Frederick and was in operation from 1907 until 1942. The white objects held by many of the miners are their lunch pails. (Courtesy of the Town of Frederick.)

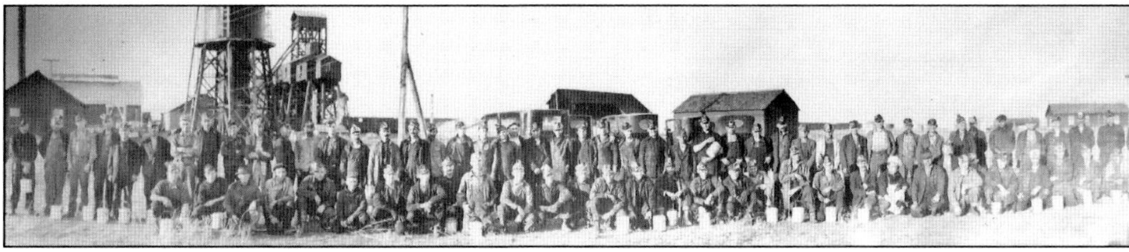

This photograph does not identify the mine in which these miners worked. Judging from the automobiles in the background, the photograph probably dates to the 1920s. Given the size and number of the buildings in the background, the mine was not a small operation. (Courtesy of the Town of Frederick.)

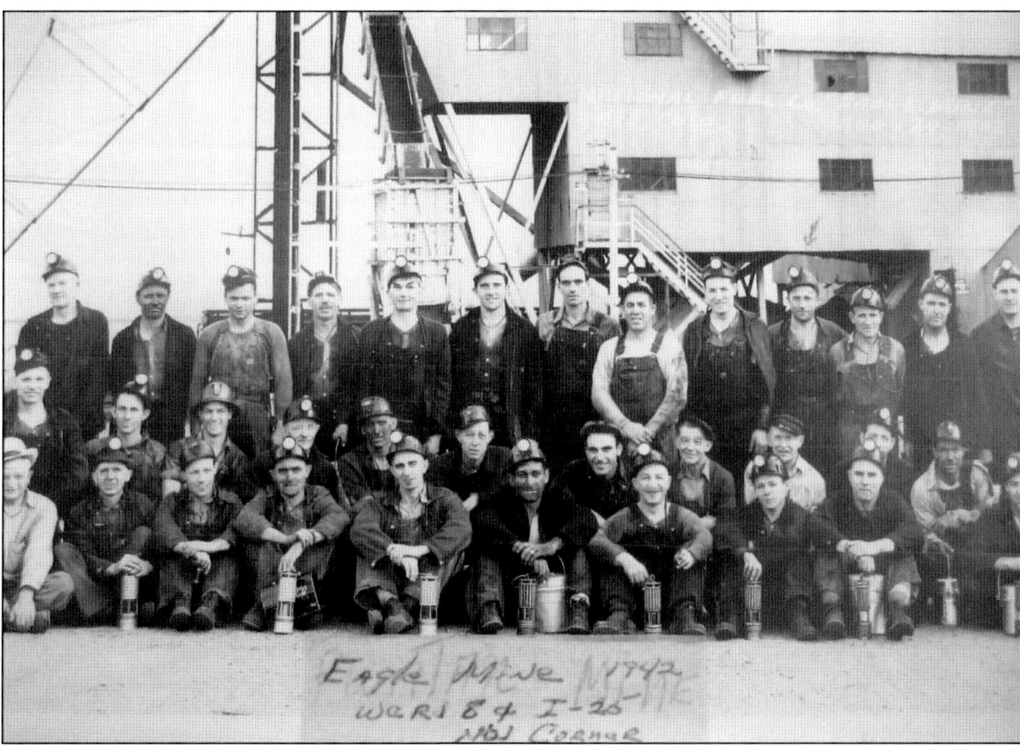

This photograph, taken in 1942, shows miners in front of the Eagle Mine. Miners filled a number of positions. Miner Jasper Maes recalls working as a gold digger and later as a mule worker and fire boss. The miners in the first row hold their carbide lamps as well as their lunch pails. The miners seem happy despite the dangerous conditions they worked under. (Courtesy of the Town of Frederick.)

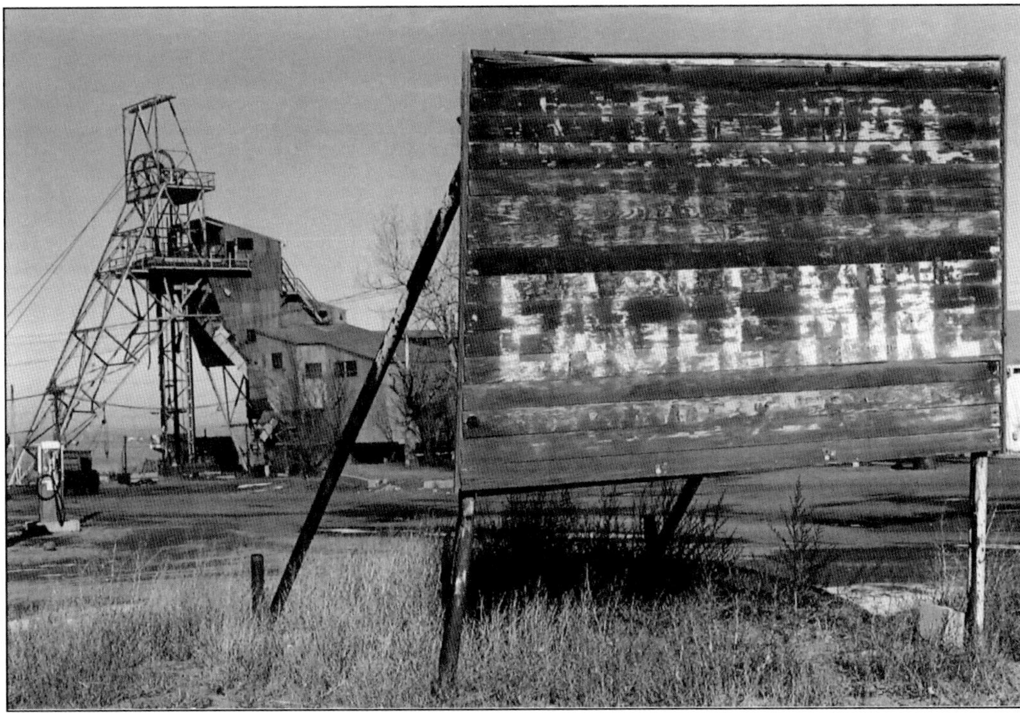

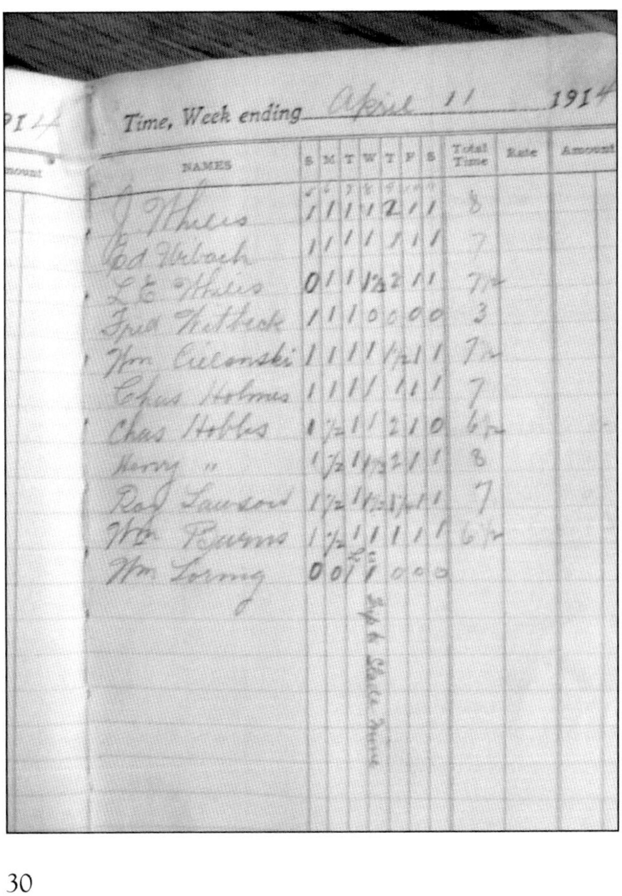

The Eagle Mine is seen here after it was closed and abandoned. The mine was torn down in the 1970s, but it appears that it had been abandoned for some time before that. (Courtesy of the Town of Frederick.)

This is the pay ledger from an unidentified mine, showing the number of hours worked for each day of the week. If work was available, miners would often work on Sundays. Despite the number of days worked, not many hours had accumulated on the ledger. The date, April 11, 1914, puts it at the end of the mine's busy season. Miner Walter J. Bourn worked in the Sterling Mine from approximately 1930 until the mine closed. He recalls being paid $1 a day during the Depression. This represented a pay raise negotiated by John L. Lewis, president of the United Mine Workers. (Courtesy of the Town of Frederick.)

This is a pay stub for Jabe Shaw, who worked at the Sterling Mine in Dacono, which was owned by the McNeil Coal Corporation. Note the entry under "wash house." Miners were expected to pay for the cost of washing their mine clothing. (Courtesy of the Town of Frederick.)

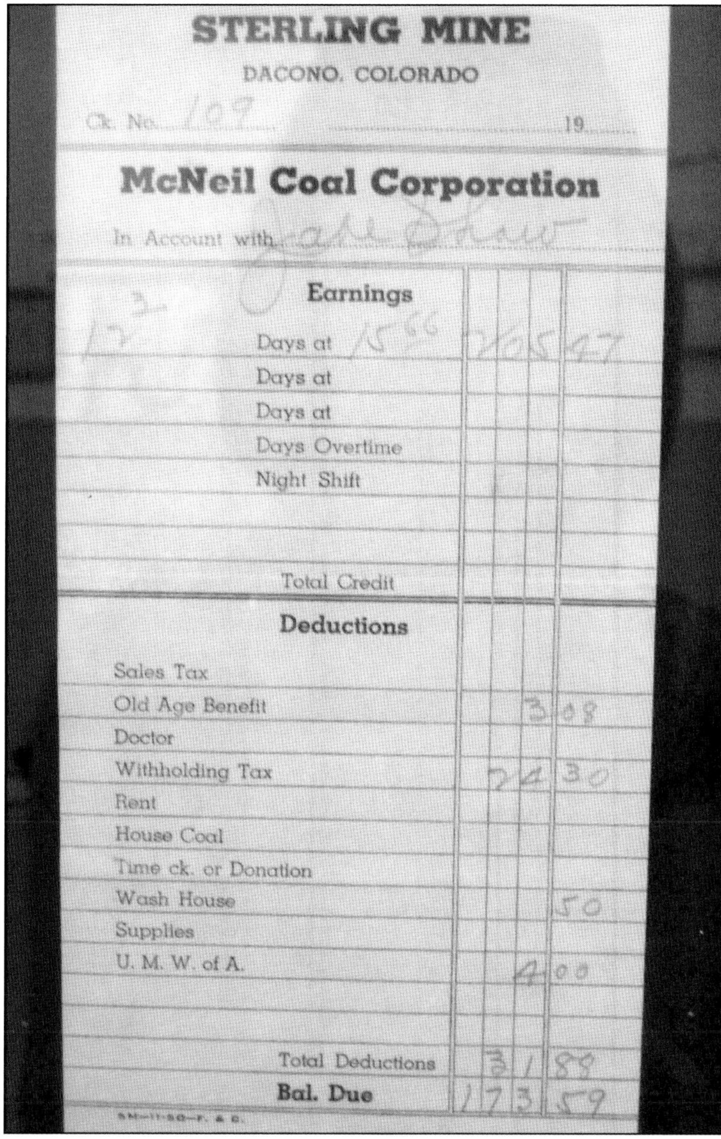
STERLING MINE

DACONO, COLORADO

Ck. No. 109 .... 19....

McNeil Coal Corporation

In Account with Jabe Shaw

Earnings	
Days at 15.66	205 47
Days at	
Days at	
Days Overtime	
Night Shift	
Total Credit	

Deductions	
Sales Tax	
Old Age Benefit	3 08
Doctor	
Withholding Tax	24 30
Rent	
House Coal	
Time ck. or Donation	
Wash House	50
Supplies	
U. M. W. of A.	4 00
Total Deductions	31 88
Bal. Due	173 59

This pay stub dates from January 15, 1937, and is for Pete Pascoff, who was working at the Baum Mine. Note that the miners were expected to pay for their blasting powder, their coal, their washing, and the check weighman, who weighed the coal cars to make sure the miners got full pay for their loads. Prior to being supplied by the unions, the weighman was an employee of the mine. The miners often felt that they were not being fully compensated for their work. However, they had to pay for their own weighman. (Courtesy of PP.)

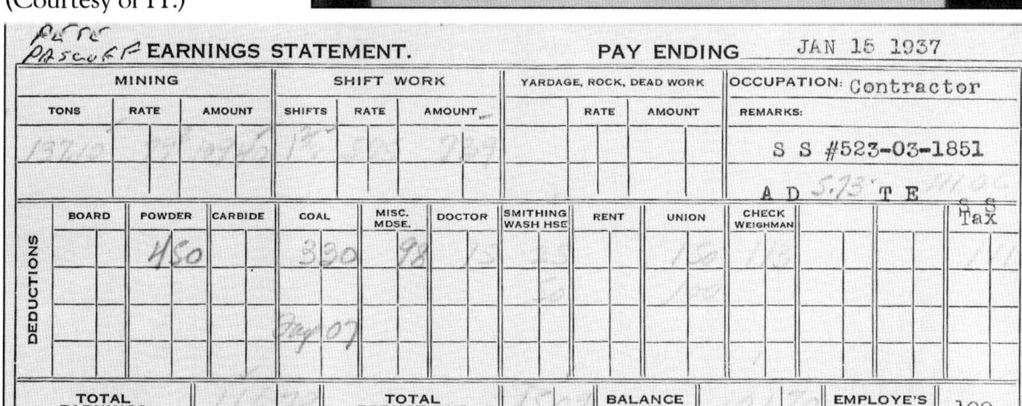
Peter Pascoff EARNINGS STATEMENT. PAY ENDING JAN 15 1937

MINING: TONS | RATE | AMOUNT — SHIFT WORK: SHIFTS | RATE | AMOUNT — YARDAGE, ROCK, DEAD WORK: RATE | AMOUNT

OCCUPATION: Contractor

REMARKS: S S #523-03-1851

A D T E

DEDUCTIONS: BOARD | POWDER 4 50 | CARBIDE | COAL 3 30 | MISC. MDSE. 98 | DOCTOR | SMITHING WASH HSE | RENT | UNION | CHECK WEIGHMAN | | S S Tax

TOTAL EARNINGS | TOTAL DEDUCTIONS | BALANCE DUE | EMPLOYE'S NUMBER 100

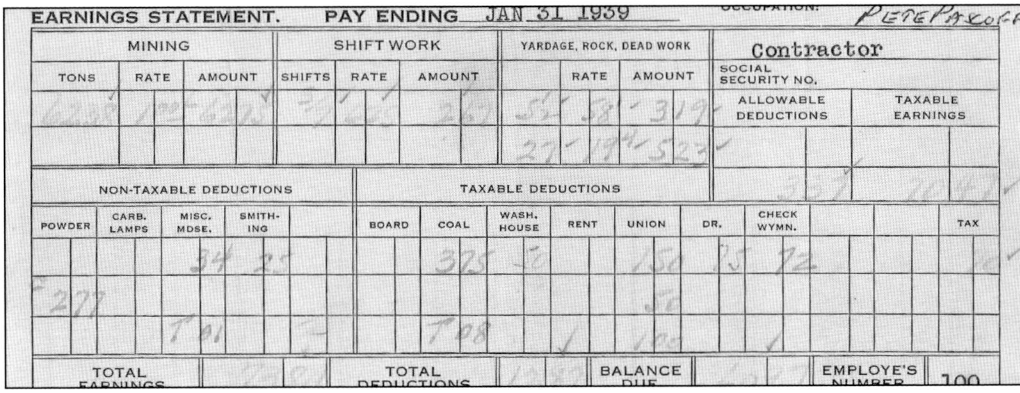

EARNINGS STATEMENT. PAY ENDING JAN 31 1939 OCCUPATION: PETE PASCOFF

MINING: TONS, RATE, AMOUNT — SHIFT WORK: SHIFTS, RATE, AMOUNT — YARDAGE, ROCK, DEAD WORK: RATE, AMOUNT — Contractor — SOCIAL SECURITY NO. — ALLOWABLE DEDUCTIONS — TAXABLE EARNINGS

NON-TAXABLE DEDUCTIONS: POWDER, CARB. LAMPS, MISC. MDSE., SMITH-ING — TAXABLE DEDUCTIONS: BOARD, COAL, WASH. HOUSE, RENT, UNION, DR., CHECK WYMN., TAX

TOTAL EARNINGS — TOTAL DEDUCTIONS — BALANCE DUE — EMPLOYE'S NUMBER 100

This is another pay stub for Pete Pascoff, dated January 31, 1939, also from the Baum Mine. Compared to the early miners, Pascoff was paid well. Jasper Maes worked at the Washington and Columbine Mines during the Depression and recalls being paid $1 per day. (Courtesy of PP.)

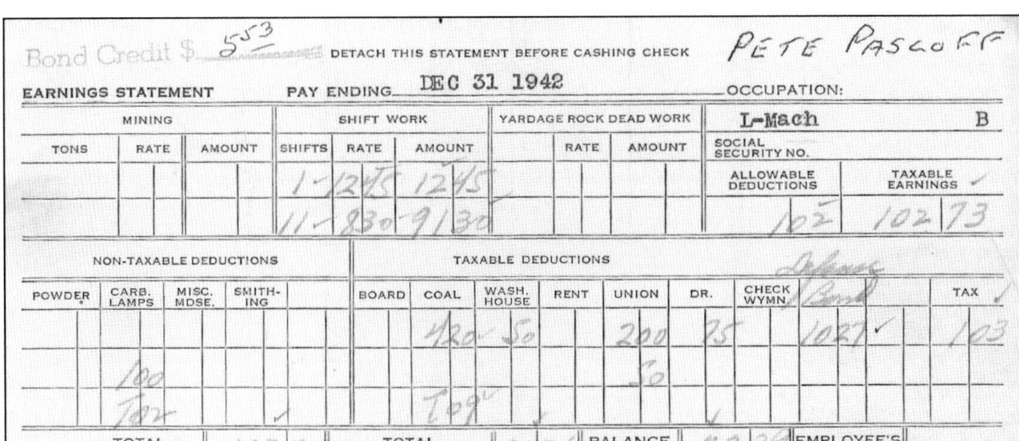

Bond Credit $ 5.53 DETACH THIS STATEMENT BEFORE CASHING CHECK PETE PASCOFF

EARNINGS STATEMENT PAY ENDING DEC 31 1942 OCCUPATION:

MINING: TONS, RATE, AMOUNT — SHIFT WORK: SHIFTS, RATE, AMOUNT — YARDAGE ROCK DEAD WORK: RATE, AMOUNT — L-Mach B — SOCIAL SECURITY NO. — ALLOWABLE DEDUCTIONS — TAXABLE EARNINGS

NON-TAXABLE DEDUCTIONS: POWDER, CARB. LAMPS, MISC. MDSE., SMITH-ING — TAXABLE DEDUCTIONS: BOARD, COAL, WASH. HOUSE, RENT, UNION, DR., CHECK WYMN., TAX

TOTAL EARNINGS — TOTAL DEDUCTIONS — BALANCE DUE — EMPLOYEE'S NUMBER P P

This pay stub for Pete Pascoff shows a bond credit in the amount of $5.53. Today, $83.39 does not seem like much for a week's work. This at least represented a steady rate of pay. Miner Antonio DeGelaranido recalls being paid according to the number of coal cars he loaded. (Courtesy of PP.)

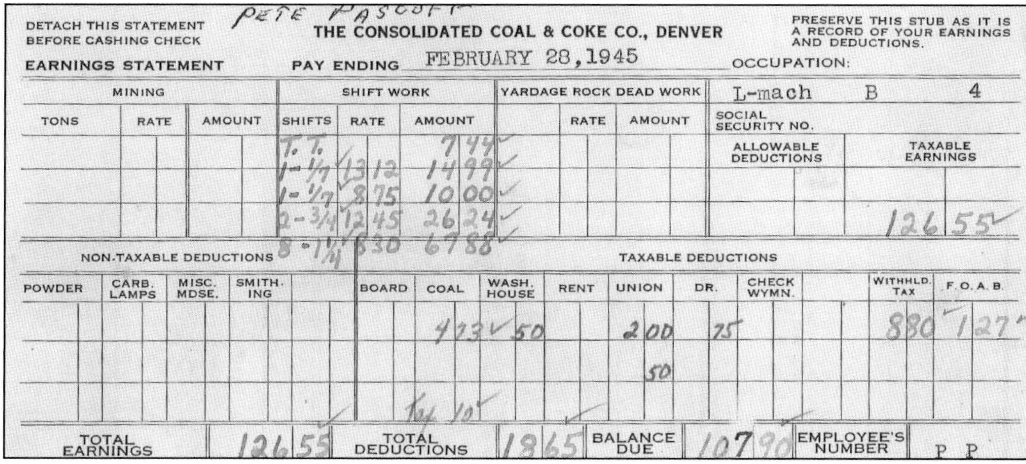

DETACH THIS STATEMENT BEFORE CASHING CHECK

Pete Pascoff

THE CONSOLIDATED COAL & COKE CO., DENVER

PRESERVE THIS STUB AS IT IS A RECORD OF YOUR EARNINGS AND DEDUCTIONS.

EARNINGS STATEMENT

PAY ENDING FEBRUARY 28,1945

OCCUPATION: L-mach B 4

MINING			SHIFT WORK			YARDAGE ROCK DEAD WORK		
TONS	RATE	AMOUNT	SHIFTS	RATE	AMOUNT		RATE	AMOUNT
			T. T.		7 44			
			1-1/7	13 12	14 99			
			1-1/7	8 75	10 00			
			2-3/4	12 45	26 24			
			8-1 1/4	8 30	67 88			

SOCIAL SECURITY NO.

ALLOWABLE DEDUCTIONS	TAXABLE EARNINGS
	126 55

NON-TAXABLE DEDUCTIONS

TAXABLE DEDUCTIONS

POWDER	CARB. LAMPS	MISC. MDSE.	SMITH-ING	BOARD	COAL	WASH. HOUSE	RENT	UNION	DR.	CHECK WYMN.	WITHHLD. TAX	F. O. A. B.
					4 23	50		2 00	75		8 80	1 27
								50				

TOTAL EARNINGS	126 55	TOTAL DEDUCTIONS	18 65	BALANCE DUE	107 90	EMPLOYEE'S NUMBER	P P

This pay stub is from the Consolidated Coal & Coke Company of Denver, who owned the Baum Mine. The miners made the most money during the busy season, which ran through the winter and into early spring. The demand for coal during the summer months was not as great. (Courtesy of PP.)

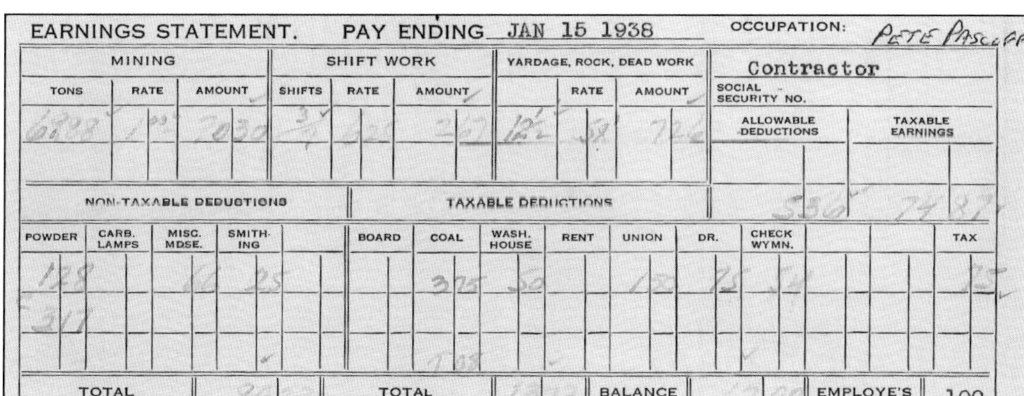

EARNINGS STATEMENT. PAY ENDING JAN 15 1938

OCCUPATION: Pete Pascoff

Contractor

MINING			SHIFT WORK			YARDAGE, ROCK, DEAD WORK		
TONS	RATE	AMOUNT	SHIFTS	RATE	AMOUNT		RATE	AMOUNT
[illegible]	[illegible]	20 30	[illegible]	[illegible]	2 62	12	[illegible]	7 26

SOCIAL SECURITY NO.

ALLOWABLE DEDUCTIONS	TAXABLE EARNINGS
5 36	74 87

NON-TAXABLE DEDUCTIONS

TAXABLE DEDUCTIONS

POWDER	CARB. LAMPS	MISC. MDSE.	SMITH-ING	BOARD	COAL	WASH. HOUSE	RENT	UNION	DR.	CHECK WYMN.	TAX
1 28		10	25		3 75	50		1 50	75	54	75
3 17											

TOTAL EARNINGS	80 23	TOTAL DEDUCTIONS	13 23	BALANCE DUE	67 00	EMPLOYE'S NUMBER	100

This is another pay stub from the Baum Mine, which was called the Golden Ash from 1906 to 1913. Afterwards, it operated as the Baum Mine until 1953. The mine site is just to the south of the current Frederick High School. Miner Thomas Dan Villani recalls working at a number of mines between 1943 and 1955. Among the mines he worked were the Evans, Sterling, Grant, Russell, Baum, Eagle, Lincoln, and Washington Mines. He worked as a machine operator and fire boss. He remembers being paid $9.25 a day. (Courtesy of PP.)

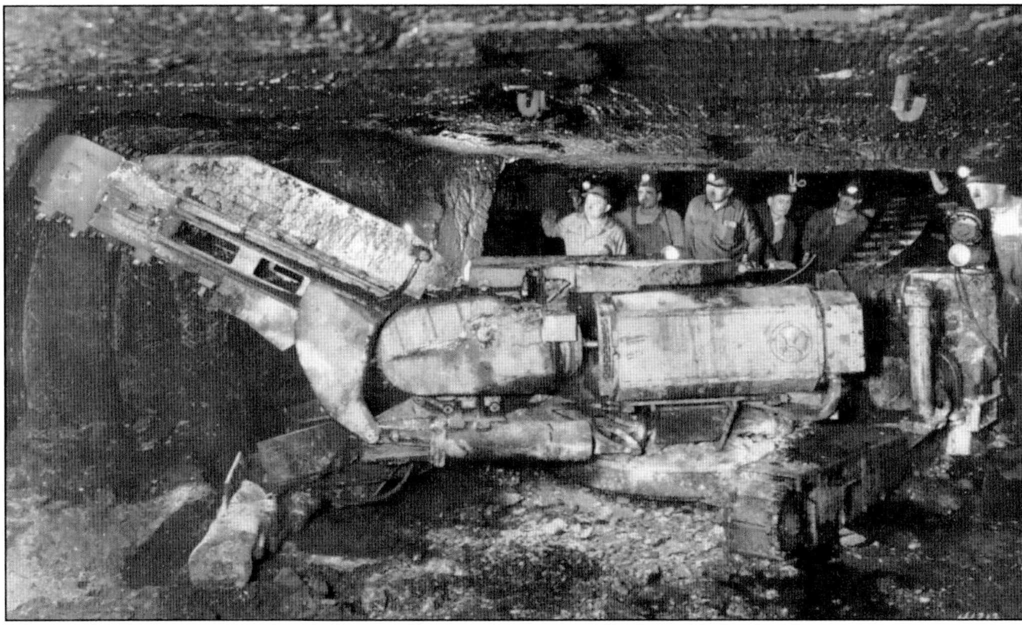

Until the mid-1940s, extracting coal was done by blasting and through the use of hand tools. This is a continuous miner machine, produced by the Joy Manufacturing Company. The first one of these machines was installed in the Baum Mine. The machine was put on rails and run to the end of the shaft, where it ground the rock and coal from the shaft face. (Courtesy of the Town of Frederick.)

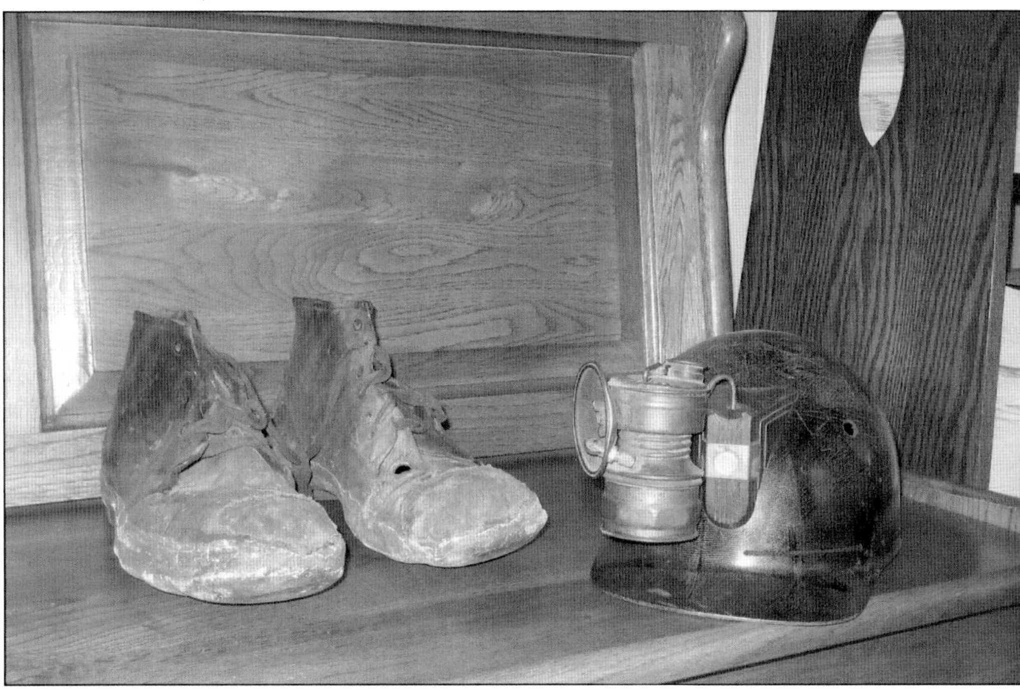

This display is in the Miners' Memorial Museum, which is located in the old city hall. The hard hat shows the carbide lamp that the miners depended on to light their way. Note the boots—there were no special shoes or boots for these miners. (Courtesy of the Town of Frederick.)

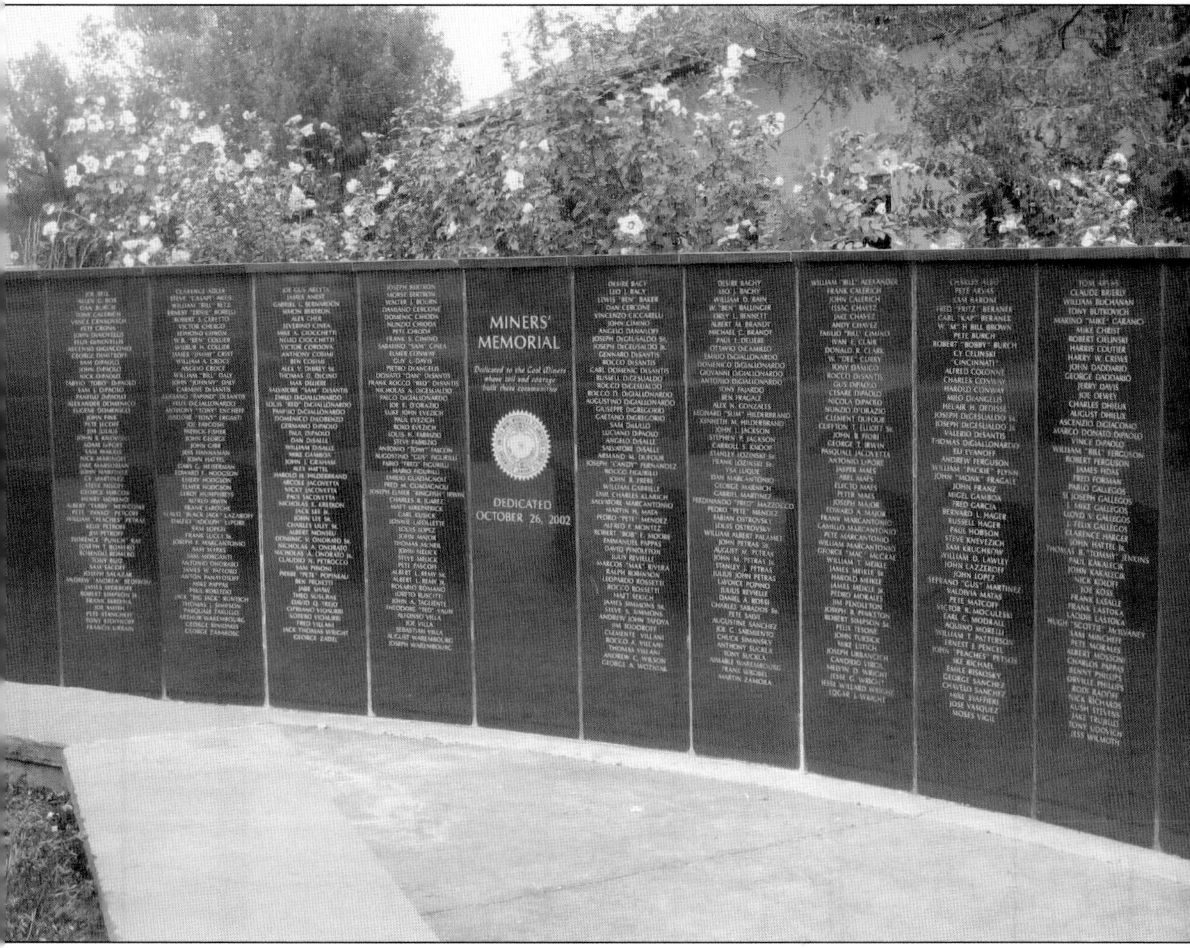

The Miners' Memorial is in Crist Park, next to the old city hall. The memorial lists the names of miners who worked in the mines. Many of the names belong to men who helped build Frederick. As the years pass, fewer and fewer of the miners listed are still alive. (Courtesy of the Town of Frederick.)

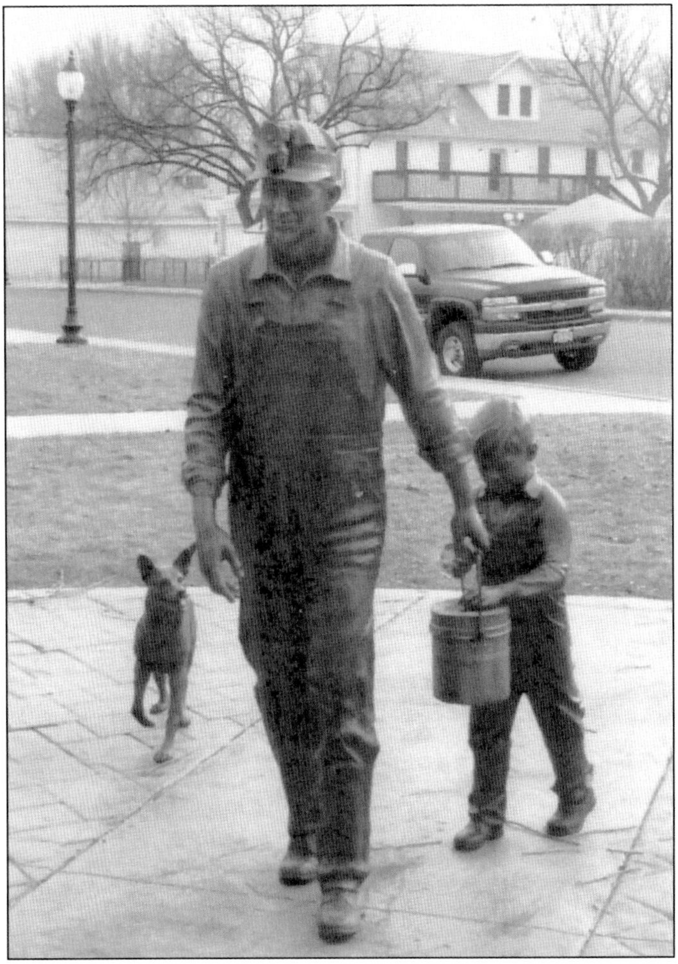

This sculpture shows a miner returning home after a day at work. In his left hand, he carries his lunch pail. On his head, he wears his hard hat with his carbide lamp. Although the sculpture includes the miner's son and his dog, there is no statue of his wife, who no doubt would have been glad to see him come home safely. The white building in the background is the old McAfee Hotel. (Courtesy of the Town of Frederick.)

This bas-relief shows the three activities that made Frederick a town. On the left are miners. The central panel shows the railway, without which there would be no town. The portion of the sculpture on the right shows farmers tending their fields. It is located in Crist Park near the old city hall. (Courtesy of the Town of Frederick.)

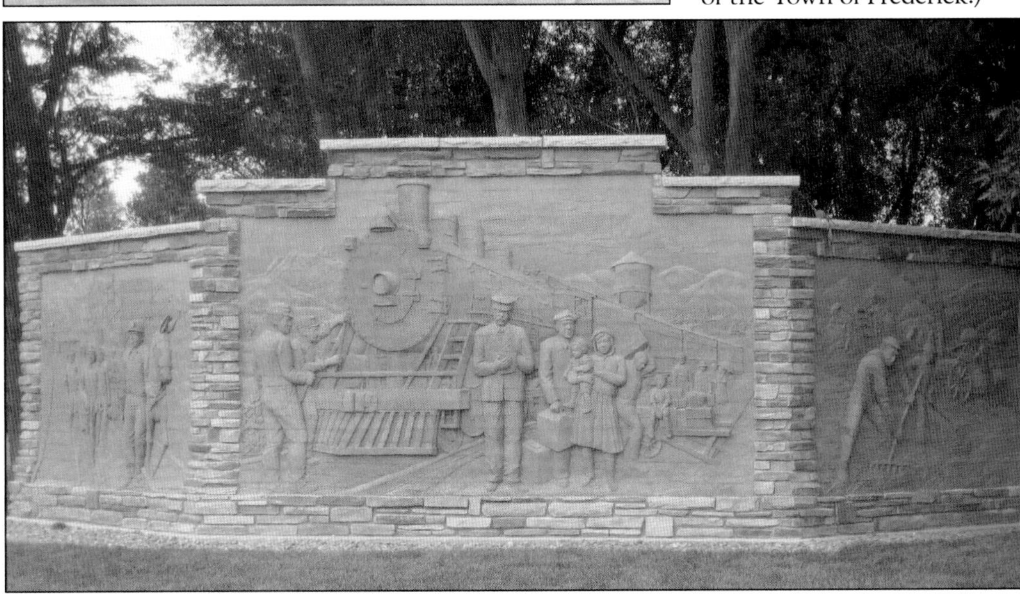

Three

Life in Frederick

Farmers and miners were not the only residents of Frederick, and shops, taverns, and grocery stores sprang up to meet the needs of all residents. Frederick was officially on the map with the opening of the post office.

As was common, the first settlers in Frederick got established and then sent for the rest of their family. Frederick and the surrounding communities quickly became home to many immigrants from Europe. Each of the three communities in the tri-town area had its own flavor. Frederick was primarily populated by Italians.

Frederick's main business district was on Fifth Street, which included Clark Lumber Company, the McAfee Hotel, Revielle's grocery, Nick's coffeehouse, Pete's barbershop, and the Sunshine Tavern. The Carbon Valley region's primary newspaper, the *Farmer and Miner,* was published in the back of the Sunshine Tavern. On the other side of the tavern, across Oak Street, were the Catholic church and the rectory. At the far end of Fifth Street was LaRoche's service station. Residences were located between the stores.

Schools have been an integral part of the Frederick community since their inception. The first school was put together from the parts of two existing buildings located at the southeast end of Seventh Street. In 1916, the area schools became part of District 76, which put them under the county's control.

The first Frederick High School was built in 1916. Since then, it has been replaced a few times. A brand new, modern high school opened in 2012. School athletics have been a constant source of pride for Frederick and the surrounding towns. Through the years, homecoming parades featured inventive floats that often carried the homecoming queen and her court.

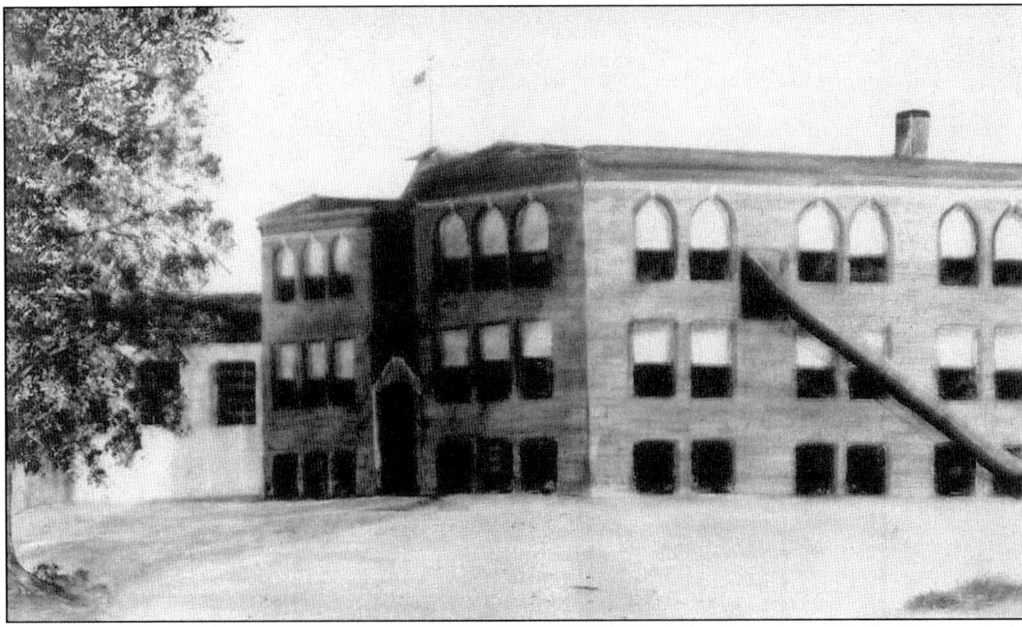

The first Frederick High School, built in 1916, is seen here. The structure in the front of the building is a fire escape, going from the third floor to the first floor. The fire escape was frequently used by students even when there was no fire. One local resident recalls himself and three other students being trapped in the bottom of the escape. The custodian had to let them out. (Courtesy of the Town of Frederick.)

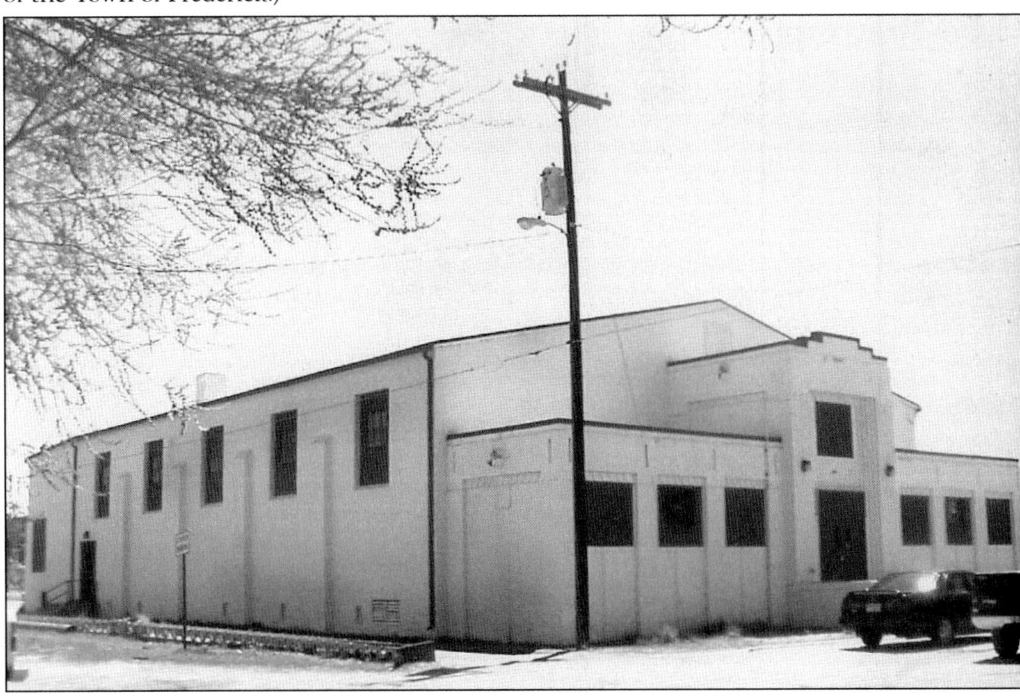

The high school gymnasium is seen here. It was built as a Works Progress Administration (WPA) project in 1935. The basketball court was in the rear of the building. (Courtesy of the Town of Frederick.)

The 1921–1922 Frederick High School basketball team is seen here. At this time, Frederick had still only been an incorporated town for 14 years. (Courtesy of the Town of Frederick.)

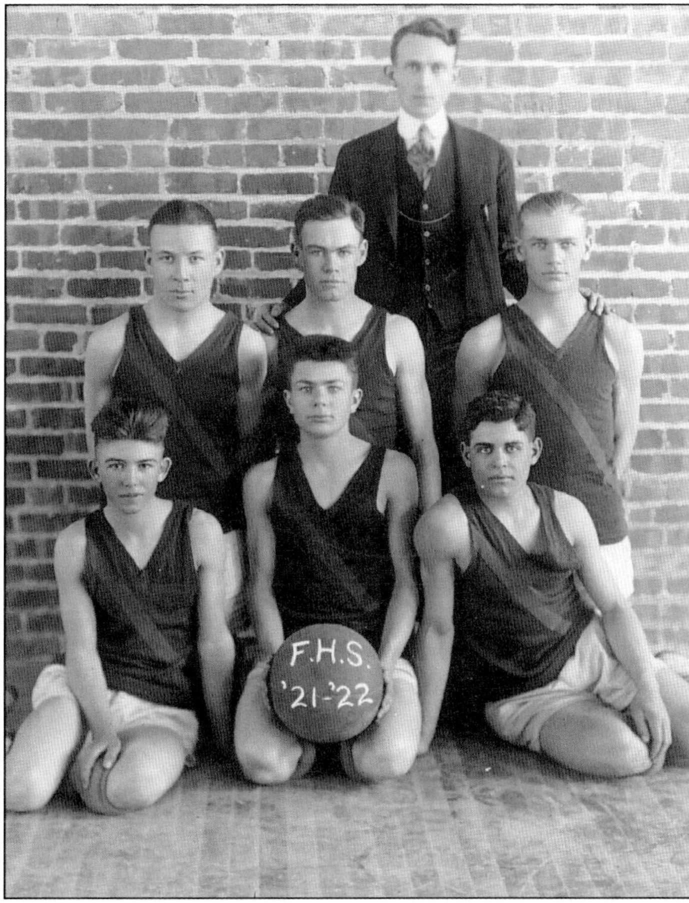

The 1924 Frederick High School basketball team is seen here. Paul Nicholson, the superintendent of the school, stands second from the right. (Courtesy of the Town of Frederick.)

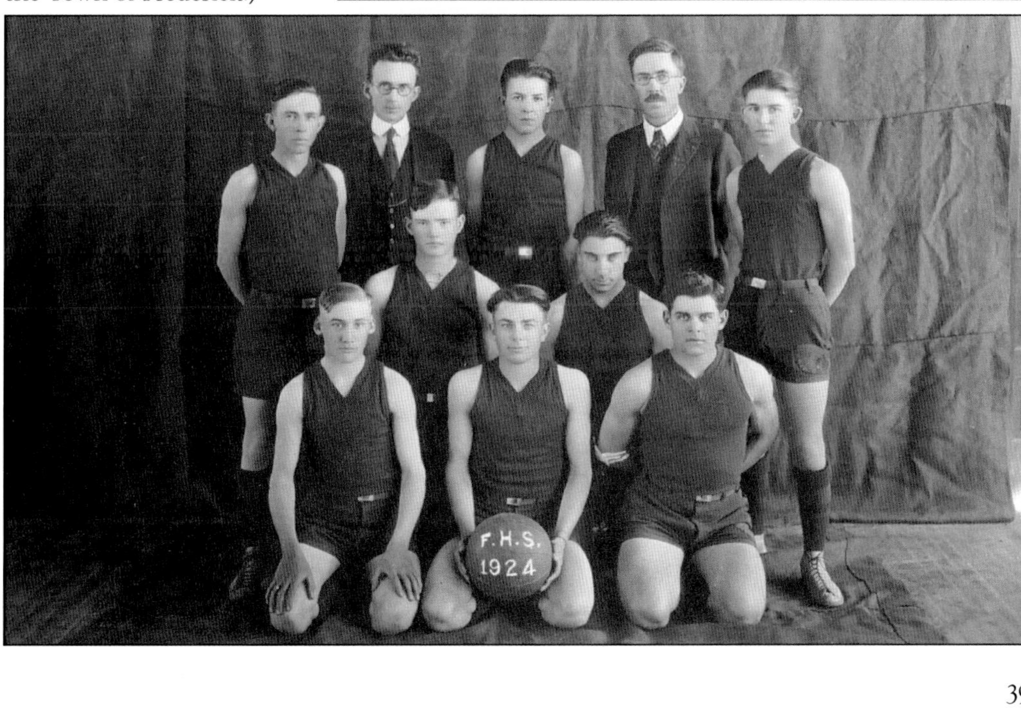

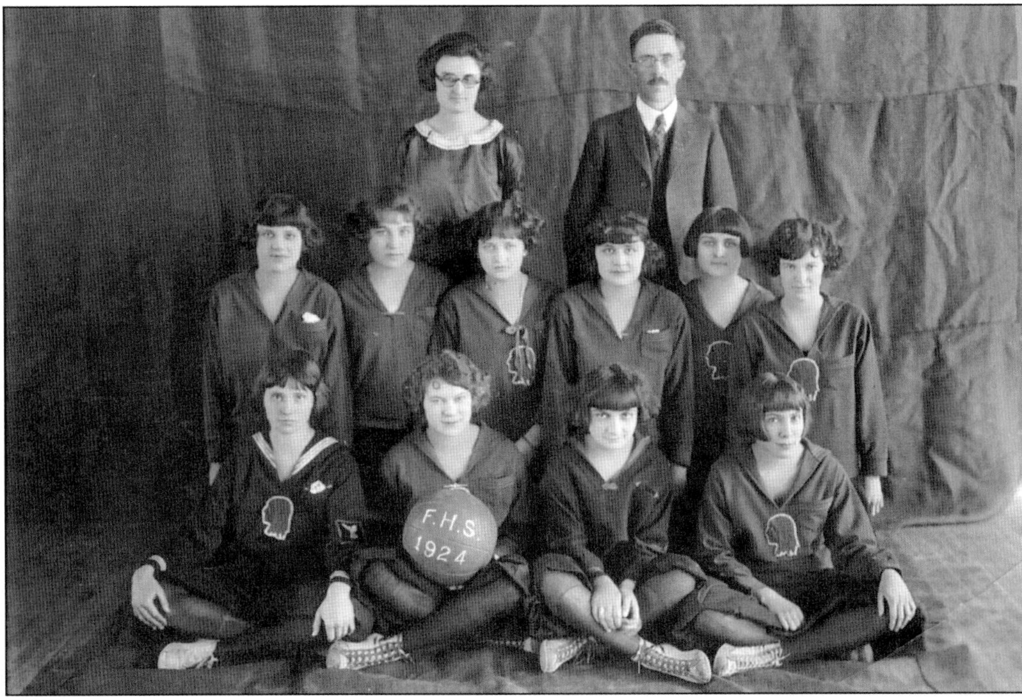

The 1924 Frederick High School girls' basketball team is seen in these two photographs. Note that the team had more players than the 1924 boys' team had. Paul Nicholson is seen again above, standing in the back right. (Both, courtesy of the Town of Frederick.)

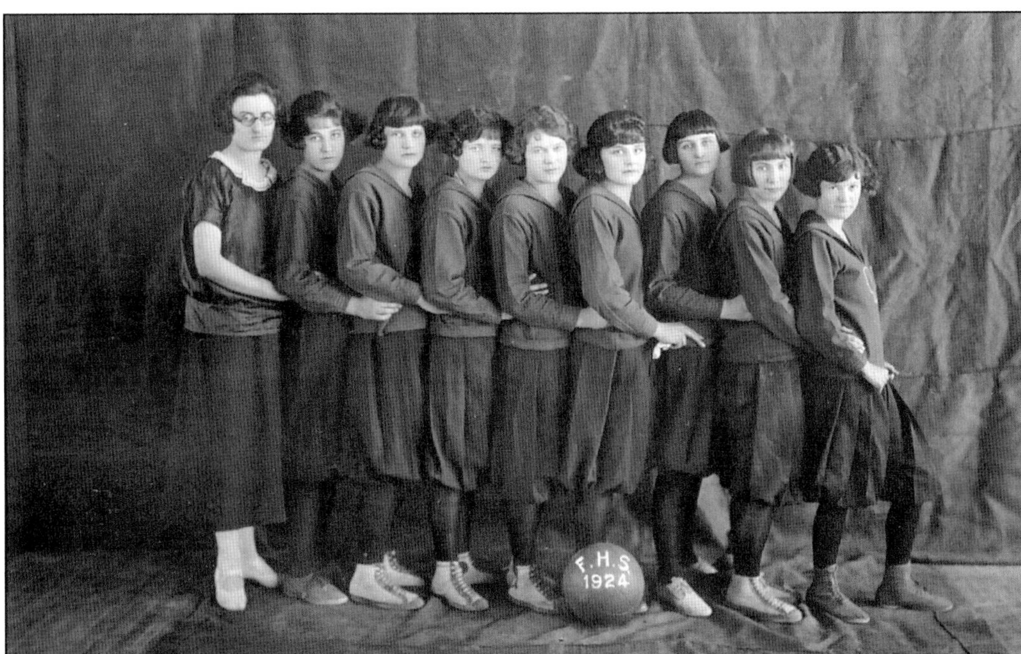

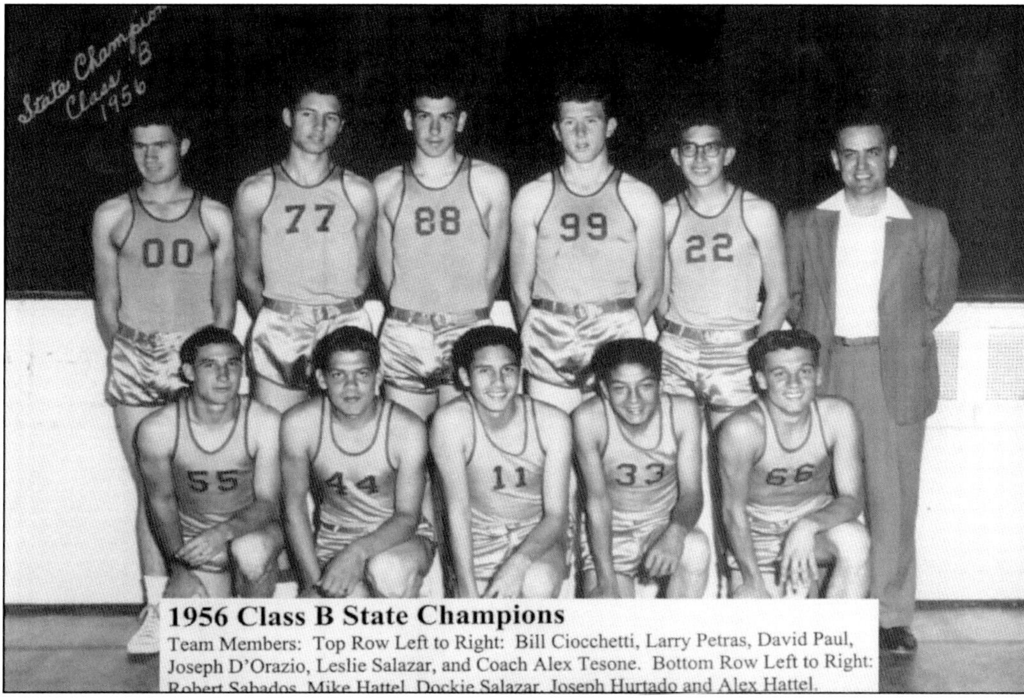

The 1956 Class B state champion Frederick High School basketball team is seen here. To date, this is the only state championship the school has ever won. The coach, Alex Tesone, coached both basketball and football at Frederick High School for many years. (Courtesy of MLH.)

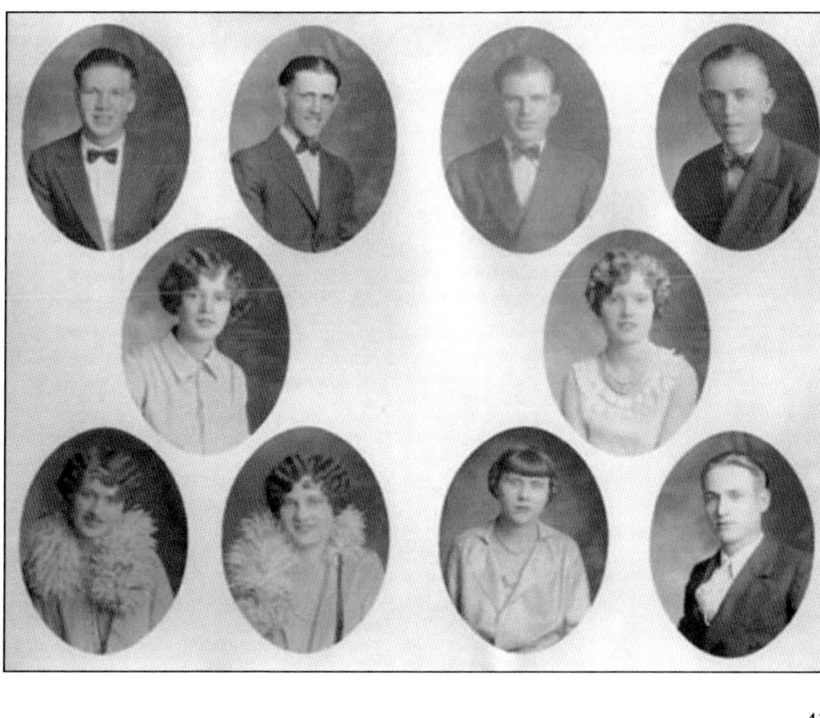

The Frederick High School graduating class of 1927 is seen here. (Courtesy of CC.)

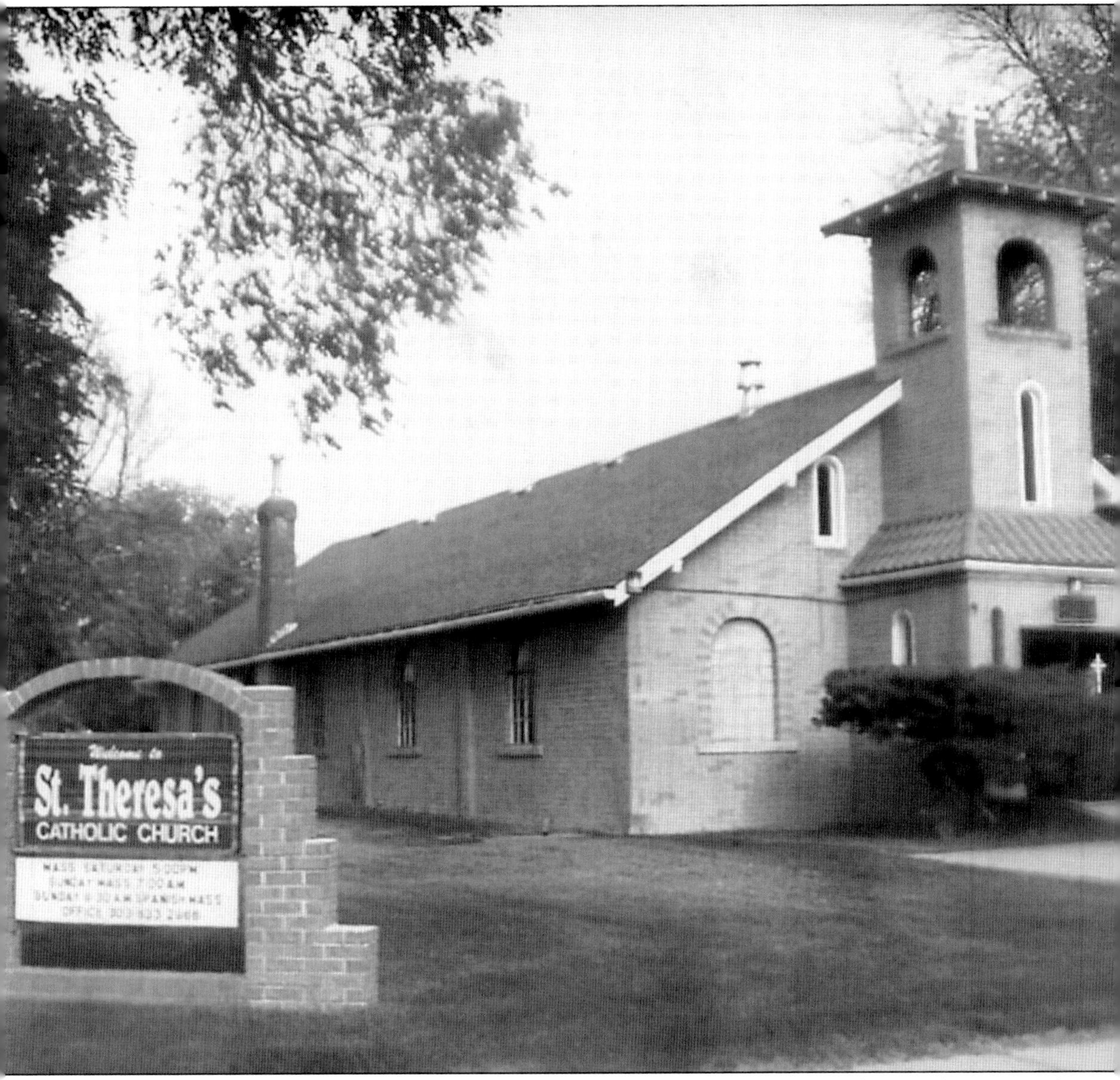

St. Theresa's Catholic Church is located at 502 Walnut Street in Frederick. The St. Theresa Parish was formed in 1923. Before that, Frederick's Catholic residents had to go to Longmont to attend St. John the Baptist Church. The lots on which the original church was built were donated by Dr. Paul Leyda. The money to build the church was raised through parishioners at socials and bazaars and by contributions from the local mines. The Catholic Extension Society of Chicago also donated $700 towards the building costs. By 1938, the congregation had outgrown the church. The new church, seen here, was built under the supervision of Fr. James Maher. The inside of the new church featured Colorado alabaster, which was used for the altar and the candlesticks. A new rectory and parish hall were also constructed. The church still serves parishioners today. (Courtesy of the Town of Frederick.)

This program is from commencement exercises for Frederick High School in 1924. Note that Paul H. Nicholson was the principal at the time and G.P. McLaughlin was the superintendent. (Courtesy of the Town of Frederick.)

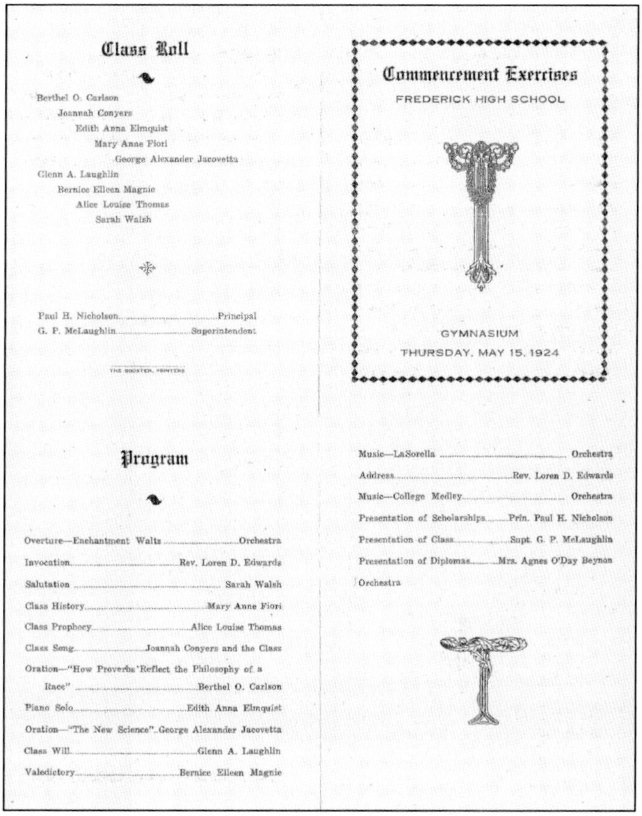

Class Roll

Berthel O. Carlson
Joannah Conyers
Edith Anna Elmquist
Mary Anne Fiori
George Alexander Jacovetta
Glenn A. Laughlin
Bernice Elleen Magnie
Alice Louise Thomas
Sarah Walsh

Paul H. Nicholson........Principal
G. P. McLaughlin........Superintendent

THE ROOSTER, PRINTERS

Commencement Exercises
FREDERICK HIGH SCHOOL

GYMNASIUM
THURSDAY, MAY 15, 1924

Program

Overture—Enchantment Waltz........Orchestra
Invocation........Rev. Loren D. Edwards
Salutation........Sarah Walsh
Class History........Mary Anne Fiori
Class Prophecy........Alice Louise Thomas
Class Song........Joannah Conyers and the Class
Oration—"How Proverbs Reflect the Philosophy of a Race"........Berthel O. Carlson
Piano Solo........Edith Anna Elmquist
Oration—"The New Science"..George Alexander Jacovetta
Class Will........Glenn A. Laughlin
Valedictory........Bernice Elleen Magnie

Music—LaSorella........Orchestra
Address........Rev. Loren D. Edwards
Music—College Medley........Orchestra
Presentation of Scholarships........Prin. Paul H. Nicholson
Presentation of Class........Supt. G. P. McLaughlin
Presentation of Diplomas........Mrs. Agnes O'Day Beynon
Orchestra

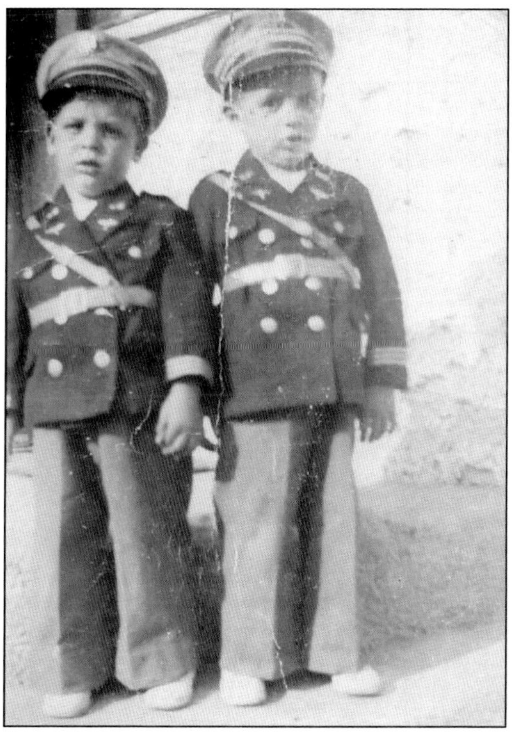

Brothers Mike (left) and Alex Hattel are seen here in 1945. The boys are dressed in military uniforms because their father was in the military. (Courtesy of MLH.)

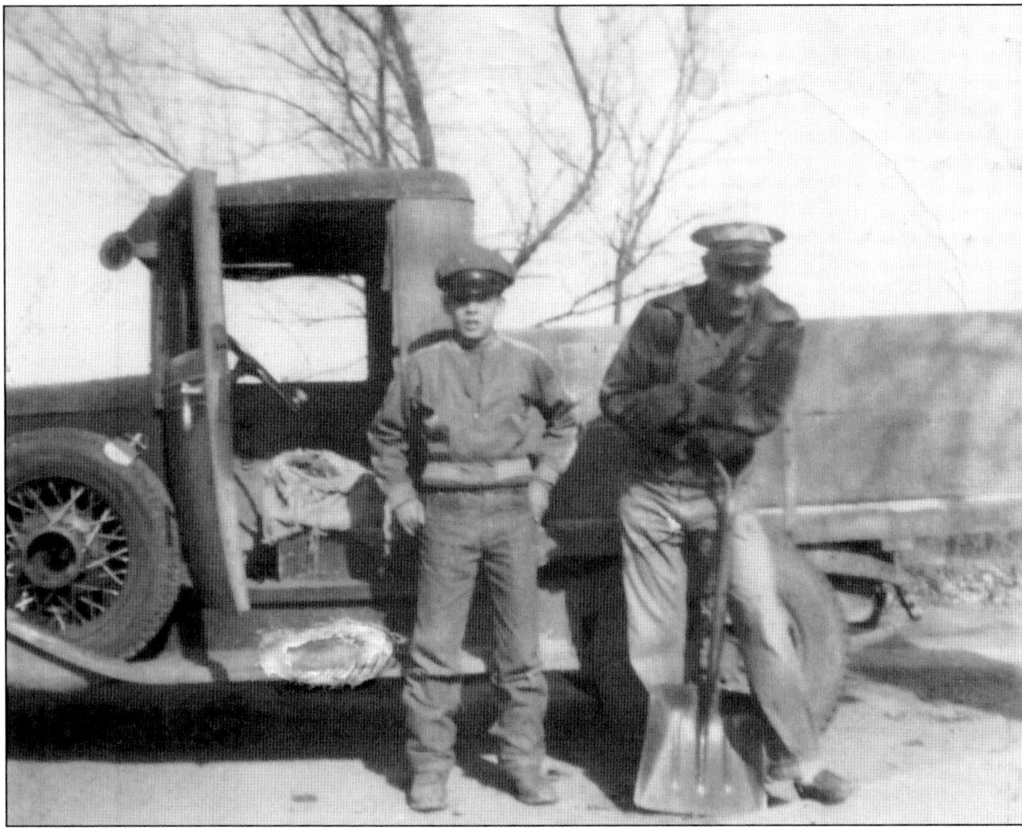

Mike Hattel is seen here with his uncle Jabe Shaw. Despite the age of the truck, this photograph was taken in the early 1950s. (Courtesy of MLH.)

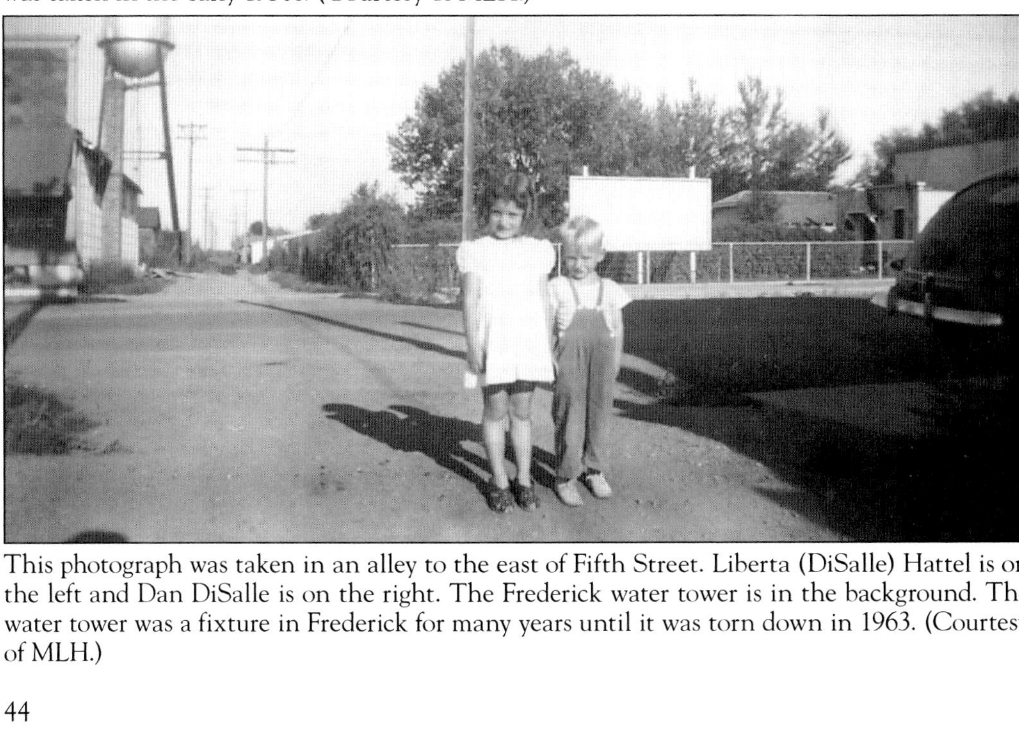

This photograph was taken in an alley to the east of Fifth Street. Liberta (DiSalle) Hattel is on the left and Dan DiSalle is on the right. The Frederick water tower is in the background. The water tower was a fixture in Frederick for many years until it was torn down in 1963. (Courtesy of MLH.)

Four

Growing Pains

Apart from issues surrounding the mines, Frederick's main problem was its growing need for a water source. Initially, water was drawn from mine shafts and carried by hand to where it was needed.

In 1913, Frederick installed its first water system, which amounted to pumps that pulled water from the mine shafts. Frederick also relied upon Firestone for its water at the time. Water quality was always an issue. The mine water was extremely hard, which made cleaning difficult. One resident remembers the water having a high concentration of fluoride.

Frederick was eventually forced to address its water supply issue. Due to its expanding population, drawing water from mine shafts proved inadequate. Frederick began looking for a source of water it could purchase, and Firestone Lake, northwest of Frederick, seemed the best possibility. However, to many of the town's residents, the cost of purchasing and upgrading water supply facilities was prohibitive. In the late 1940s and early 1950s, the issue became a point of contention in Frederick politics.

Periodically, Frederick and the surrounding areas would experience floods. They came not from overflowing rivers but from persistent rainfall. Frederick, Firestone, and Dacono sit in a shallow valley, so during intense summer thunderstorms, water would collect and have no place to go. The result was destructive flooding. There was no way to divert storm water, however, and persistent flooding became a fact of life in the Carbon Valley area.

The flood of 1957 brought matters to a head. Flood damage was extensive and widespread, but the flooding also destroyed Frederick's water supply, leaving Frederick needing to either find a new water source or somehow upgrade its facilities. The choices facing the town became more acute when the state refused to declare Frederick a disaster area and provide funds for cleanup and reconstruction.

In the late 1950s, Frederick decided, by vote, to authorize the funds necessary to purchase Firestone Lake. Since that affirmative vote, what is now Milavec Reservoir has provided water and flood control for the Frederick area.

Frederick's streets were not paved until the early 1960s, and the paving project vastly improved life in the town center, as residents no longer had to deal with dust and mud in the streets.

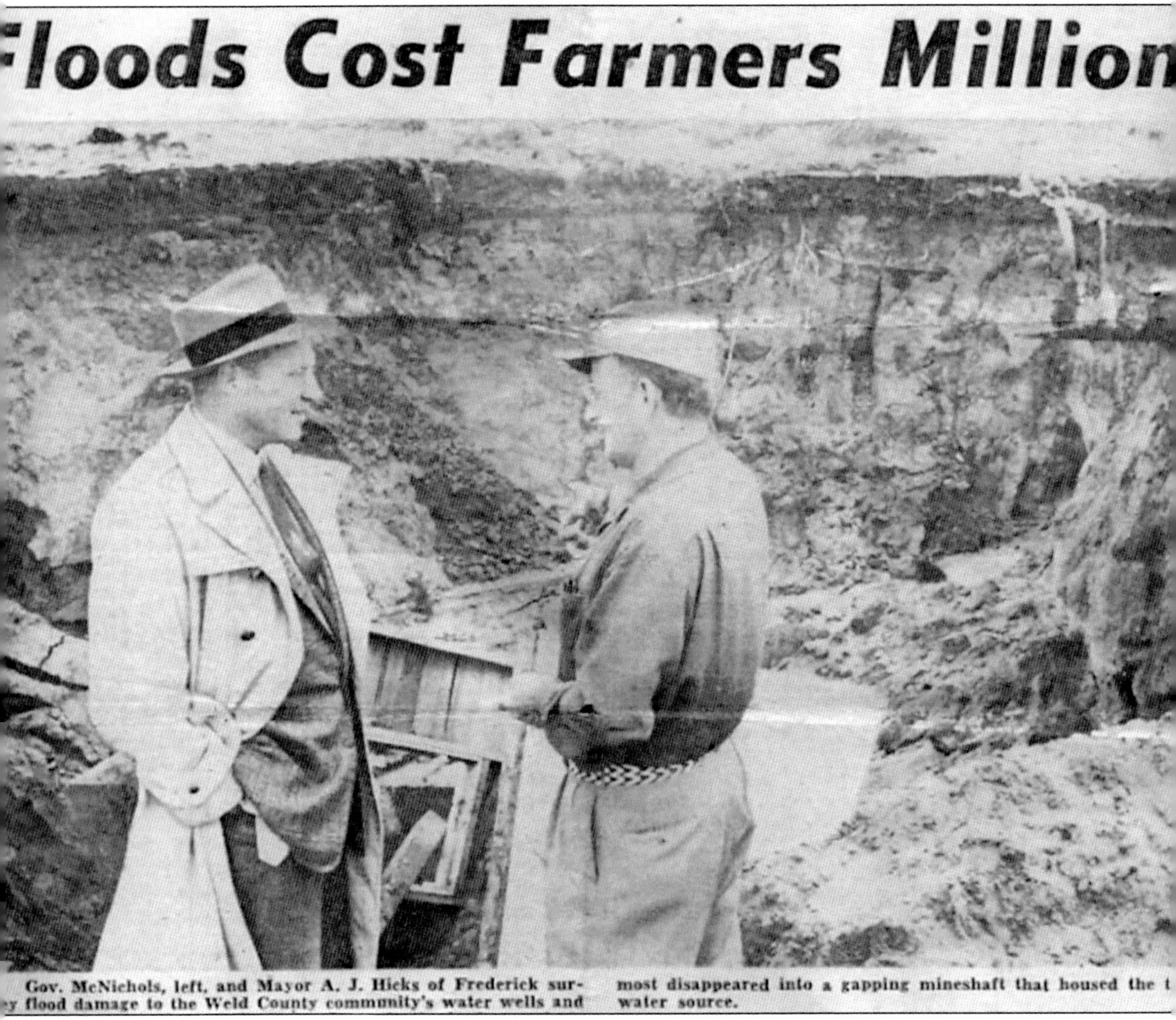

Floods Cost Farmers Millio

Gov. McNichols, left, and Mayor A. J. Hicks of Frederick sur- y flood damage to the Weld County community's water wells and most disappeared into a gapping mineshaft that housed the t water source.

This newspaper photograph shows Colorado governor Stephen McNichols (left) conferring with Frederick mayor A.J. Hicks after the 1957 flood. Despite numerous requests for assistance, the state refused to declare Frederick a disaster area, leaving the cost of the cleanup to local residents. (Courtesy of the Town of Frederick.)

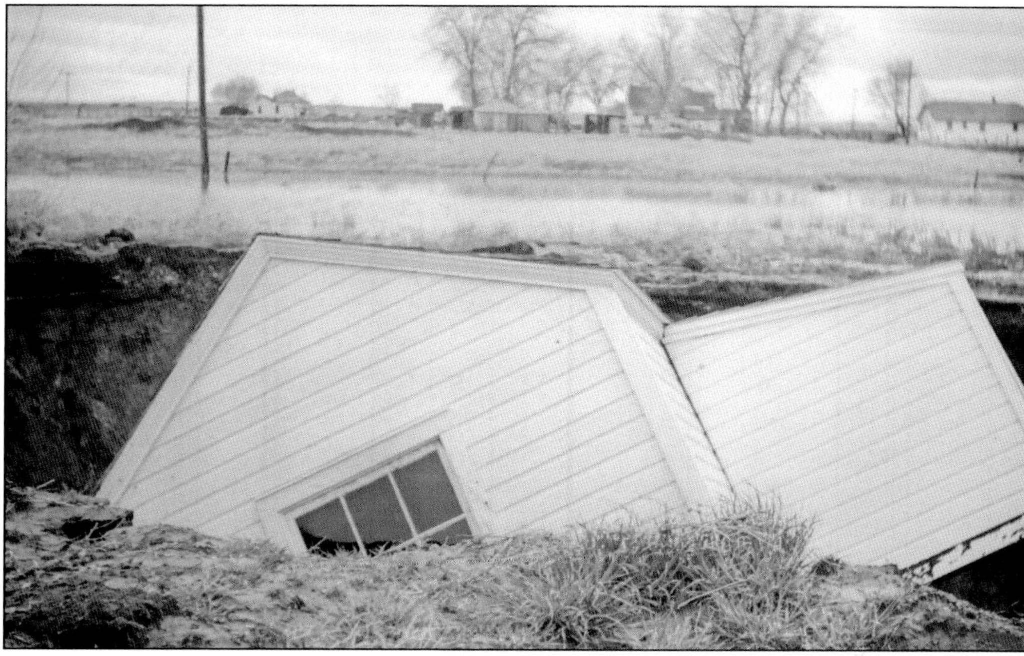

During the 1957 flood, the Frederick pump house fell into this mine shaft after the shaft collapsed due to the flooding. Prior to the flood, the pump house pumped water out of the mines and supplied all of the water for Frederick. After the flood, Frederick was without water for some time. The flood prompted the construction of a new water system as well as the purchase of a secure water supply. (Courtesy of BTB.)

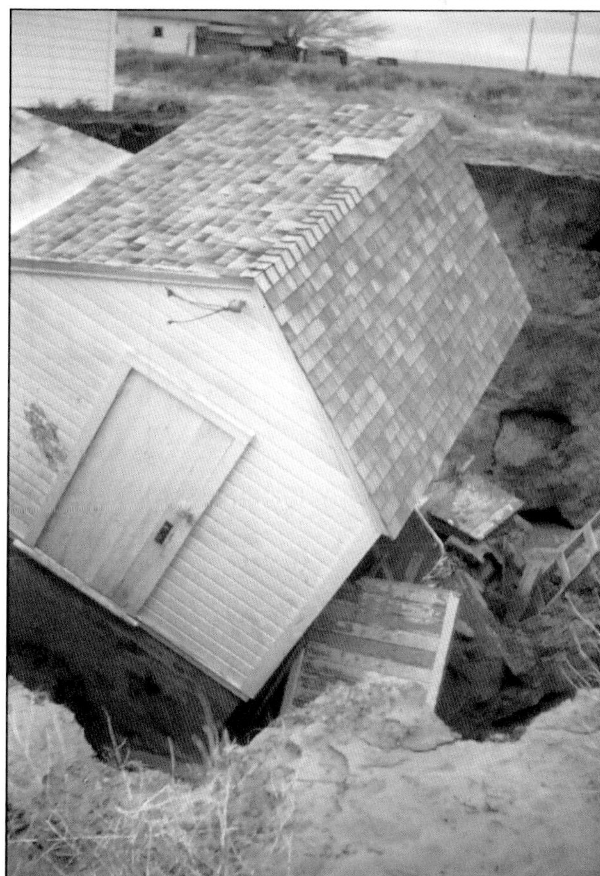

This is another view of the collapsed pump house. Because of the many mine shafts that ran under Frederick, Firestone, and Dacono, there were occasional cave-ins. Even today, local builders must be aware of the locations of old mines. (Courtesy of BTB.)

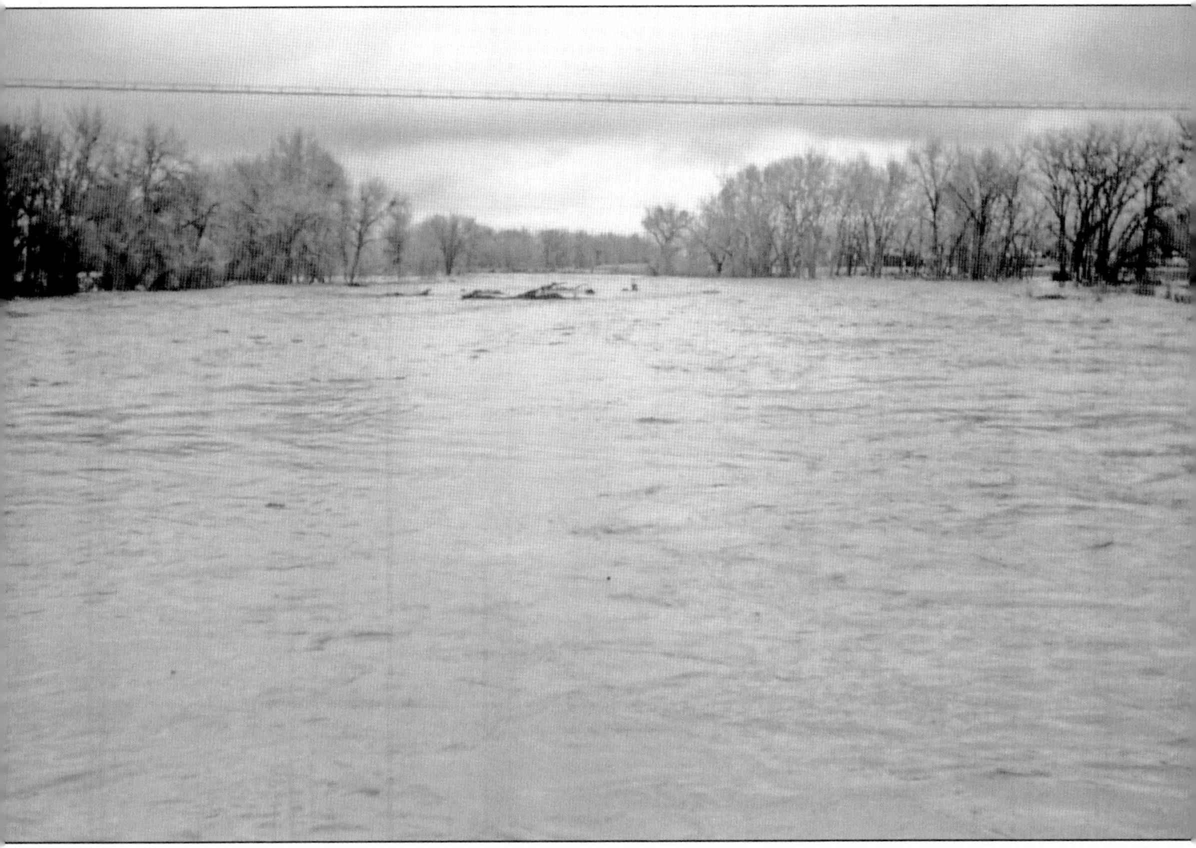

The South Platte River is seen here in full flood in 1957. The Platte is one of the major rivers of eastern Colorado and Nebraska. This photograph was taken near Fort Lupton, which is to the east of Frederick on Highway 52. Under normal conditions, the river is a fraction of the size it is in this photograph. (Courtesy of BTB.)

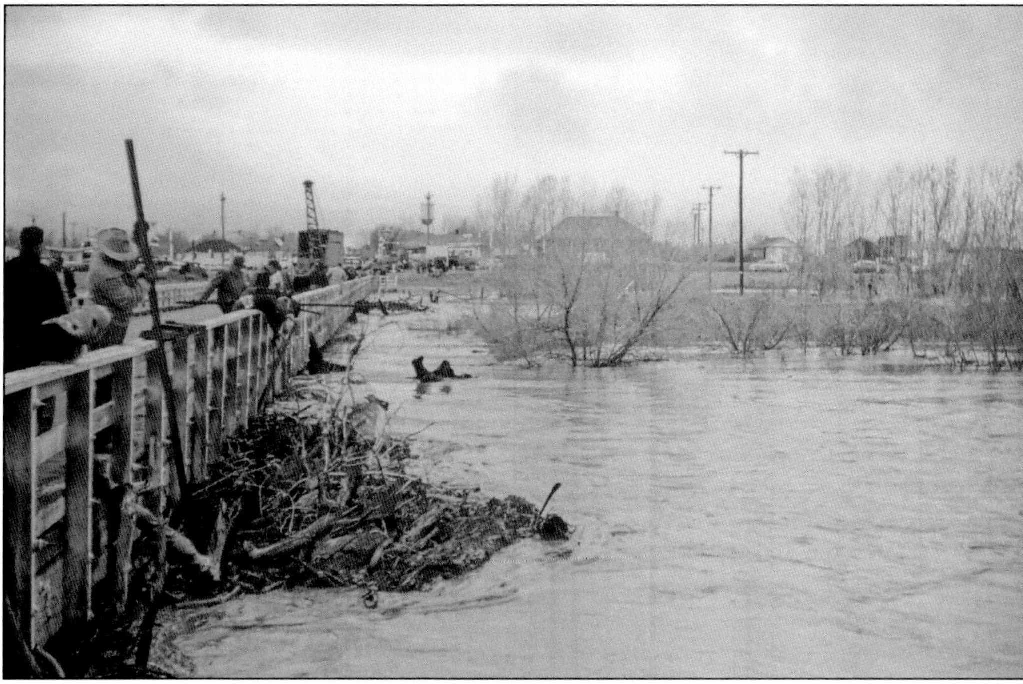

This is another view of the South Platte River at Fort Lupton. The river is normally quite shallow and not very wide, but this image shows how that completely changes during a flood. People are on the bridge trying to clear debris so that the bridge does not wash away. (Courtesy of BTB.)

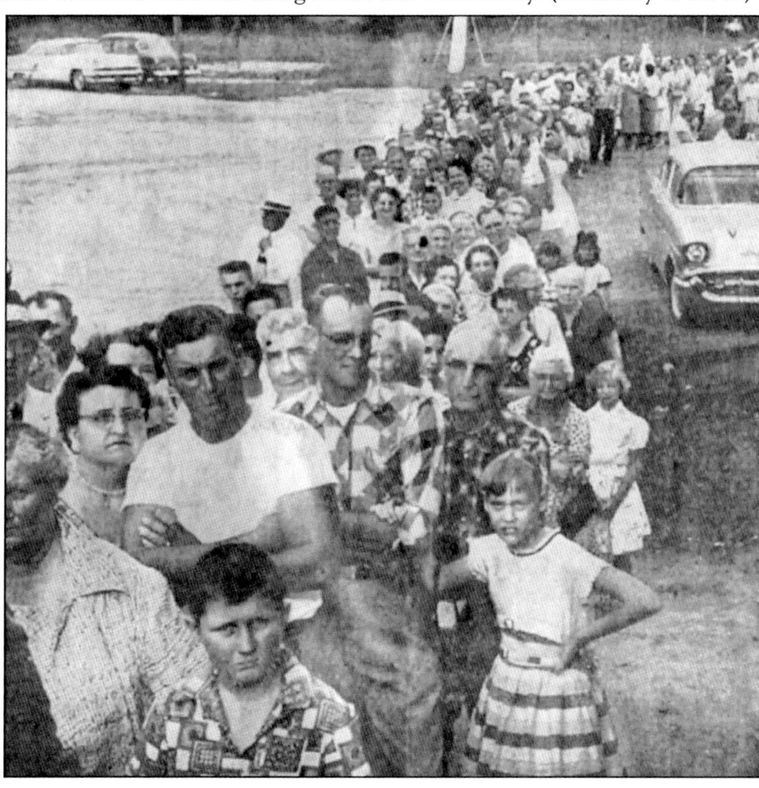

Frederick residents assembled to provide assistance after the 1957 flood. Since no financial assistance was available from the state, the townspeople had to do the best they could with their own resources. (Courtesy of the Town of Frederick.)

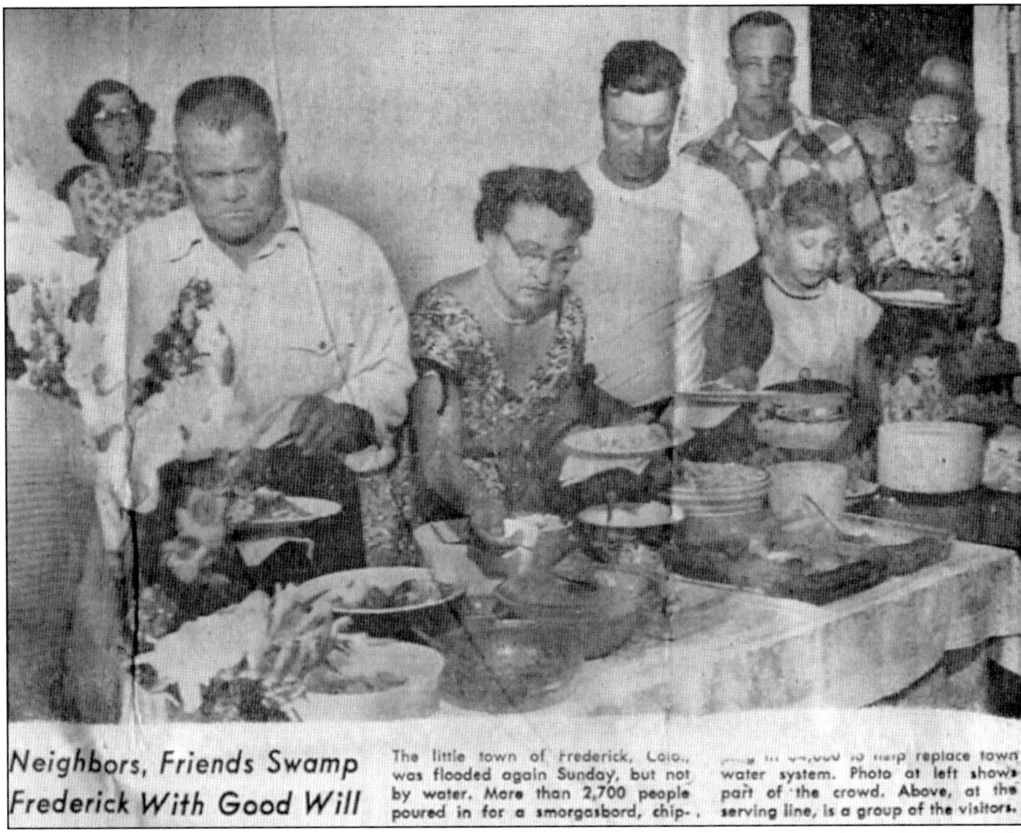

Neighbors, Friends Swamp Frederick With Good Will

The little town of Frederick, Colo., was flooded again Sunday, but not by water. More than 2,700 people poured in for a smorgasbord, chip- [illegible] to help replace town water system. Photo at left shows part of the crowd. Above, at the serving line, is a group of the visitors.

This newspaper photograph shows Frederick residents during a fundraiser after the 1957 flood. The flood damage was not limited to destroyed homes and the pump house. Many other residents had their basements flooded and lost many of their belongings. (Courtesy of the Town of Frederick.)

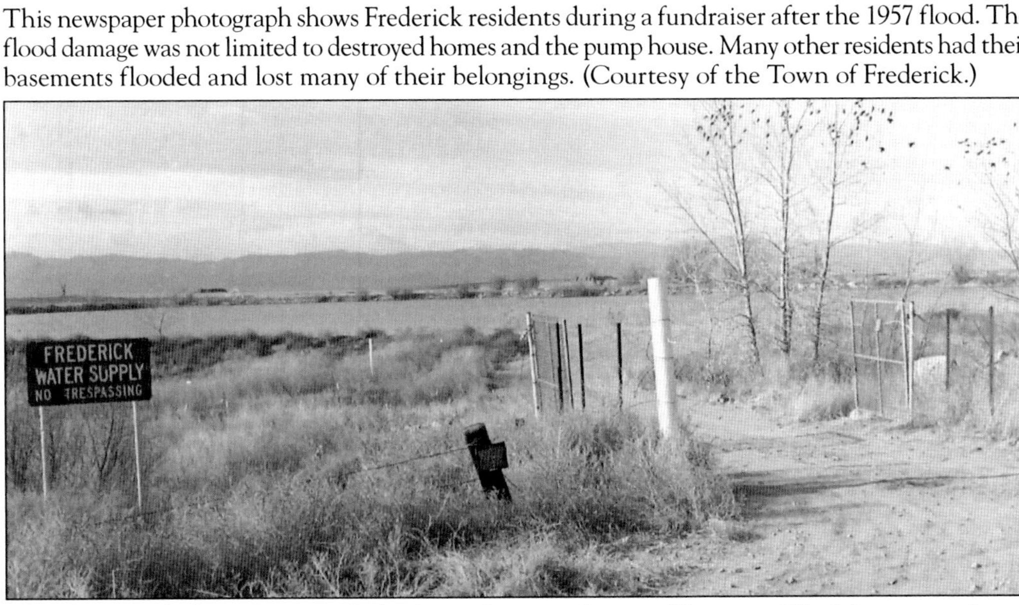

This photograph shows Firestone Lake, located just northwest of Firestone. The lake was purchased by the town of Frederick after the 1957 flood in order to provide an untainted source of water and to help with flood-control problems. Note that the sign designates the lake as "Frederick Water Supply." The lake is now known as Milavec Reservoir. (Courtesy of the Town of Frederick.)

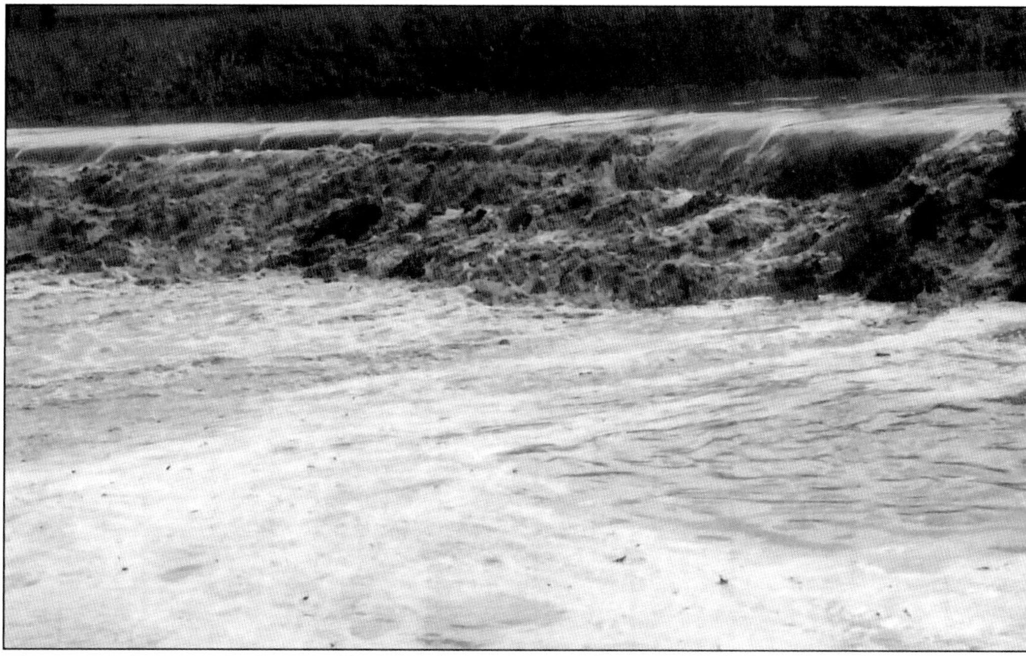

This 1960 photograph shows a flooded ditch overflowing onto Eighth Street during yet another flood. Despite all efforts to counteract flooding, Frederick is still prone to floods during periods of excessive rain. (Courtesy of the Town of Frederick.)

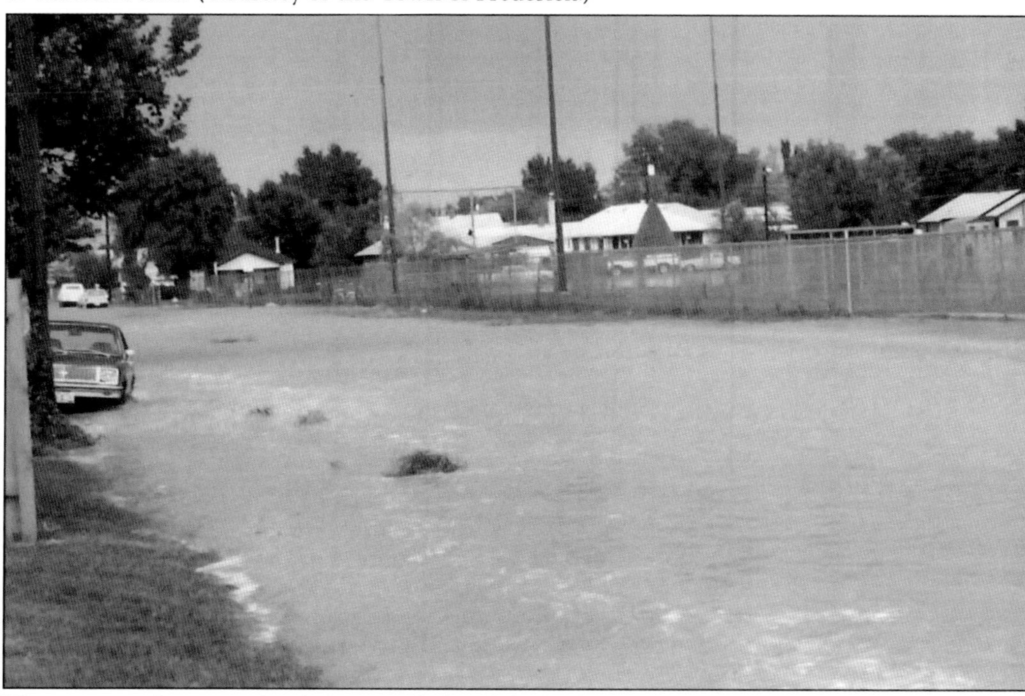

This image, taken near Sixth Avenue, behind the high school, also shows the effects of the 1960 flood. The streets around the baseball field were completely flooded. One unintended consequence of flooding was an explosion of the mosquito population, which added to the misery suffered by the town residents. (Courtesy of the Town of Frederick.)

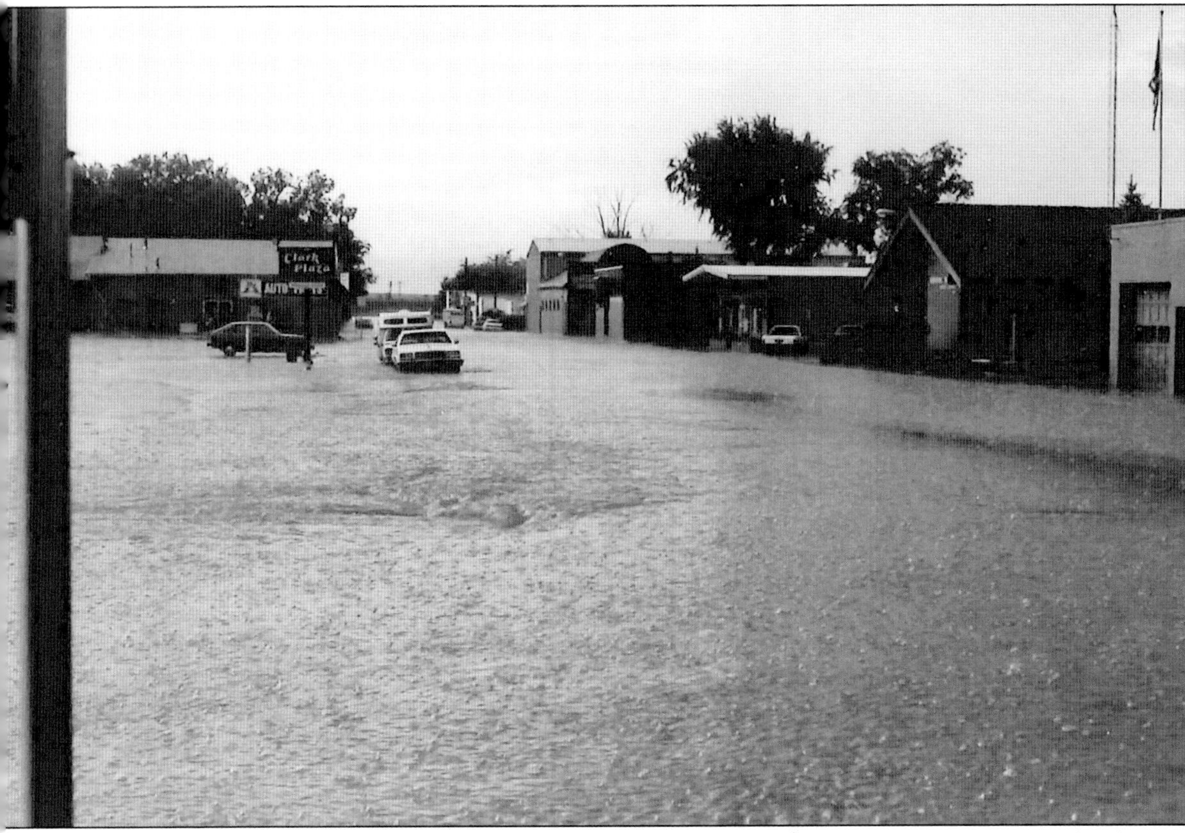

This view looks down Fifth Street during the 1998 flood. The building in the right foreground is the Frederick Police Department. To the left is Clark Plaza, the former home of Clark Lumber Company. It was still raining when the photograph was taken. (Courtesy of the Town of Frederick.)

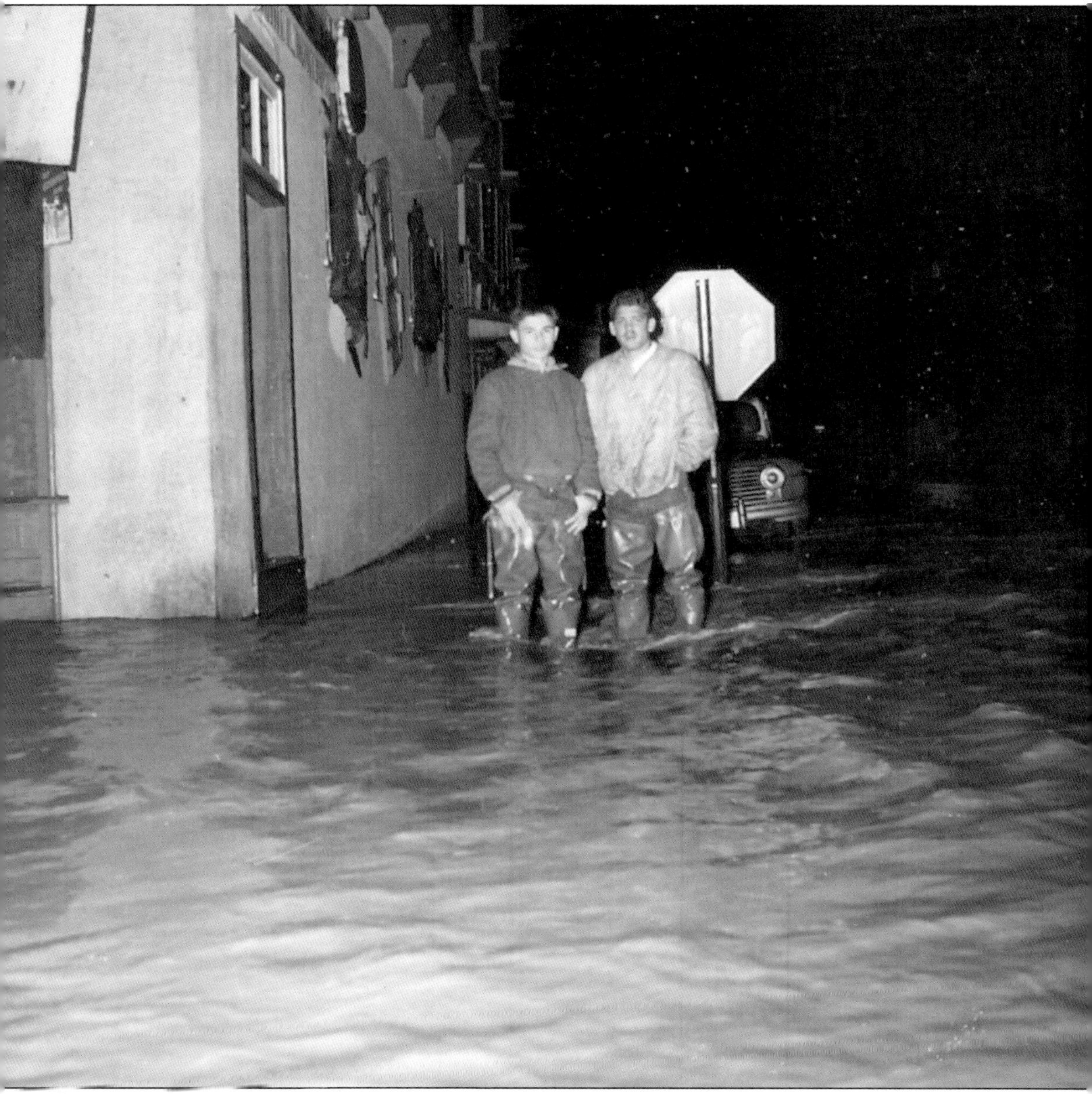

Downtown Frederick is seen here again during the 1957 flood. As evidenced, a substantial amount of water ran through Frederick. Images like this show just how floods have been so damaging to the town. Jimmy Phoutides is on the left, and Mike Hattel is on the right. (Courtesy of MLH.)

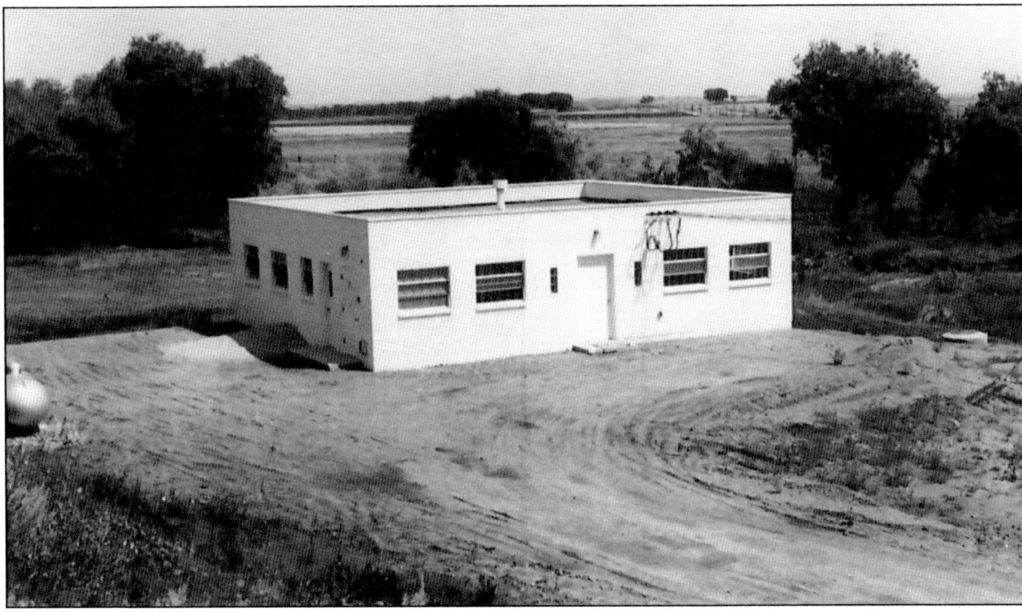

This photograph shows Frederick's new pump house, located next to Milavec Reservoir. This pump house has served the needs of Frederick residents since its construction. The field in the background was formerly the Missing Link Golf Course. Several of the greens on the nine-hole course were made of Astroturf laid on top of cement. If nobody was at the clubhouse to take greens fees, players simply put them in a box. Later, Bella Rosa Golf Course was built on the site. It is a vast improvement over the Missing Link. (Courtesy of the Town of Frederick.)

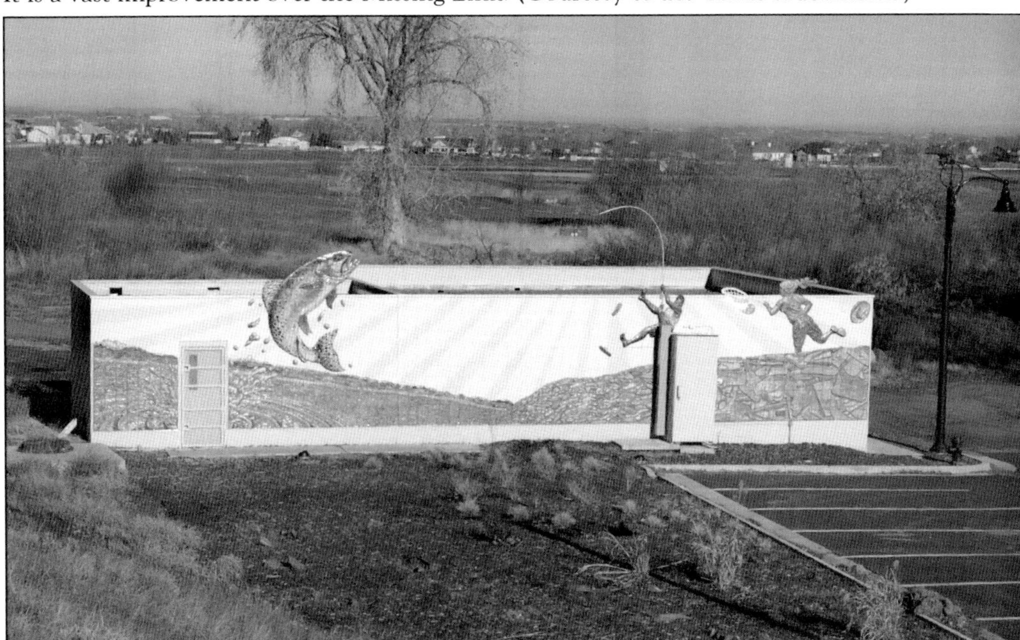

This photograph shows the pump house in 2012. This tile mural was designed by Mario Echevarria. In the background is Bella Rosa Golf Course, which is owned and maintained by the Town of Frederick. The general manager of the course, Pete Bain, is responsible for its upkeep.

Five

Expansion and Growth

In the 1930s, Frederick's population was approximately 2,000. Growth was slow, and even as late as the mid-1970s, Frederick's population was no more than 4,000 people. However, beginning in the late 1970s and continuing to the present day, Frederick has benefited from the growth of northern Colorado.

The land between the northern limits of the Denver metropolitan area and Frederick used to consist of only farms and ranches. To Frederick's north, the largest cities were Loveland and Fort Collins. To the west, the largest city was Boulder. All of these blank spaces began to fill in.

At first, businesses began to locate along the Interstate 25 corridor. With the growth of businesses came residential expansion, which worked its way north from Denver.

In the late 1990s and early 2000s, Frederick experienced a housing boom. People were drawn to the Frederick area because of its quiet and simple lifestyle. Of course, these new residents also needed additional services. New businesses relocated to the Carbon Valley area to service the needs of its new residents. Despite the growth, Frederick has retained its small-town appearance and feel.

At the present time, Frederick's population is approaching 10,000, and that figure is expected to keep growing larger. Soon, the area from northern Denver to Frederick and on to Loveland and Fort Collins will no longer have farms and ranches but will be mainly businesses and homes.

Expansion and growth have brought new challenges. The first challenge is increasing the amount of cooperation between Frederick, Firestone, and Dacono. For the most part, each community has its own distinct sets of services. Each community has its own police department, its own mayor, and its own board of trustees. While fire and rescue are a shared service, not much else is. Increasing the level of cooperation will be a constant challenge but is the goal of each town.

Annexation is the flip side of cooperation. Through the years, each town has sought to expand its boundaries through flagpole annexations. This has resulted in a crazy quilt of annexed land that makes community maps look odd indeed. The towns are driven by the lure of commercial expansion.

The biggest anomaly is the section of unincorporated Weld County called Evanston. All attempts at making this section part of either Frederick or Firestone have been fruitless, as Evanston has resisted annexation for the time being. There are no immediate plans to change its status.

One example of community members banding together to establish and provide a key service was the tri-town ambulance service. A purely volunteer organization funded through donations, the service operated since 1970. It provides an essential service to members of the tri-town communities despite facing constant funding issues.

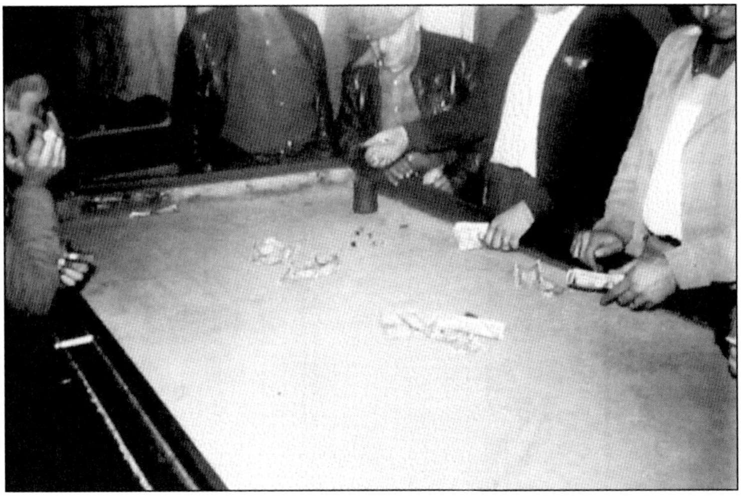

This photograph shows gambling occurring in Nick's Place in 1952. The cup in the center of the image identifies the game as some variation of dice. The gentleman wearing the hat with the cigar has been identified only as Nick or Pappas, the proprietor. This was not the only place where gambling could be found in Frederick. (Courtesy of PP.)

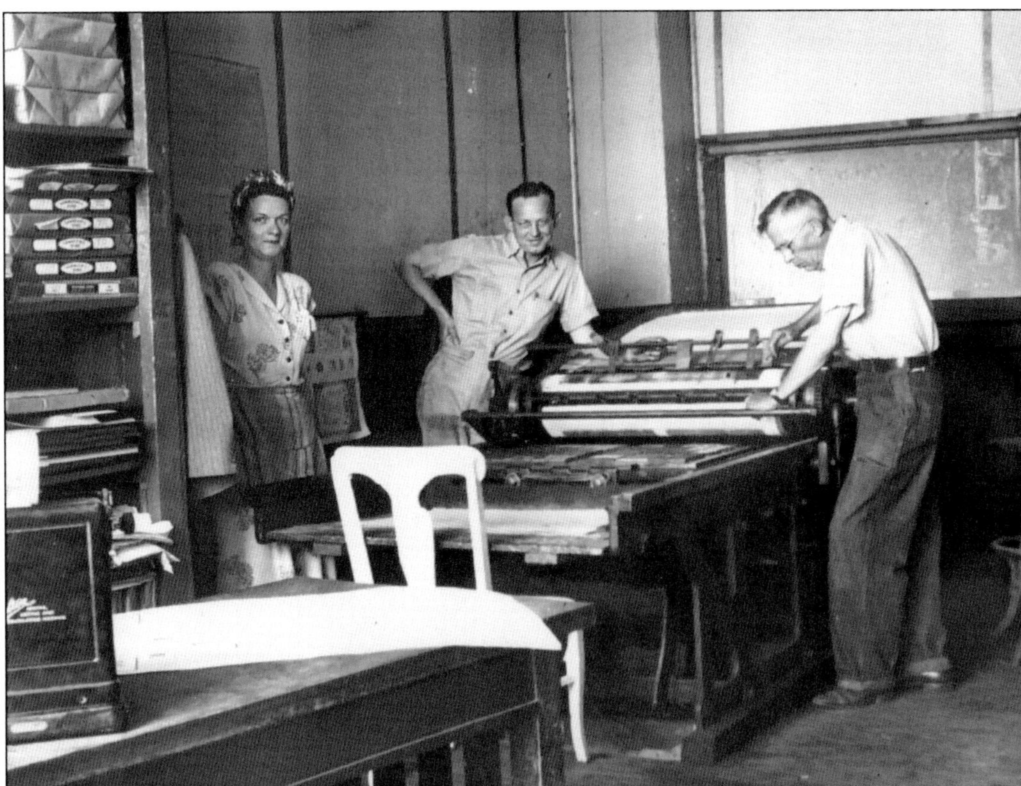

The original office of the *Farmer and Miner* newspaper is seen here. The paper was later sold but was still published in Frederick for many years. (Courtesy of the Town of Frederick.)

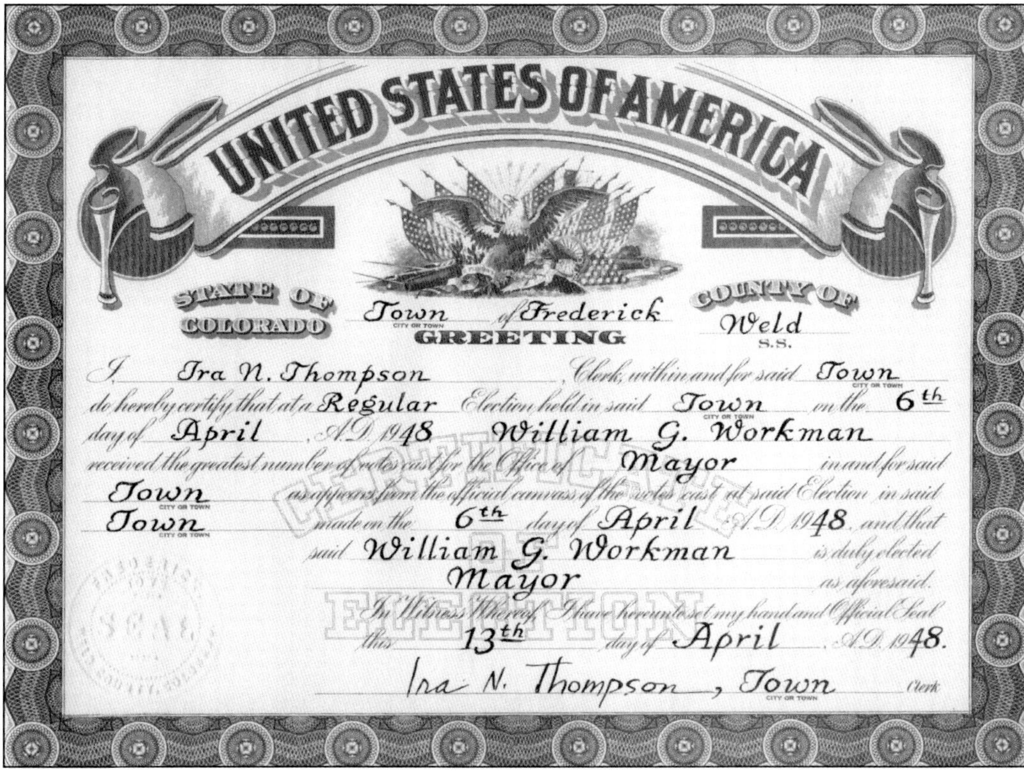
UNITED STATES OF AMERICA

STATE OF COLORADO — Town of Frederick (CITY OR TOWN) — COUNTY OF Weld S.S.

GREETING

I, Ira N. Thompson, Clerk, within and for said Town (CITY OR TOWN) do hereby certify that at a Regular Election held in said Town (CITY OR TOWN) on the 6th day of April, A.D. 1948 William G. Workman received the greatest number of votes cast for the Office of Mayor in and for said Town (CITY OR TOWN) as appears from the official canvass of the votes cast at said Election in said Town (CITY OR TOWN) made on the 6th day of April A.D. 1948, and that said William G. Workman is duly elected Mayor as aforesaid.

CERTIFICATE OF ELECTION

In Witness Whereof, I have hereunto set my hand and Official Seal this 13th day of April A.D. 1948.

Ira N. Thompson, Town (CITY OR TOWN) Clerk

This certificate, signed in 1948, memorialized William G. Workman as the mayor of the town of Frederick. Note that the town clerk was Ira N. Thompson, whose father, I.W. Thompson, was mayor both before and after Workman's one year as mayor. I.W. Thompson was mayor from July 1945 to 1948 and then from 1949 to 1955. (Courtesy of the Town of Frederick.)

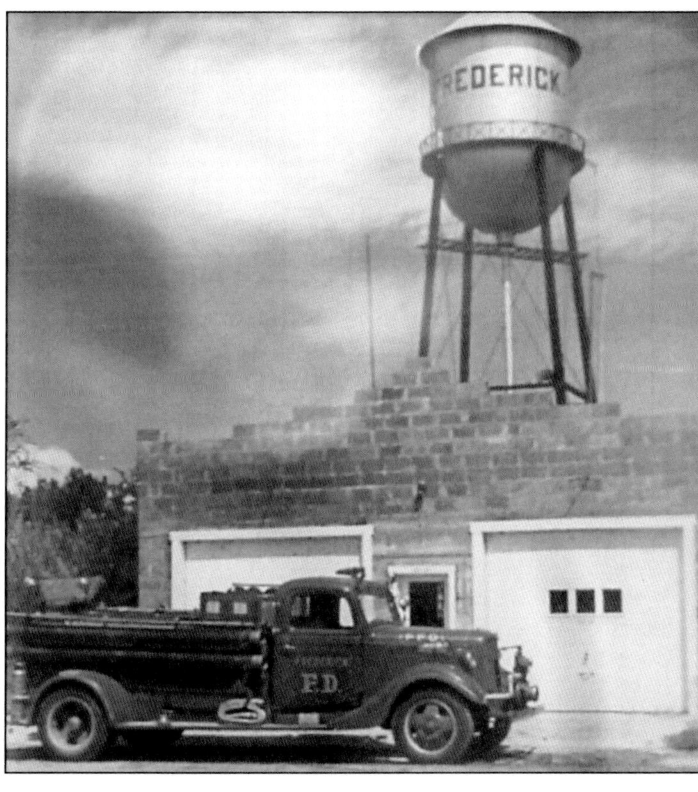

The Frederick Volunteer Fire Department's garage is seen here on Oak Street. The town water tower is behind it. The fire engine in front of the building was purchased by the town and later destroyed in a fire. (Courtesy of the Town of Frederick.)

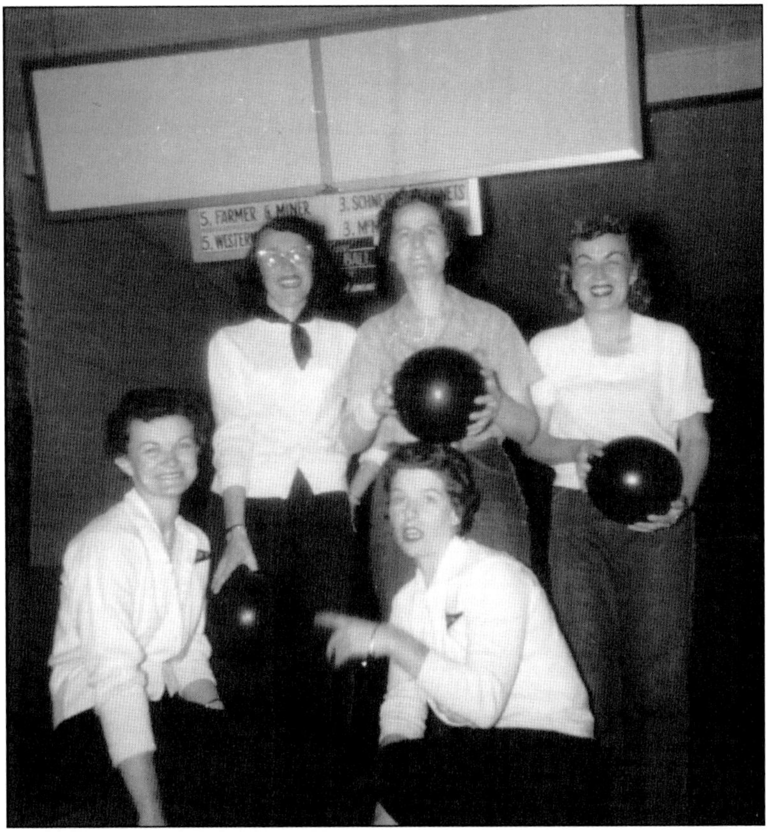

These bowlers in the Farmer and Miner Bowling League pose for a team photograph in 1957. They are, from left to right, (kneeling) Mary Lepore and Leona Dixon; (standing) Gloria Betron, Dorothy Phillips, and Betty Maes. (Courtesy of CC.)

Frederick's seventh-grade class poses for their class picture with teacher Jim Harrison in 1965. (Courtesy of CC.)

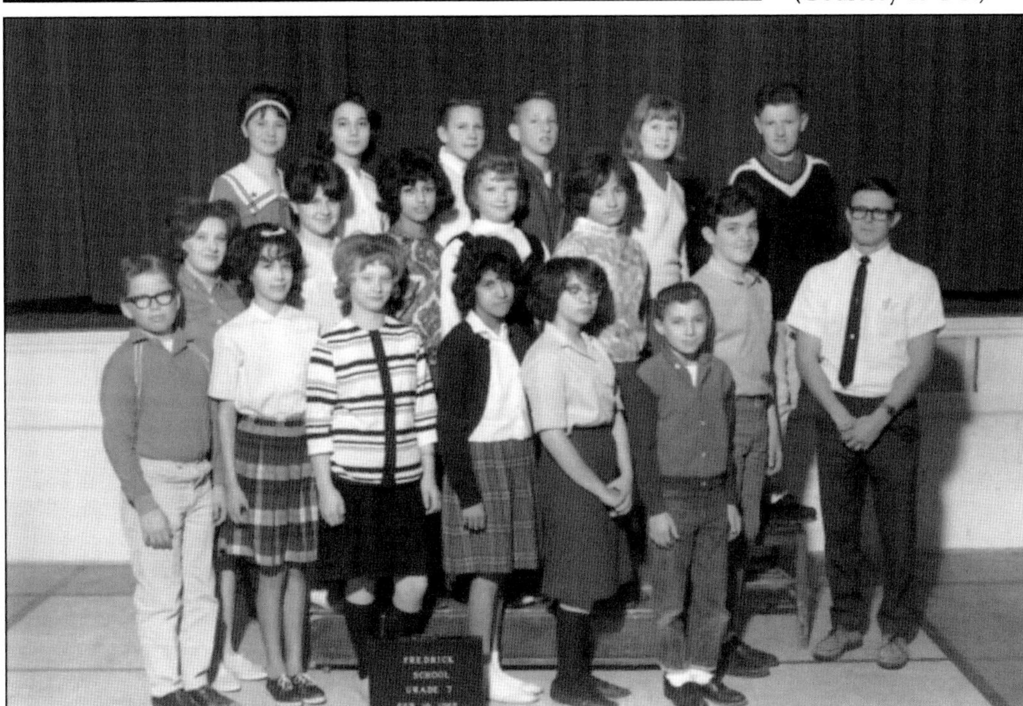

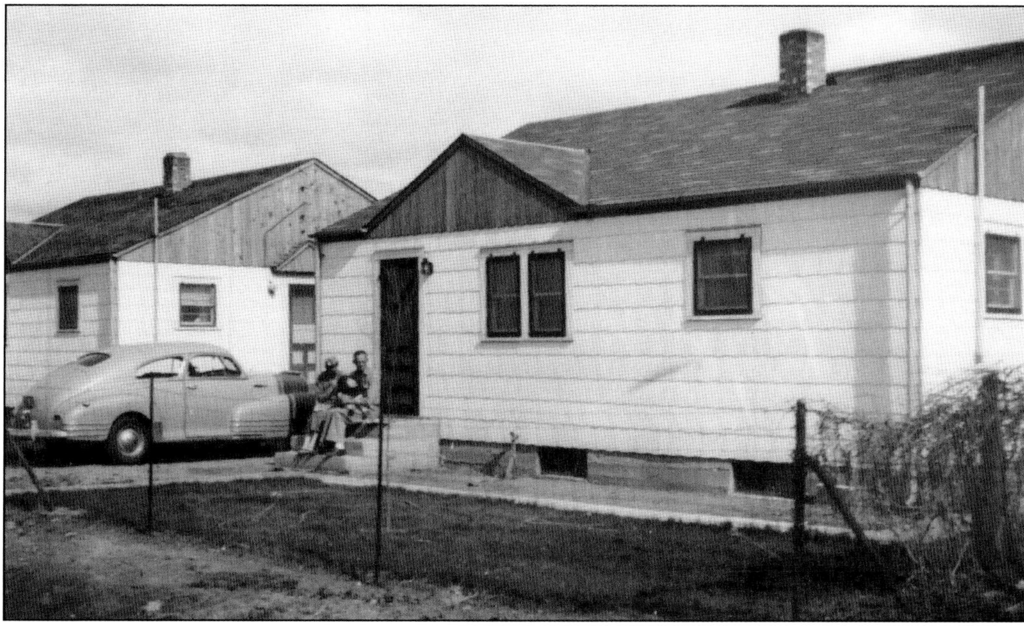

This photograph shows the Workman family home in Frederick. This photograph was taken around 1950. (Courtesy of WF.)

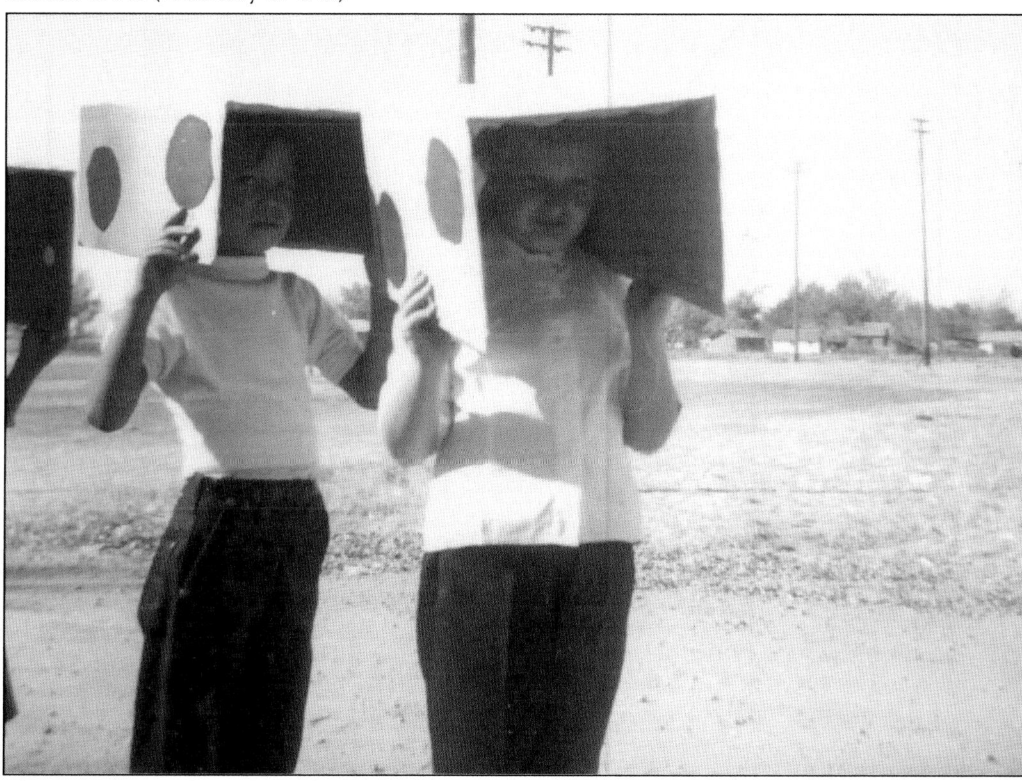

These young students form the head of the caterpillar parade, one of the many parades held in Frederick. Standing from left to right are Gloria Morales and Cathy Dixon. This photograph was taken in 1958. (Courtesy of CC.)

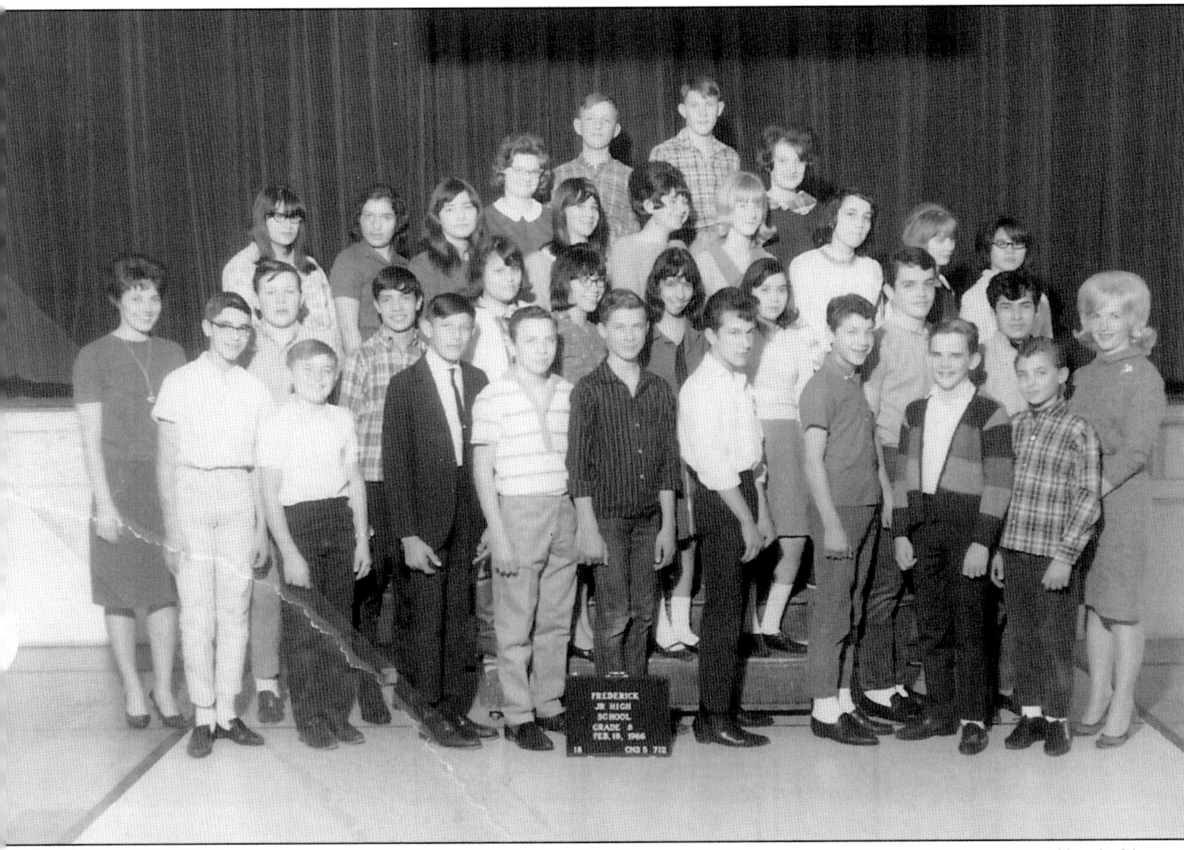

Frederick's eighth-grade class poses for their picture in 1966 with teachers Nancy Best (far left) and Mary Lou Waitz (far right). (Courtesy of CC.)

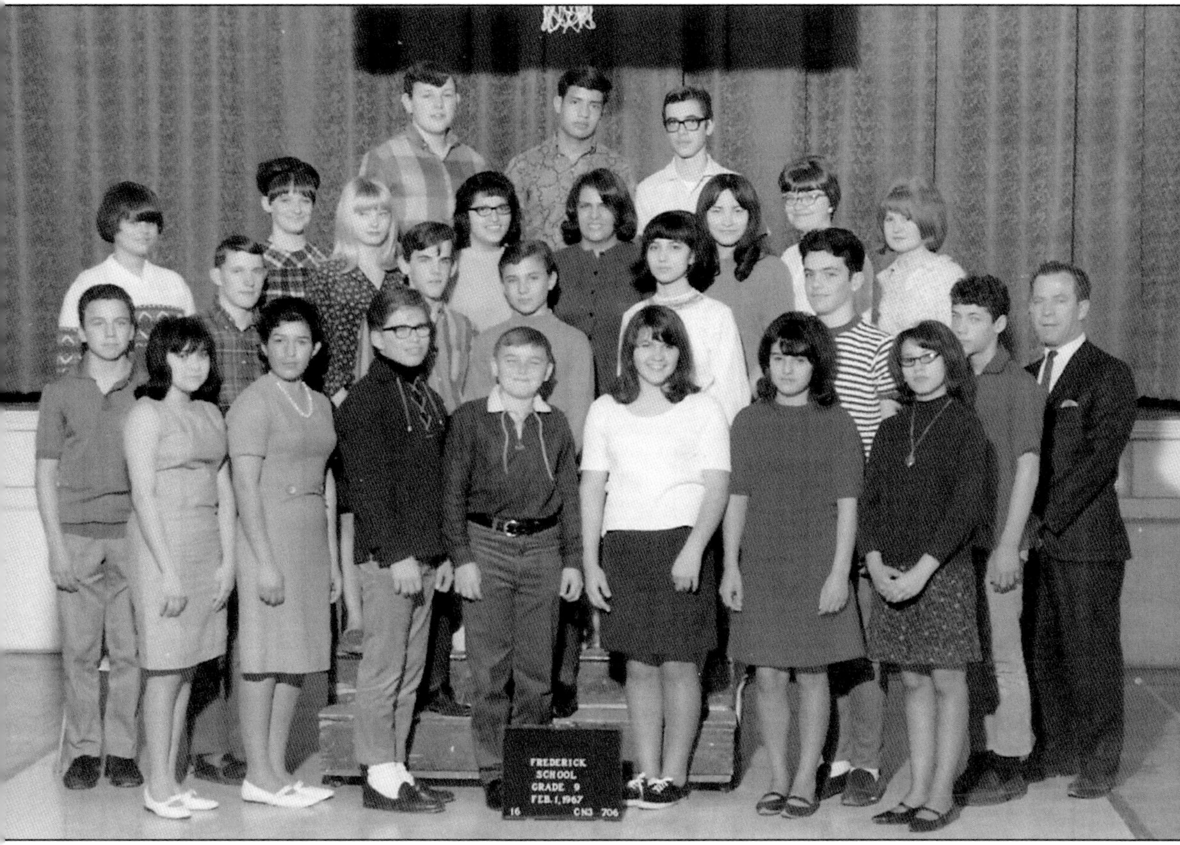

Frederick High School's ninth-grade class is seen here in 1967. On the far right is longtime Frederick resident Carmen DeSantis. At various times, DeSantis has served as a school custodian, bus driver, and teacher. (Courtesy of CC.)

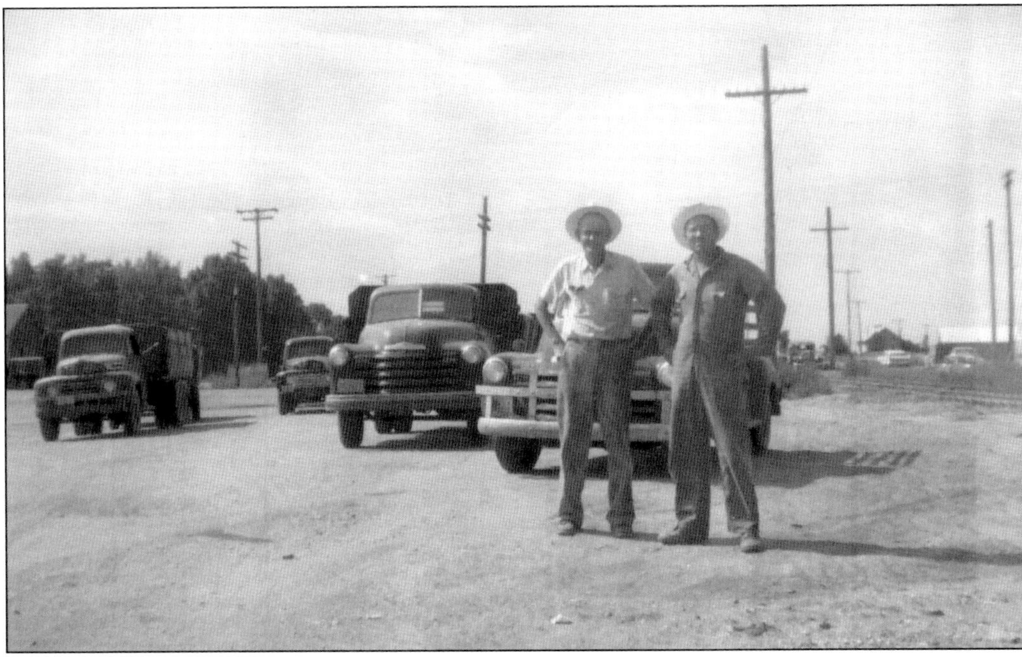

With the demise of coal mining, farming became the chief industry in Frederick and throughout northern Colorado. In one respect, the two occupations were similar: in order to get paid, the product had to be weighed. This photograph shows farmers waiting to weigh their grain at the Denver Elevators during harvest time in 1958. (Courtesy of CC.)

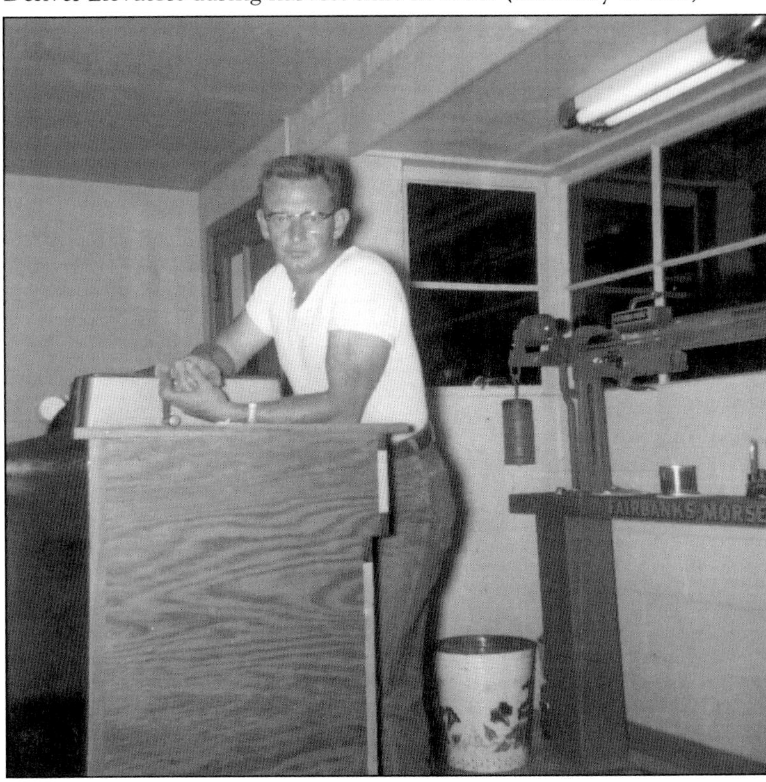

The Dixon family purchased Denver Elevators in the early 1960s, and the name changed to Dixon Feed & Grain. Marvin Dixon is seen here at the scale in the grain elevator office in 1955. (Courtesy of CC.)

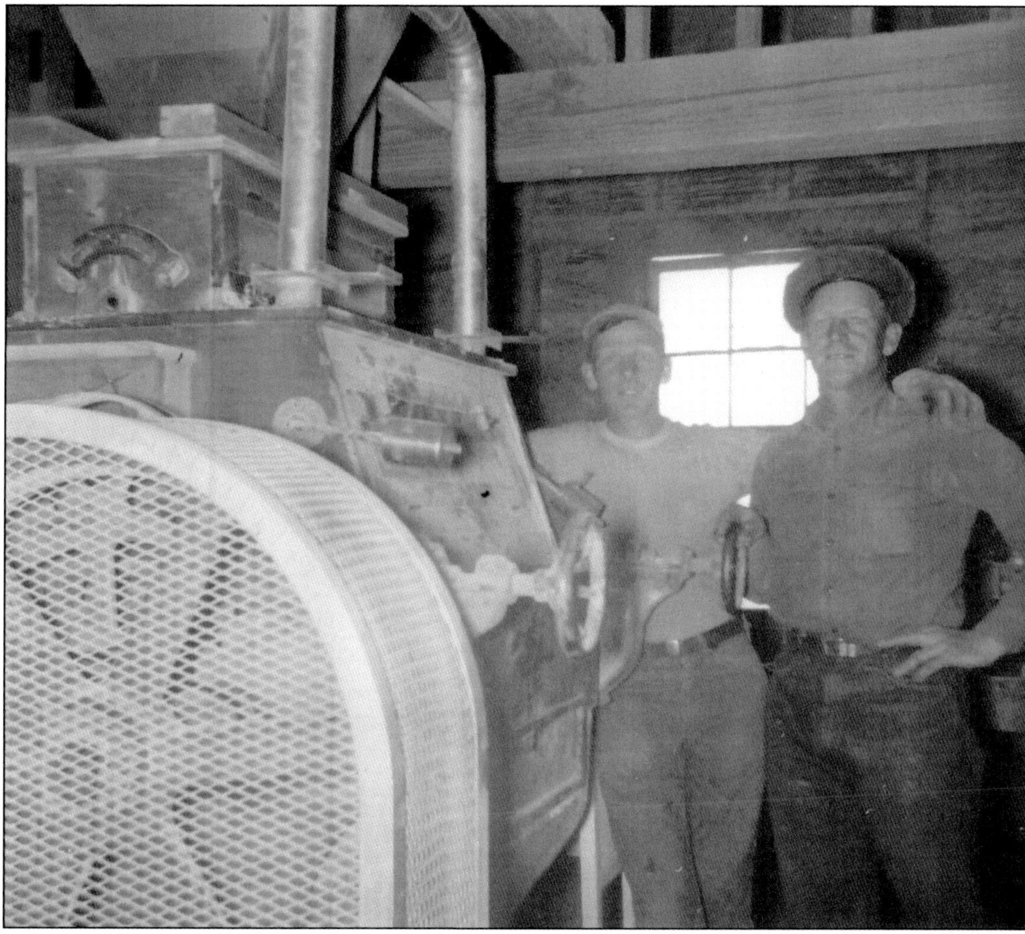

Sam Cook (left) and Harold McKaye, employees at Denver Elevators, stand in front of the boiler. This photograph was taken in 1955. (Courtesy of CC.)

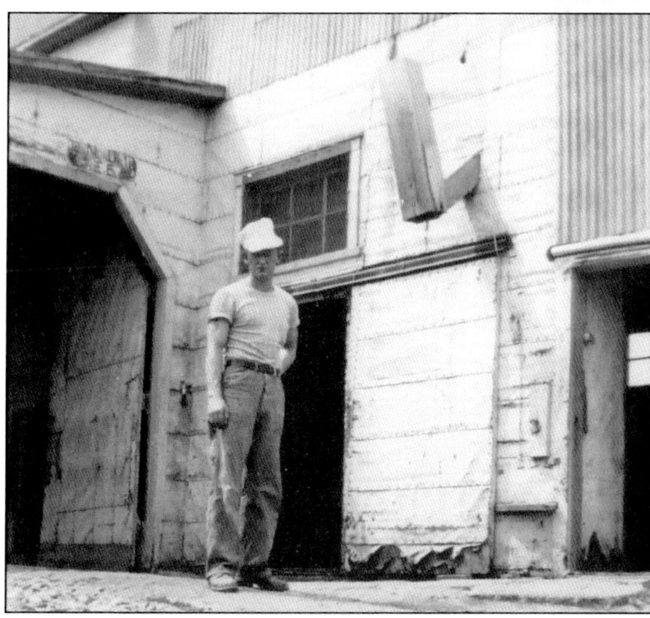

Ed Gero, an employee at the grain elevator, is seen here in 1946. Gero died of complications from a work injury in 1948. Mining was not the only hazardous occupation in Frederick. (Courtesy of CC.)

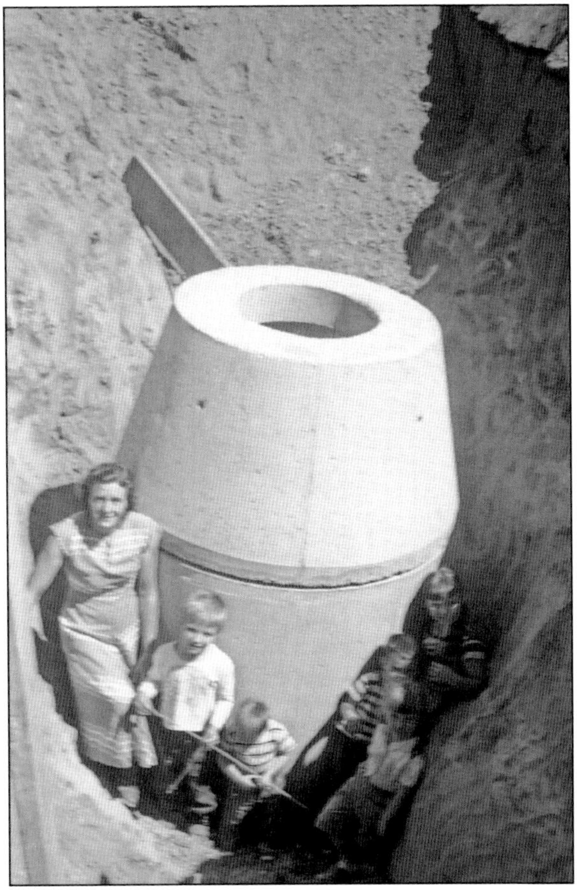

This photograph shows a completed manhole structure. From left to right are Elvera Melavick, David Irwin, Bud Baker, Trudy Chuck, and Linda Baker. It is hard to imagine anyone today being allowed this close to a construction site. (Courtesy of BTB.)

Frederick's streets were not paved until the early 1960s. This photograph shows sewer installation and street paving in Frederick. (Courtesy of BTB.)

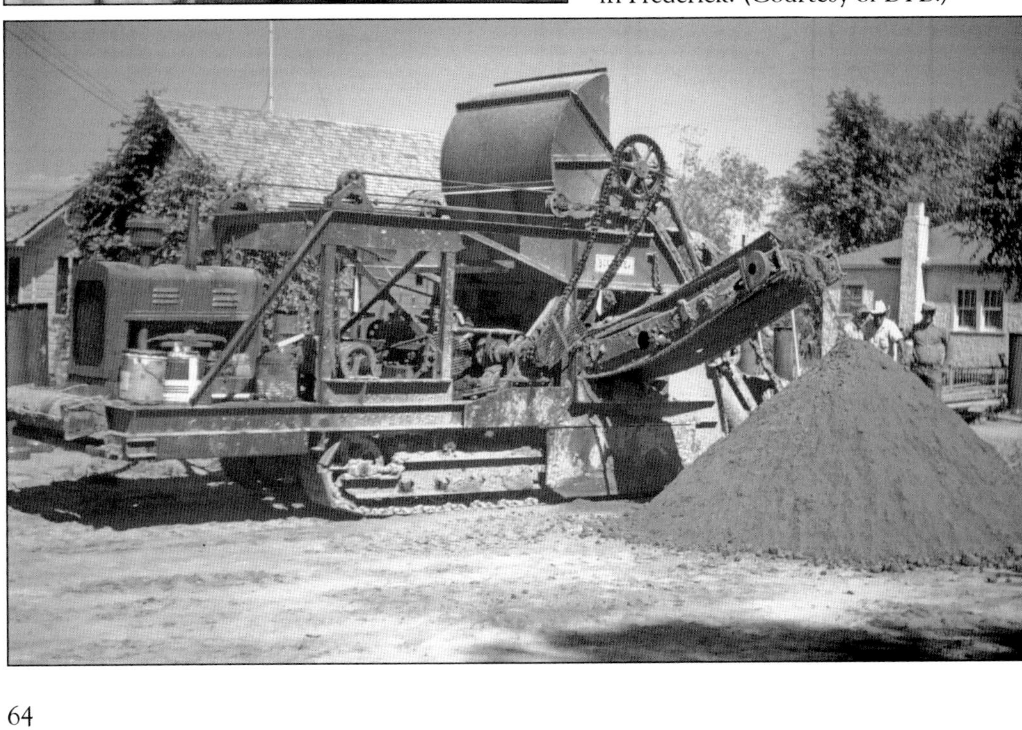

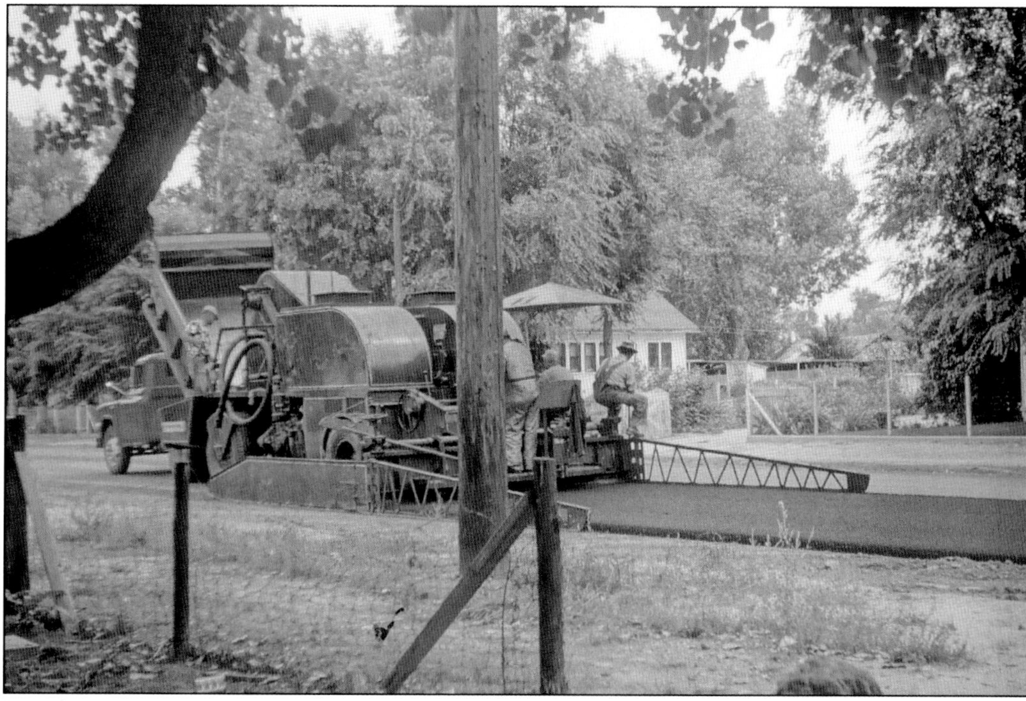

Paved streets were a vast improvement over the gravel and dirt streets residents had endured until the early 1960s. The installation of sewer lines was also greatly appreciated. (Courtesy of BTB.)

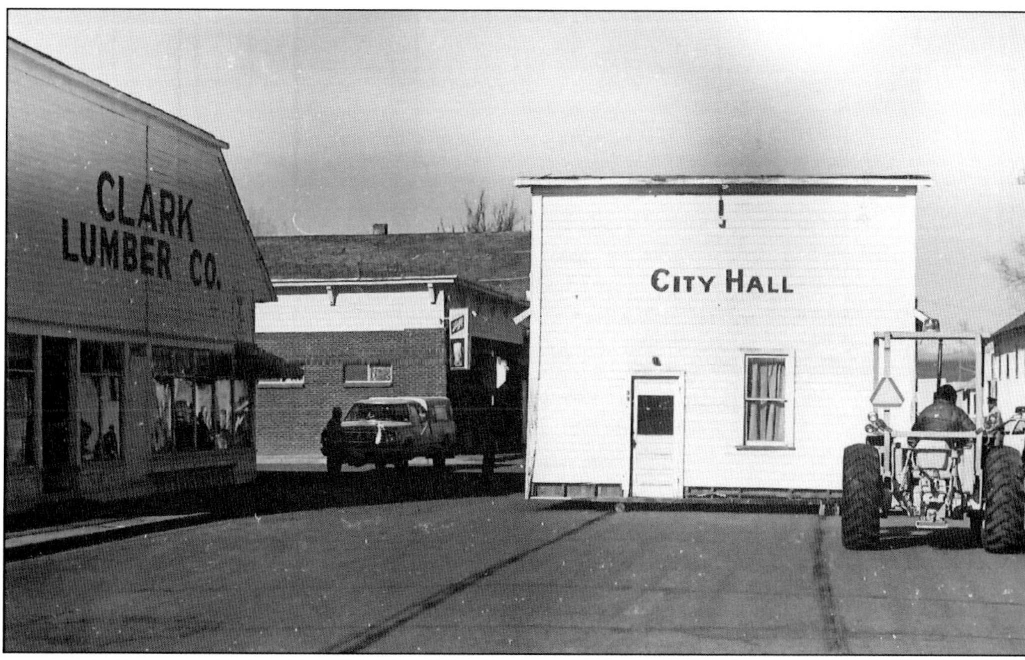

The old city hall was moved to make room for the Frederick Police Department. The false front has been removed in this photograph, but it was later replaced. The city hall was headed to its new home in Crist Park. On the left is Clark Lumber Company, one of the oldest businesses in Frederick. (Courtesy of the Town of Frederick.)

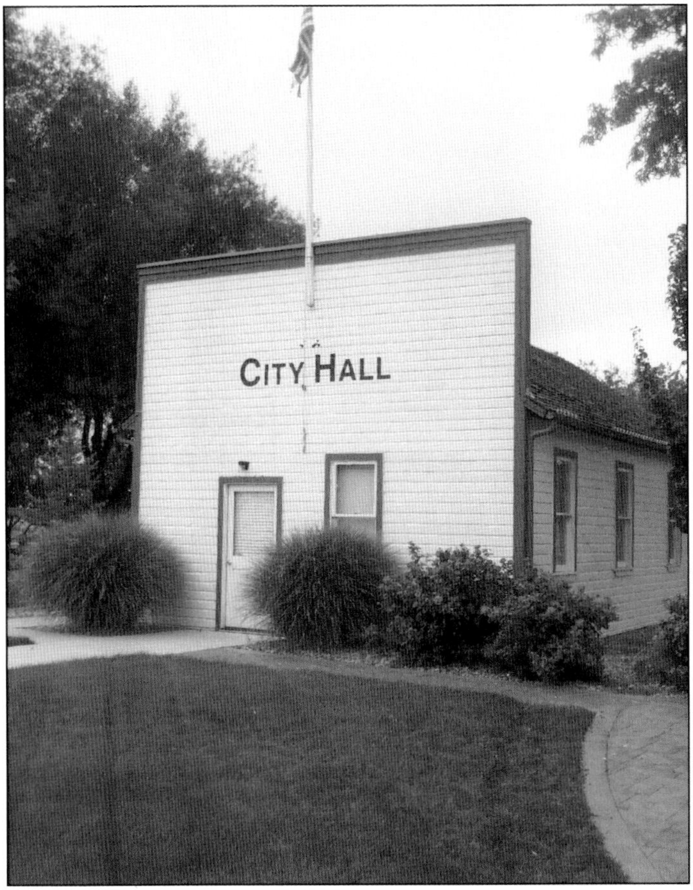

The old city hall is seen here in its new home. The false front was reinstalled and the area around it was landscaped. To the right of the city hall is the Miners' Memorial. Prior to city hall being refurbished in 1999, it was used to store Christmas decorations. In the late 1990s, local interest in preserving the structure grew. The old city hall was designated a state historical landmark on January 26, 2012. (Courtesy of the Town of Frederick.)

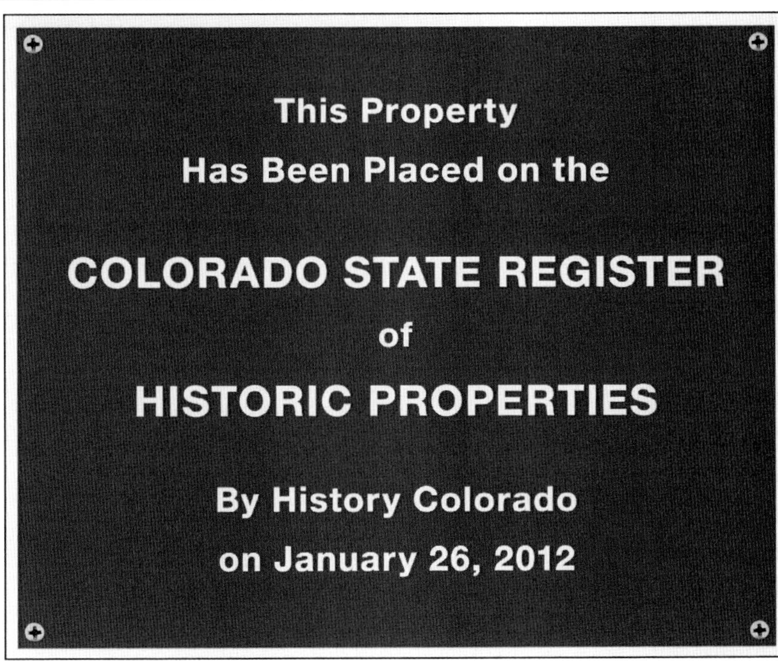

This plaque, designating the old city hall as a state historical landmark, was unveiled during the Miners Day celebration in September 2012. The designation was awarded in recognition of the unique architecture of the building., as well as the city hall's role in the history of Frederick and the surrounding areas. (Courtesy of the Town of Frederick).

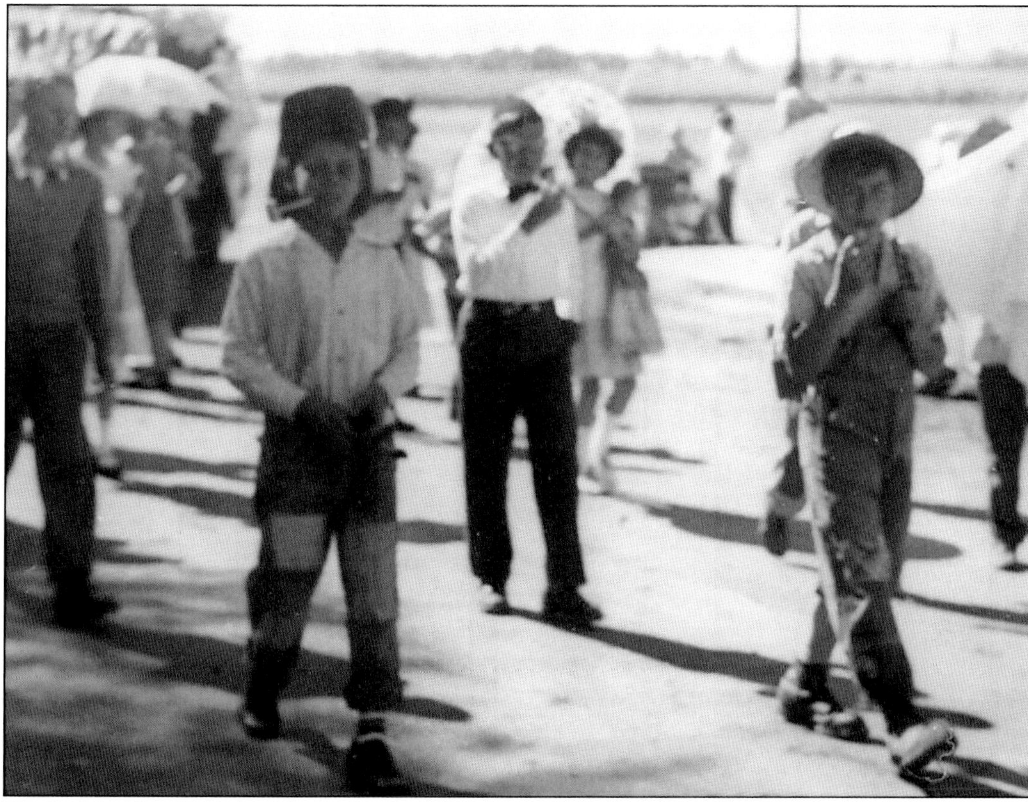

This 1948 photograph shows a Frederick parade featuring Tom Sawyer and Huck Finn. The part of Huck Finn (the boy with the corncob pipe) was played by Mike Hattel, who still lives in Frederick today. (Courtesy of the MLH.)

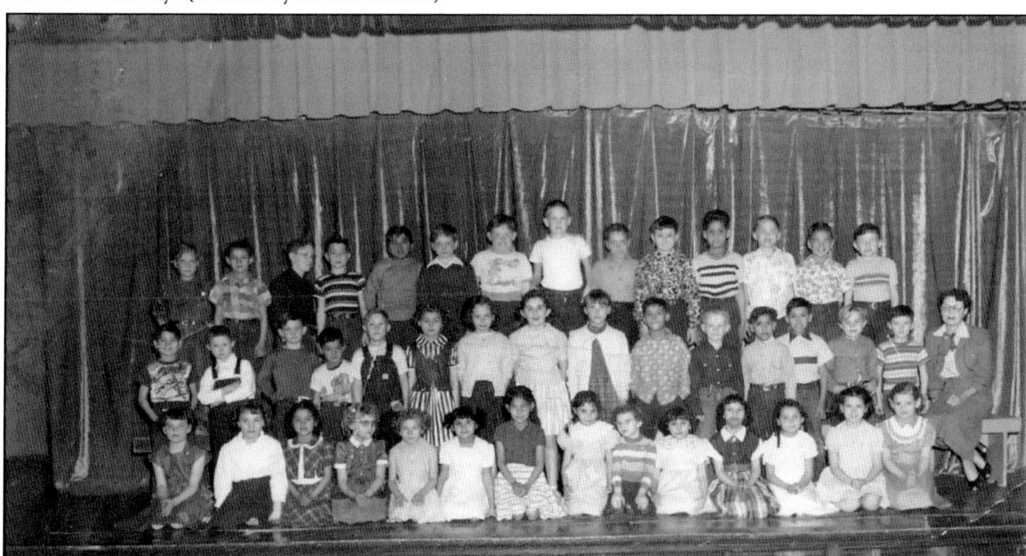

This is an undated photograph of a Frederick Elementary School class. Frederick Elementary School closed in 2013. (Courtesy of the Town of Frederick.)

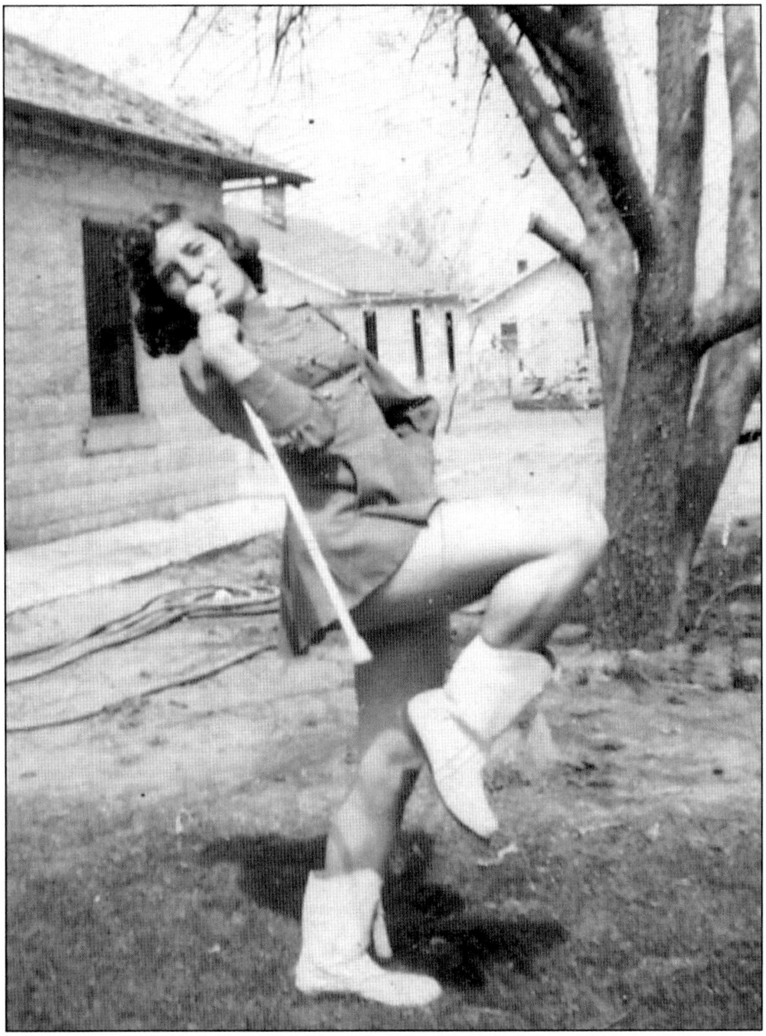

Cheerleader Liberta Hattel performs her routine for the camera in 1955. (Courtesy of MLH.)

Downtown Frederick has hosted many high school parades. This parade is forming in front of the Sunshine Tavern, which was also known as the El Patio Inn. To the left is the town barbershop. (Courtesy of the Town of Frederick.)

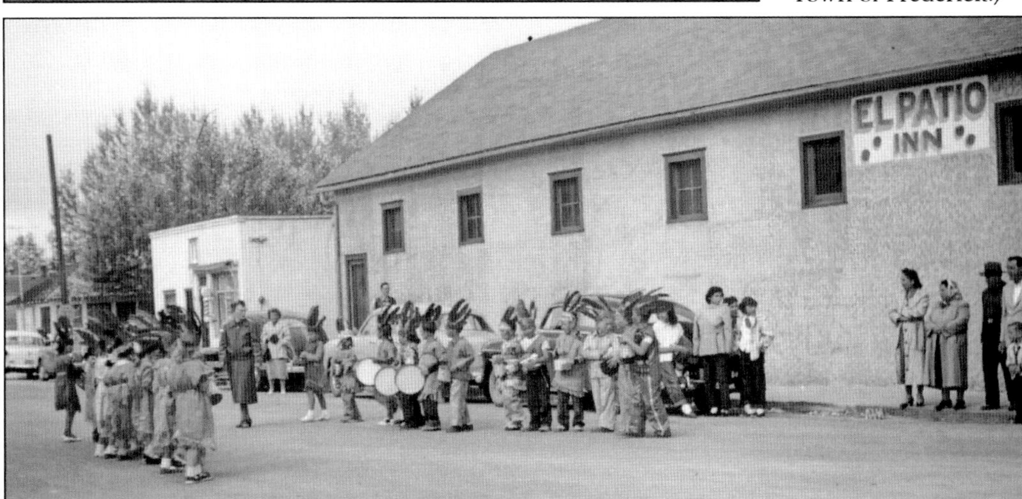

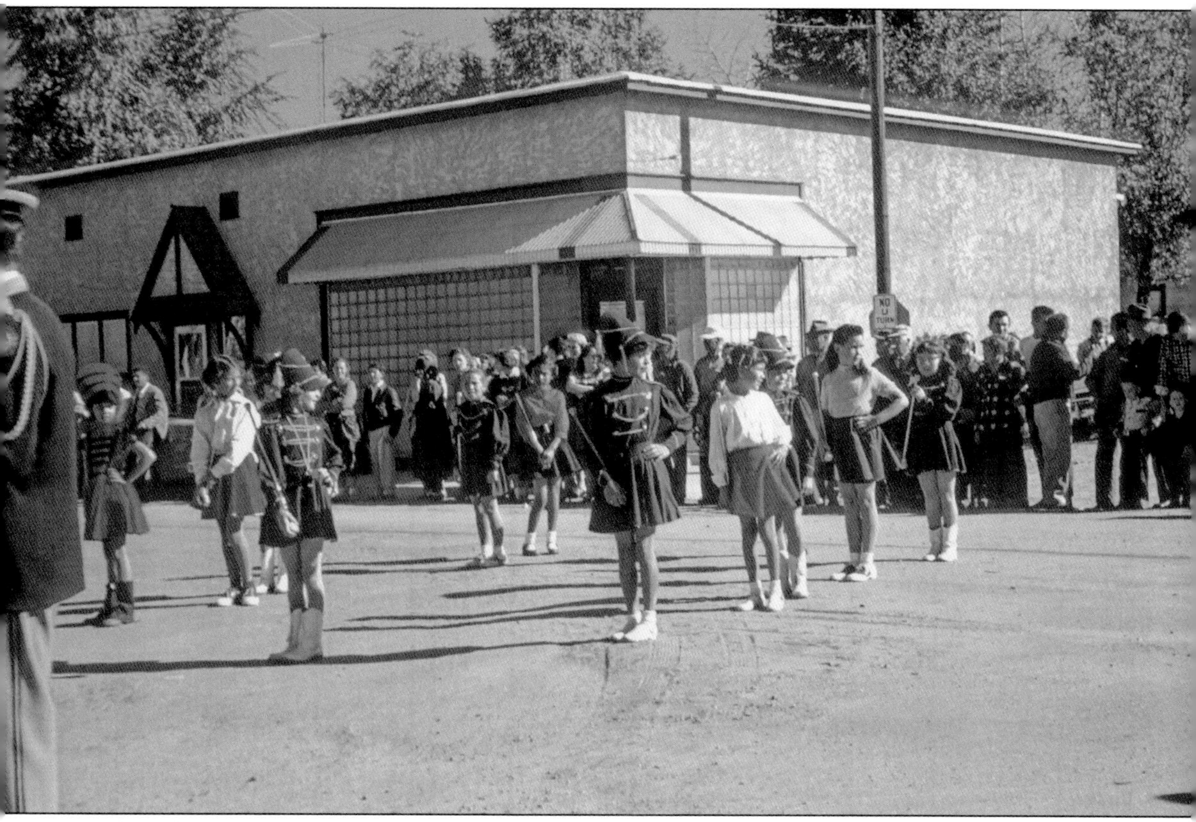

Another school parade is seen here. The building in the background is the rectory for St. Theresa's Catholic Church. School parades were always well attended by town residents. (Courtesy of the Town of Frederick.)

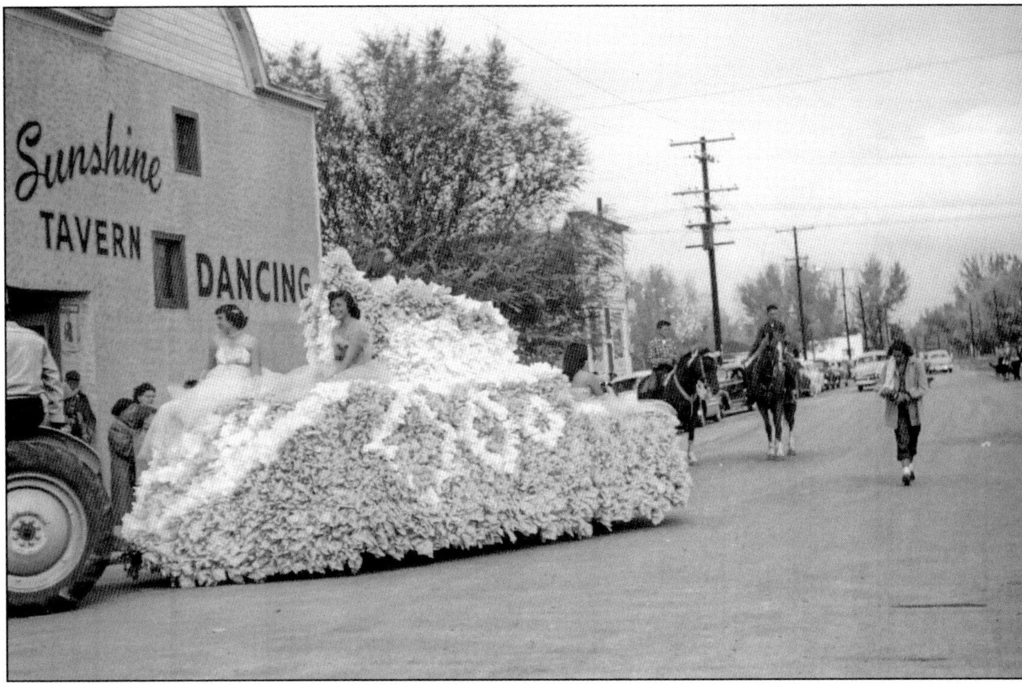

A homecoming parade float makes the turn around the Sunshine Tavern. The building in the left background is the former office of the *Farmer and Miner* newspaper. (Courtesy of the Town of Frederick.)

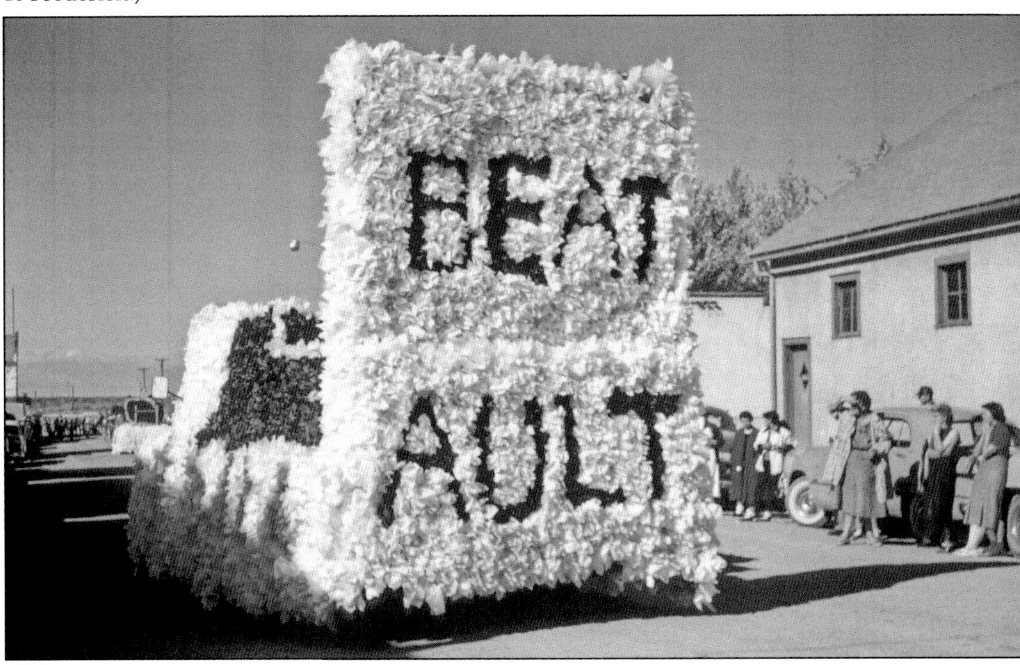

The picture of this homecoming float, heading west along Fifth Street, offers a view of the mountains west of Frederick in the left background. Ault is a town northeast of Frederick. To play against Ault, the Frederick High School football team had to travel at least an hour. (Courtesy of the Town of Frederick.)

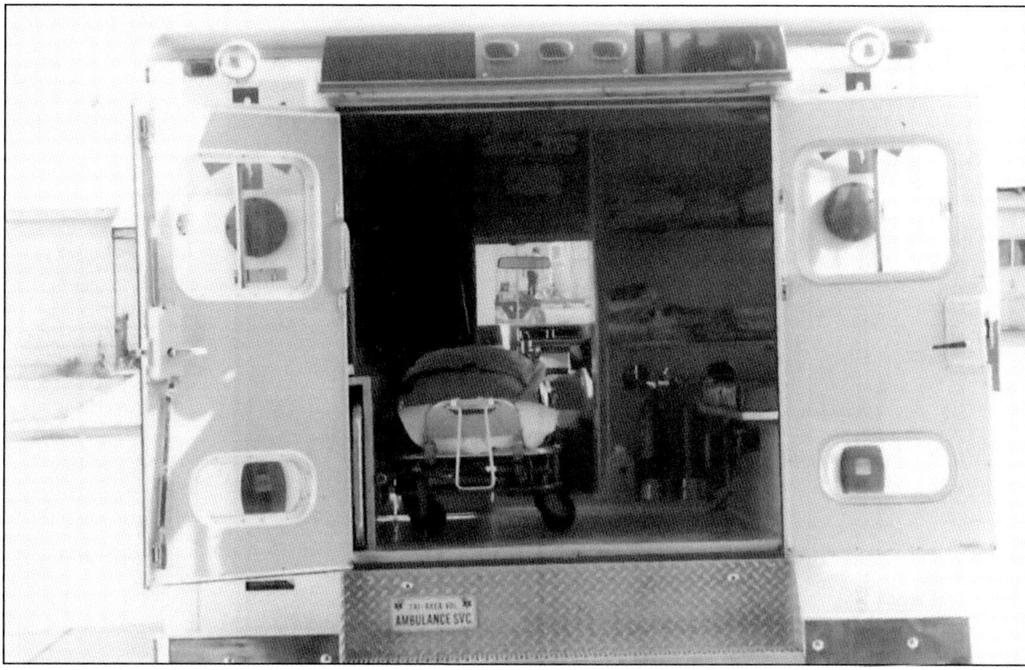

This ambulance was used by the Tri-Area Valley Ambulance Service (TAVAS). The purely voluntary service was established in 1971. In its first year of operation, the service answered 300 calls. (Courtesy of the Town of Frederick.)

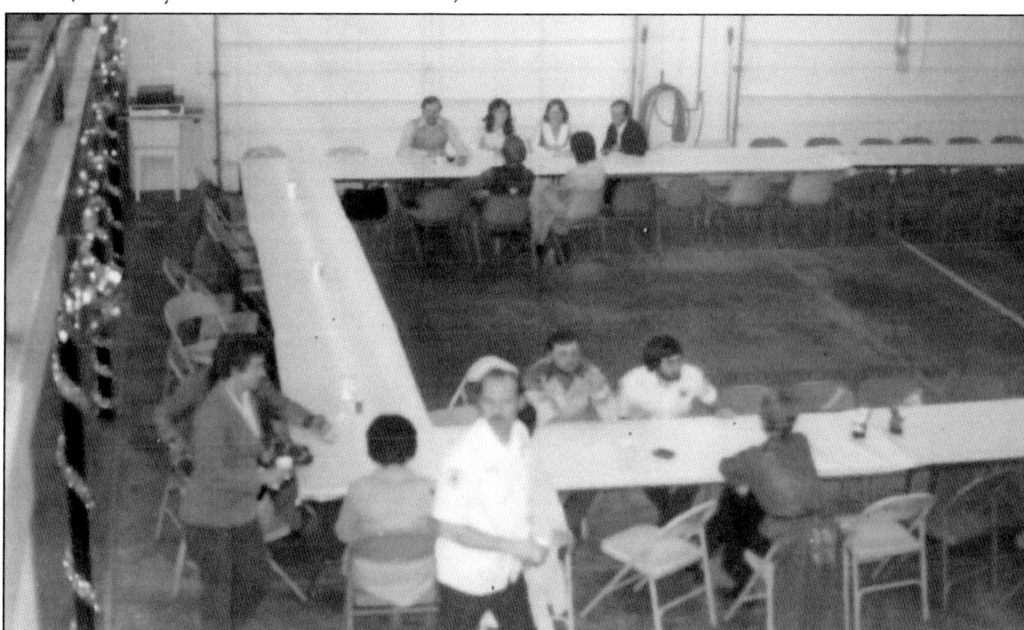

This image shows one of the many fundraising events used to keep TAVAS in operation. At first, people went from door to door to raise money. A community picnic served as its first organization meeting. Within two months, $2,200 was collected, which represented one half of what was needed. In order to obtain funding, TAVAS sold $10 family memberships. (Courtesy of the Town of Frederick.)

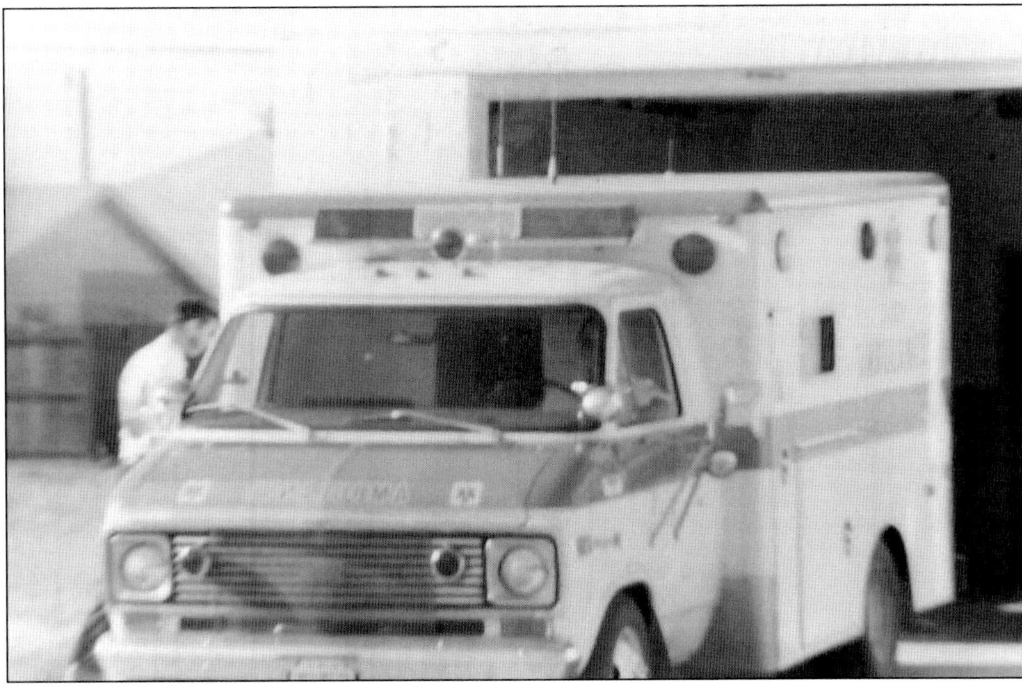

This is another ambulance used by TAVAS. A great deal of time and effort went into finding appropriate ambulances for the service. It was hoped that the service could receive state and federal funds. However, in order to receive funds, it needed to be associated with a town government. Legal liability discouraged any of the town governments from associating with TAVAS. In order to overcome this hurdle, the group incorporated as a nonprofit organization. This allowed donations to be tax deductible and helped donations grow. (Courtesy of the Town of Frederick.)

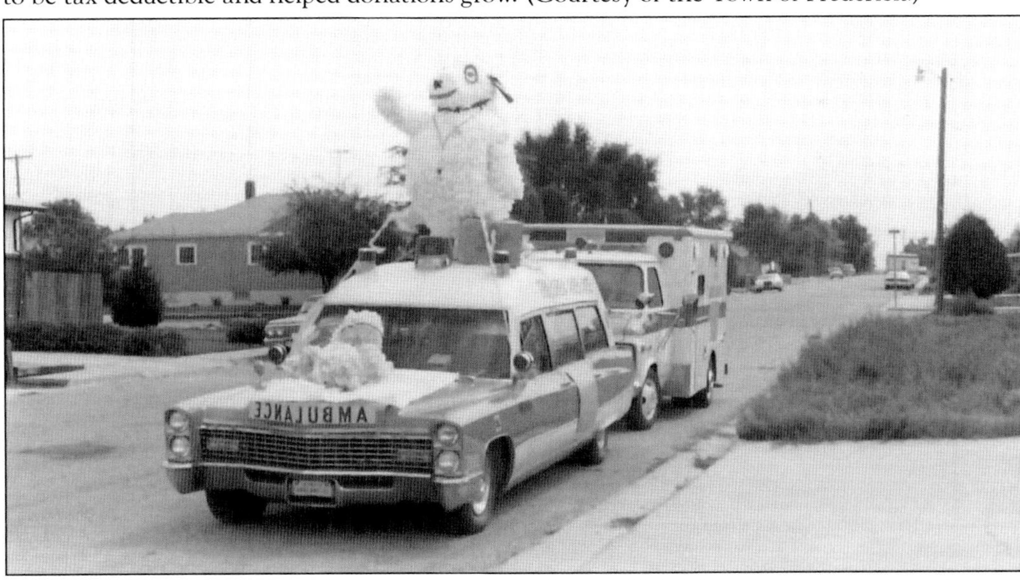

This photograph shows a fundraising event using the two TAVAS ambulances. The ambulance service depended solely on donations from residents and local towns. Still today, none of the volunteers receive payment. By 1980, the service had 14 emergency medical technicians and 30 certified first-aid workers and EMT observers. (Courtesy of the Town of Frederick.)

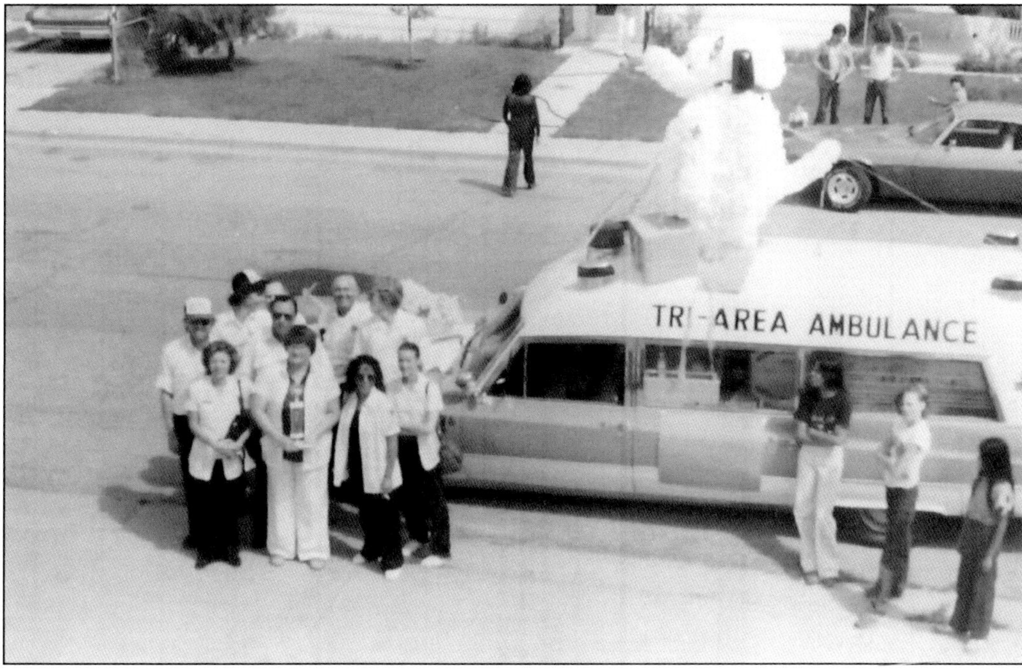

Volunteers stand in front of one of the TAVAS ambulances. Note the dog on the roof of the ambulance during this fundraising event. (Courtesy of the Town of Frederick.)

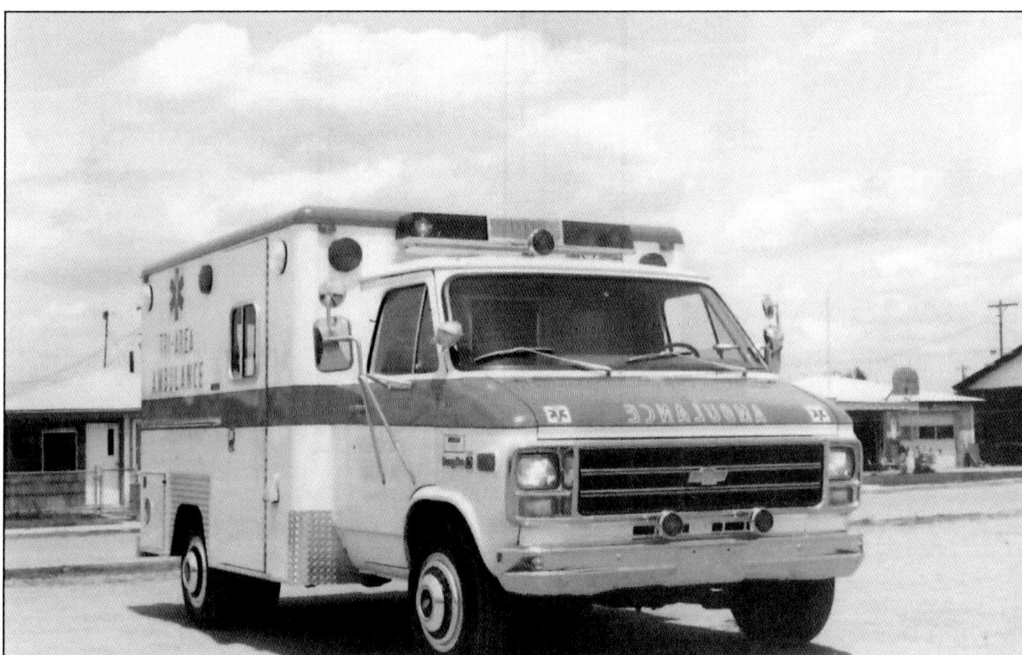

One of the TAVAS ambulances is seen here. By 1980, the service required an annual budget of $28,000 to provide medical supplies and maintain the ambulances. Money was a constant problem, but contributions came from the local towns and were greatly appreciated. (Courtesy of the Town of Frederick.)

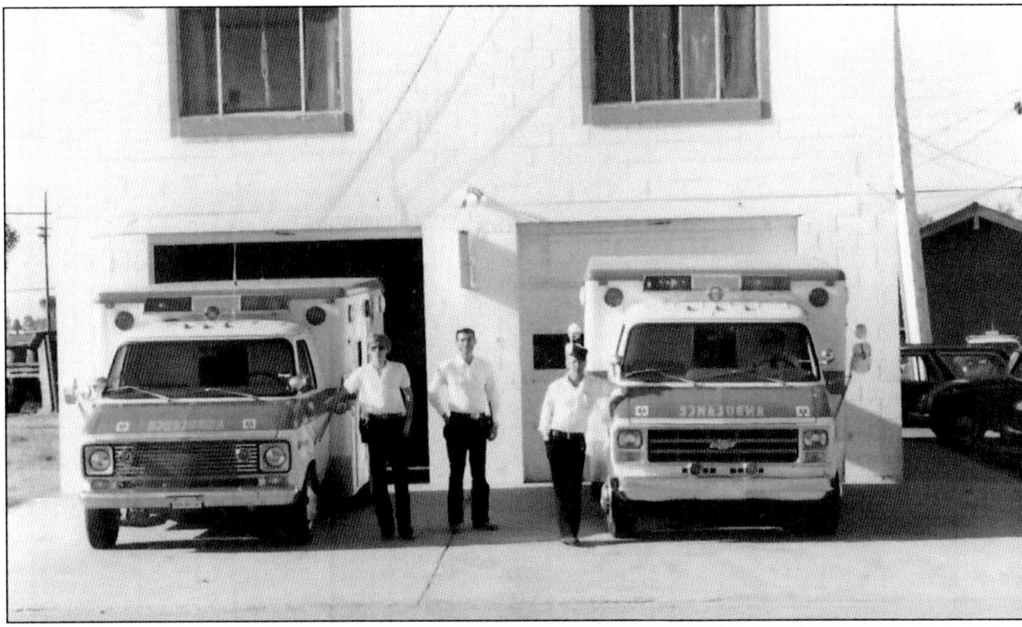

By 1980, TAVAS had two ambulances and its own place to keep them. The service was created after an emergency involving a small child. The existing service took nearly two hours to respond. The residents of Frederick, Firestone, and Dacono felt this was too long. They recognized the need for a local service that would provide faster service. (Courtesy of the Town of Frederick.)

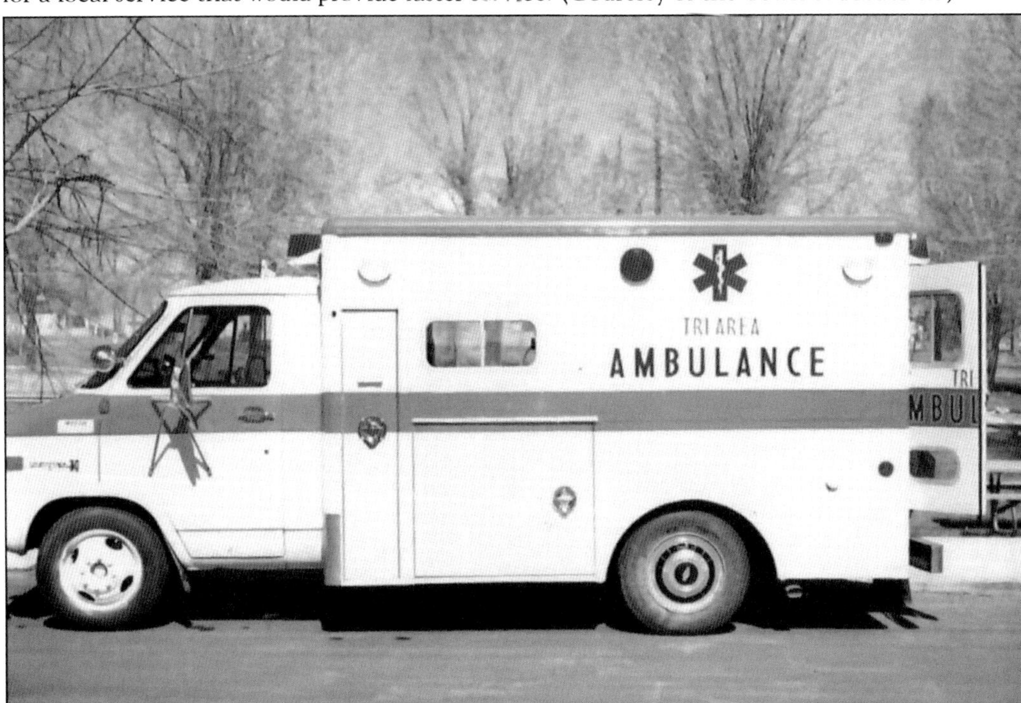

One of the TAVAS ambulances is seen here on display. Originally planned to service only towns in the tri-town area, it soon began servicing areas outside of the town boundaries. Most patients were transported to Longmont United Hospital. (Courtesy of the Town of Frederick.)

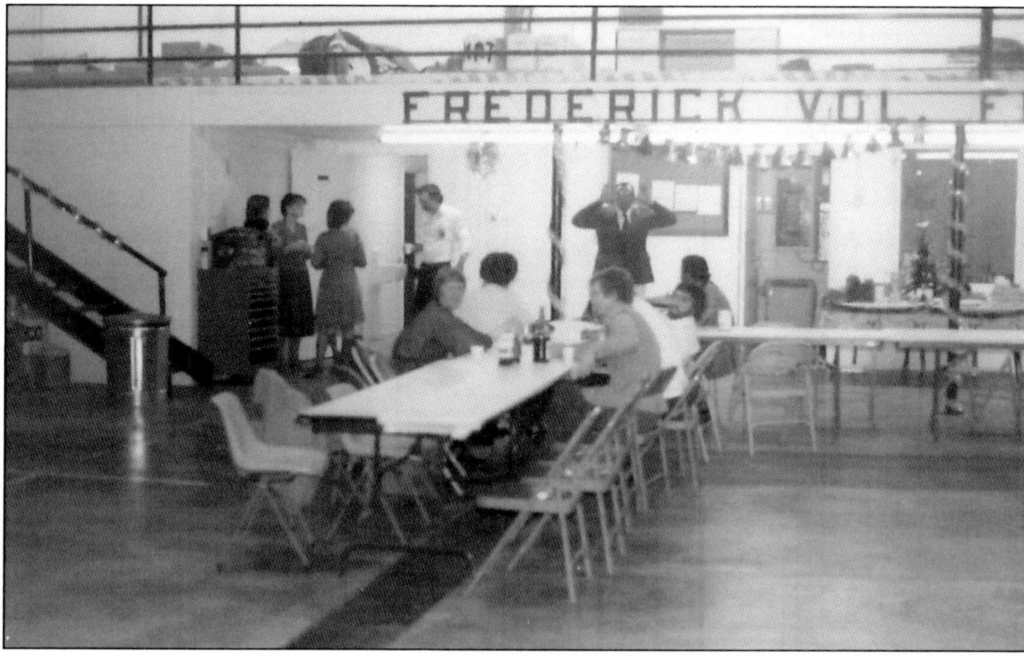

The pressure of constantly having to raise funds finally brought TAVAS to an end in 1983, when the service was forced to close. (Courtesy of the Town of Frederick.)

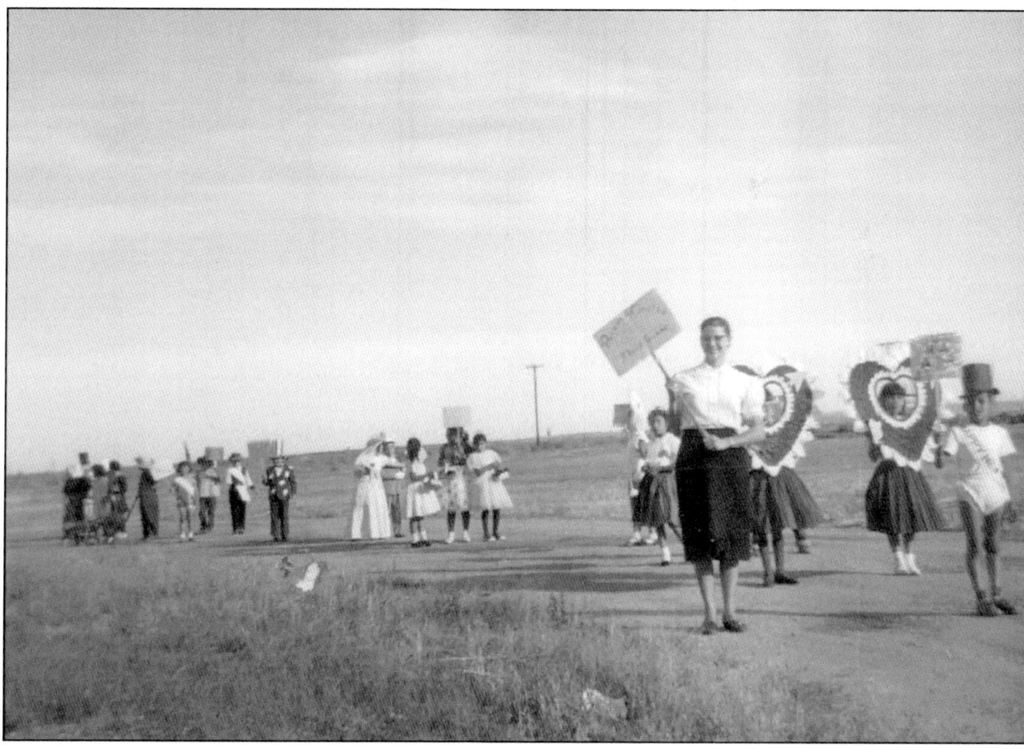

Frederick Elementary School students parade around town in 1960. The students each represented a different month of the year. The child wearing the top hat to the right represents January, and the students holding the hearts represent February. (Courtesy of BTB.)

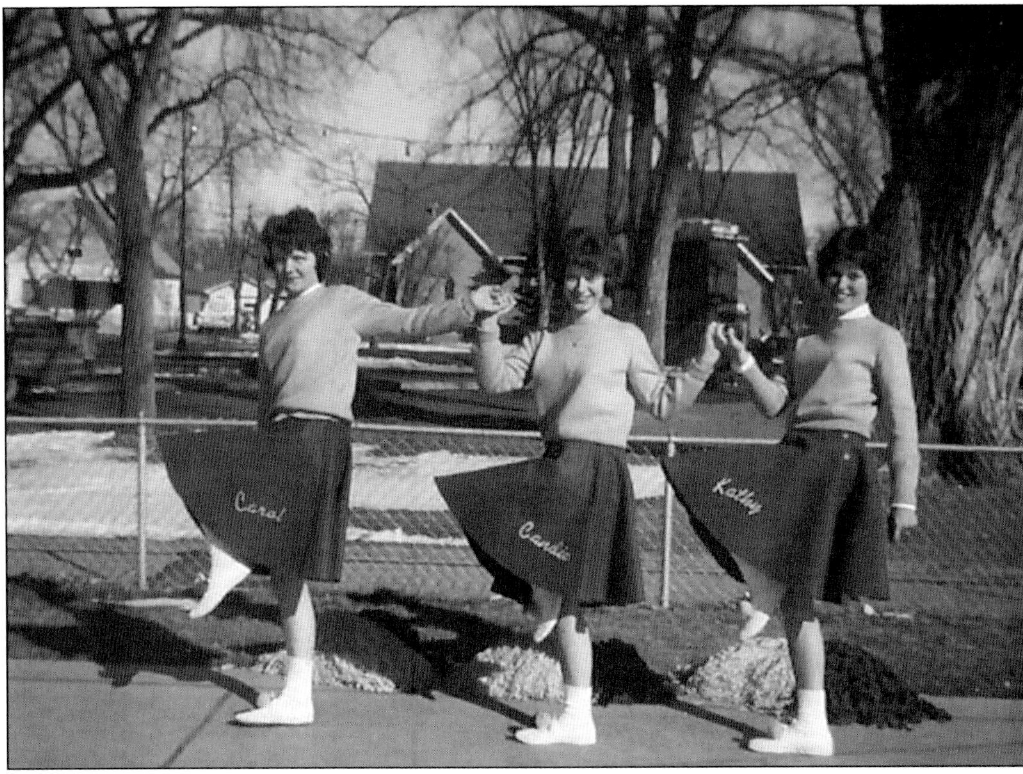

Everyone participated in school parades. This photograph shows Frederick High School cheerleaders posing in April 1963. From left to right are Carol Monseau, Candie Dixon, and Kathy Kuretich. (Courtesy of BTB.)

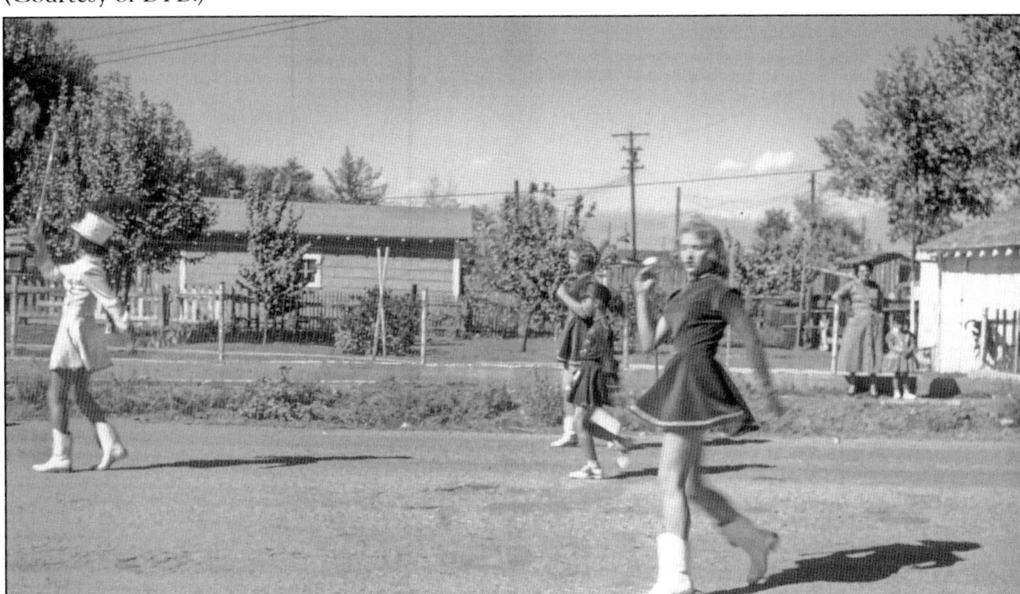

The 1959 homecoming parade is seen here. Note that the streets are not paved. The girl marching closest to the camera is Beverly Spellings. (Courtesy of BTB.)

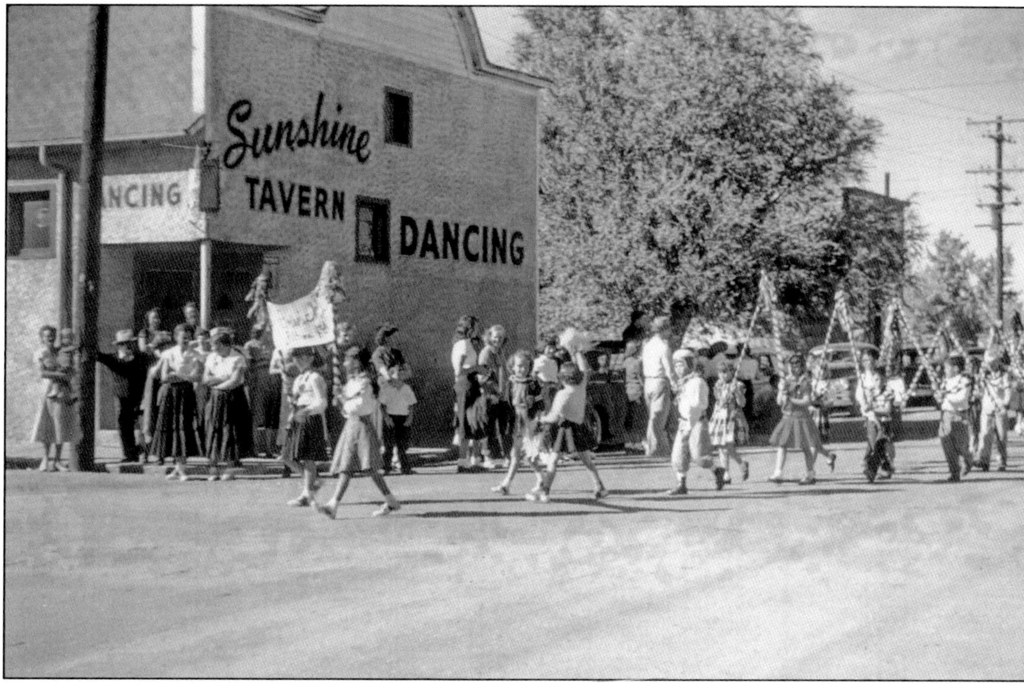

The homecoming parade passes in front of the Sunshine Tavern. The man in the dark clothes with the white hat on the far left is Carmen DeSantis's father. (Courtesy of BTB.)

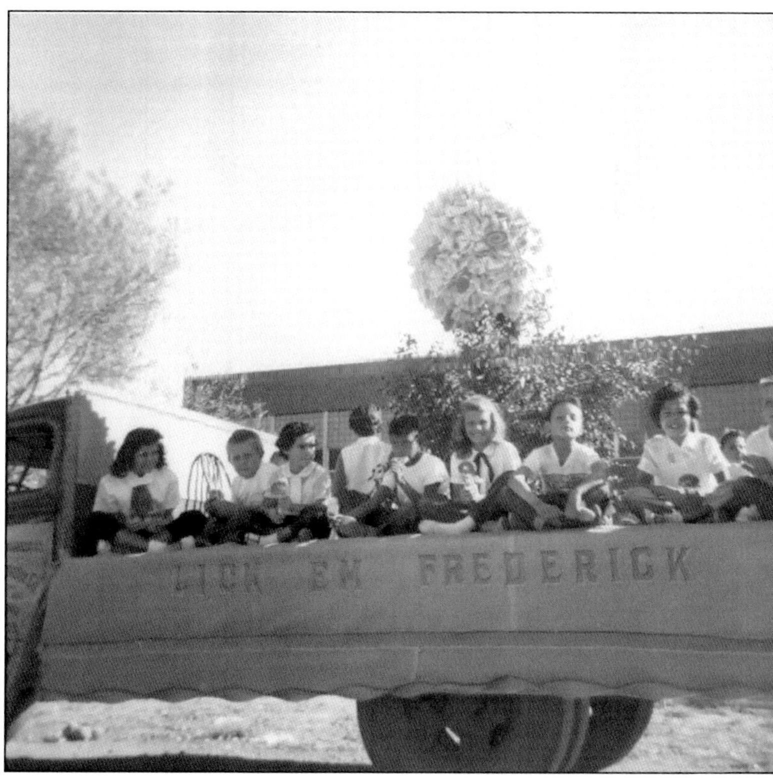

The Frederick Elementary School fourth-grade class float is seen here in 1958. (Courtesy of CC.)

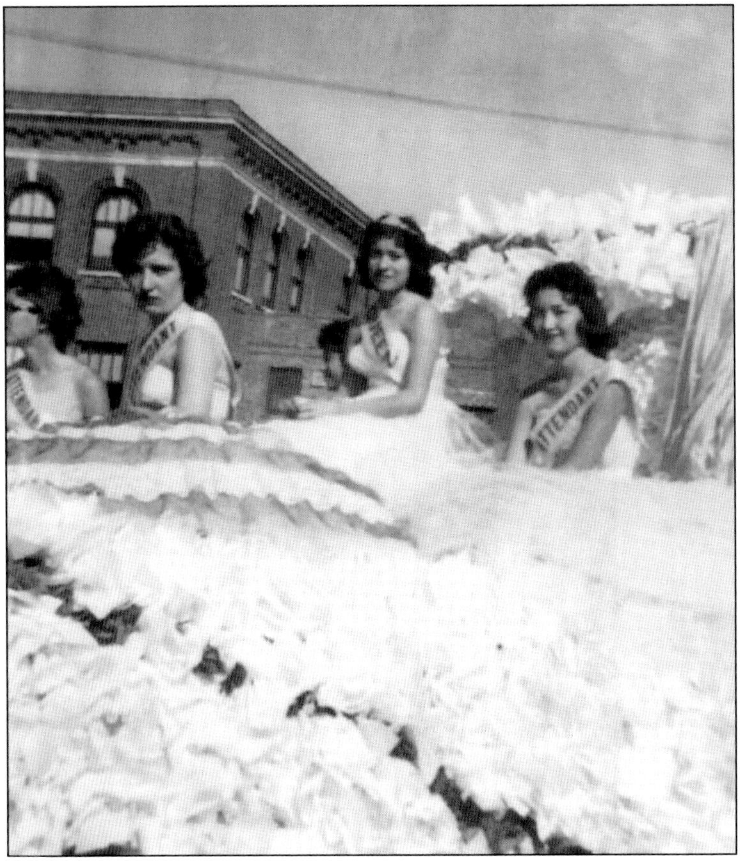

The Frederick homecoming float is seen here. Seated from left to right are Kathleen Stanakz, Laberta DiSalle, Josephine Luque, and Lucille Marquez. (Courtesy of CC.)

High school students gather around the homecoming float. The building in the background is the old Frederick High School. Seen here are, from left to right, Joe Hurtado, Gene Tagliente, Bobby Jackson Stadler, Bill Cevetti, and Mike Hattel. The two boys standing in the back right are unidentified. (Courtesy of MLH.)

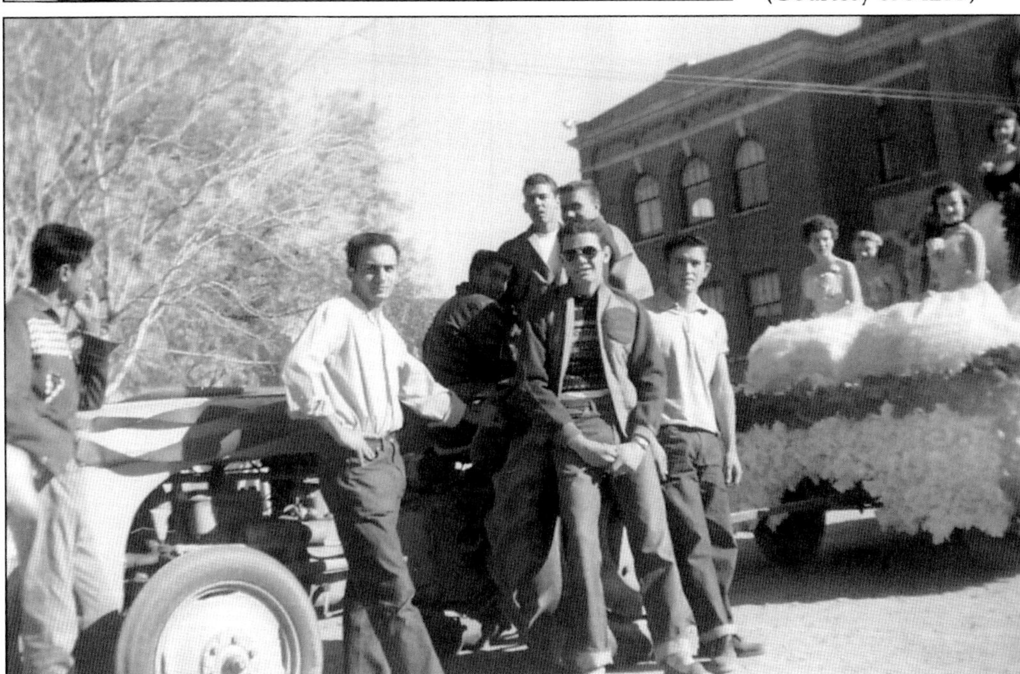

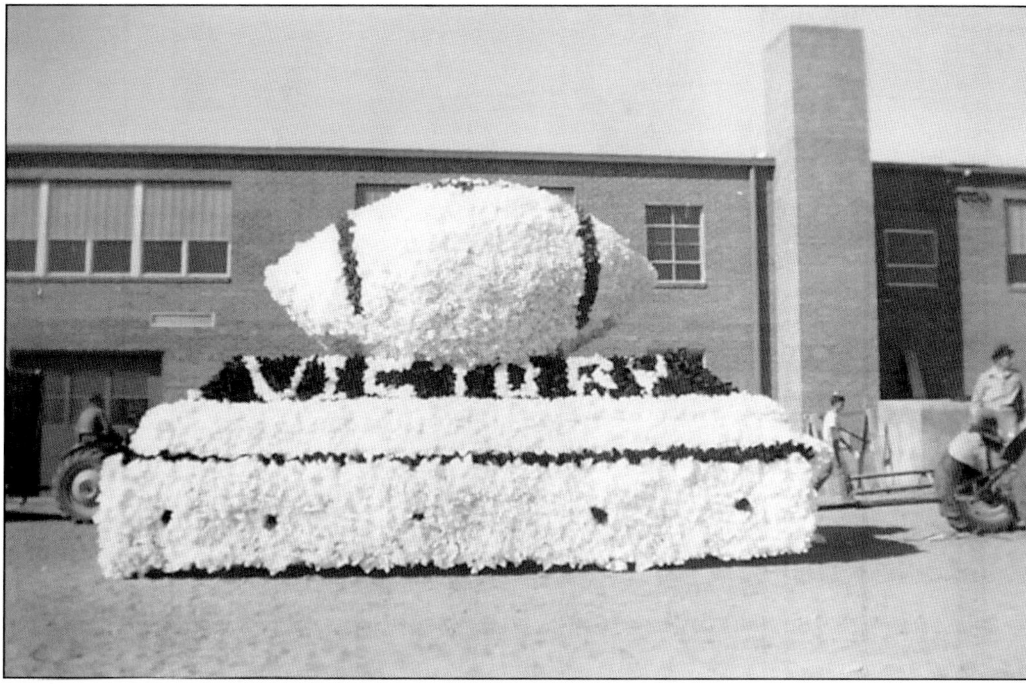

Students invested a lot of time making homecoming floats like this one. Frederick was and is very interested in school activities, and school parades were well attended. This float was designed to inspire victory. (Courtesy of the Town of Frederick.)

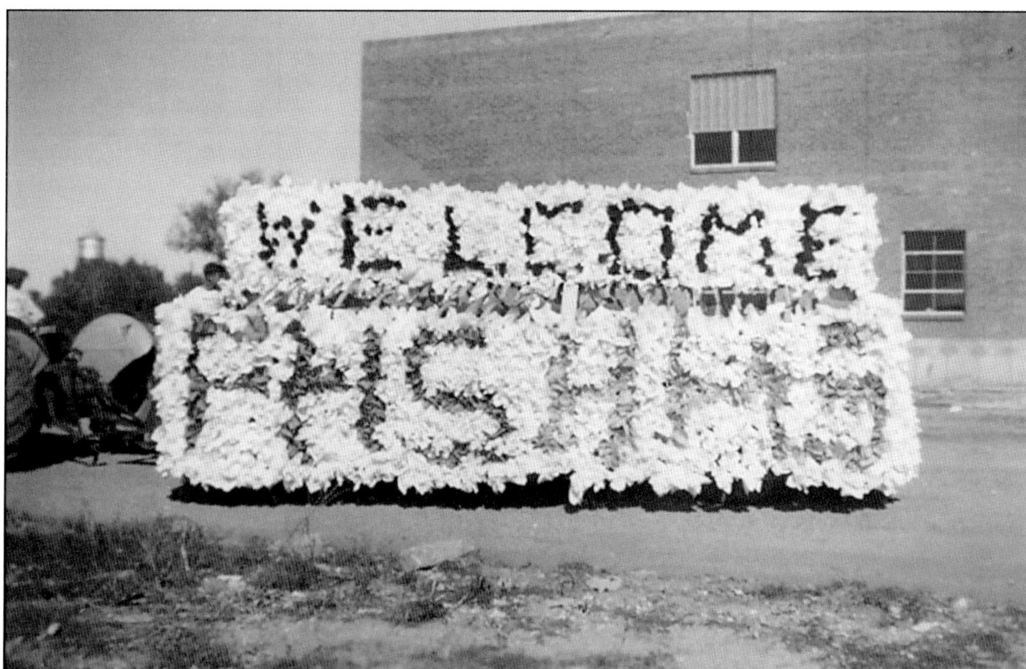

This Frederick High School homecoming float reads, "Welcome FHS HHS." (Courtesy of the Town of Frederick.)

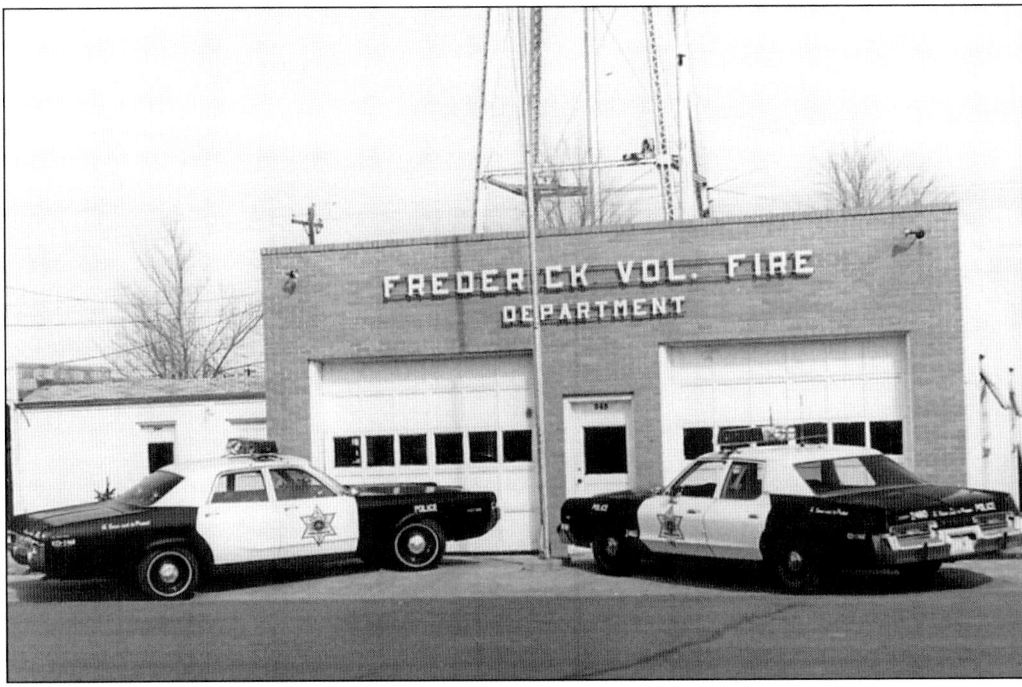

This building served as the headquarters of both the Frederick Volunteer Fire Department and the police department, until the police department moved to Fifth Street, across from Clark Plaza. (Courtesy of the Town of Frederick.)

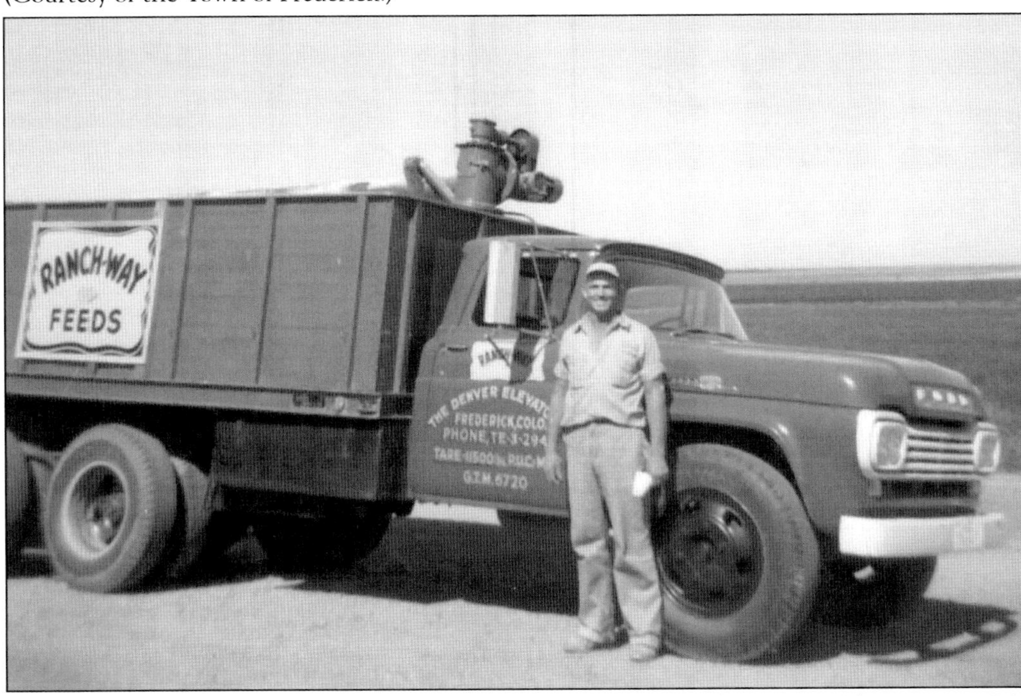

Bob Thornton stands in front of the Ranch-Way Feeds truck at the Denver Elevators in 1961. It was about this time that the elevators were purchased by the Dixon family. Ranch-Way Feeds refers to the brand of feed sold by the elevators. (Courtesy of CC.)

The boiler at the Denver Elevators is seen here in 1957. It looks to be extremely well tended. (Courtesy of CC.)

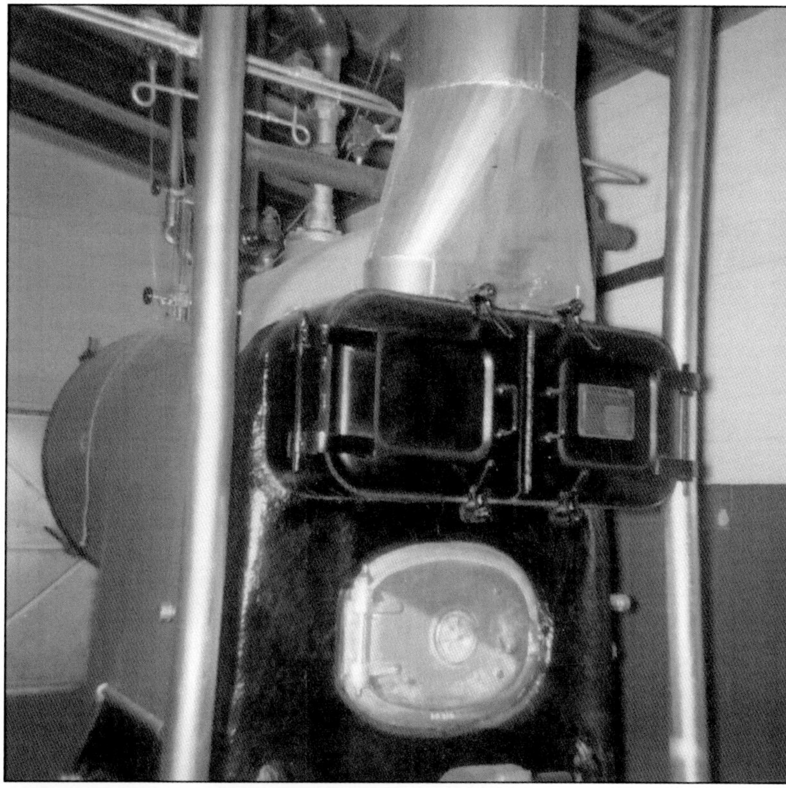

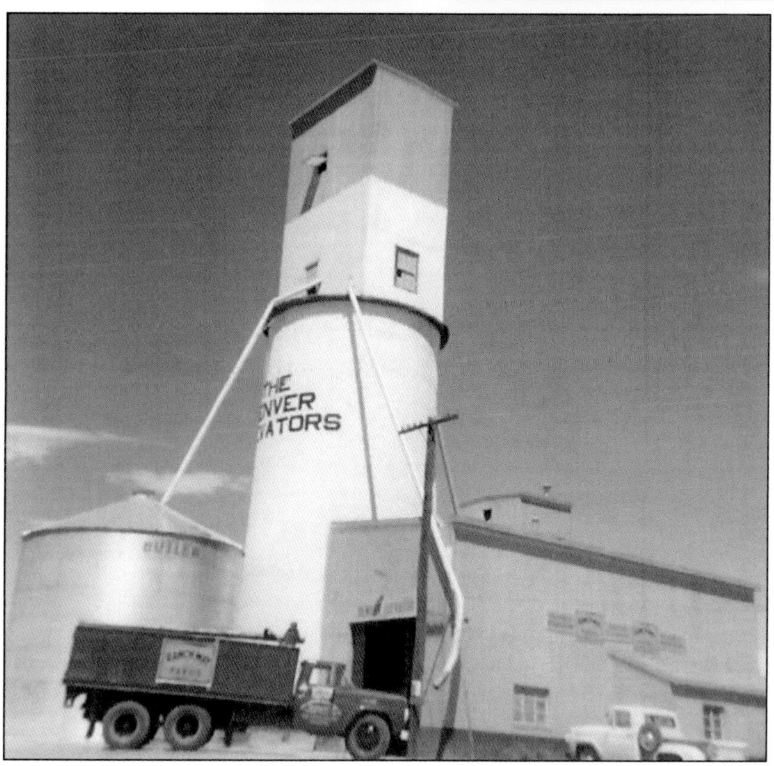

The Ranch-Way Feeds truck is seen here parked in front of the Denver Elevators in 1961. (Courtesy of CC.)

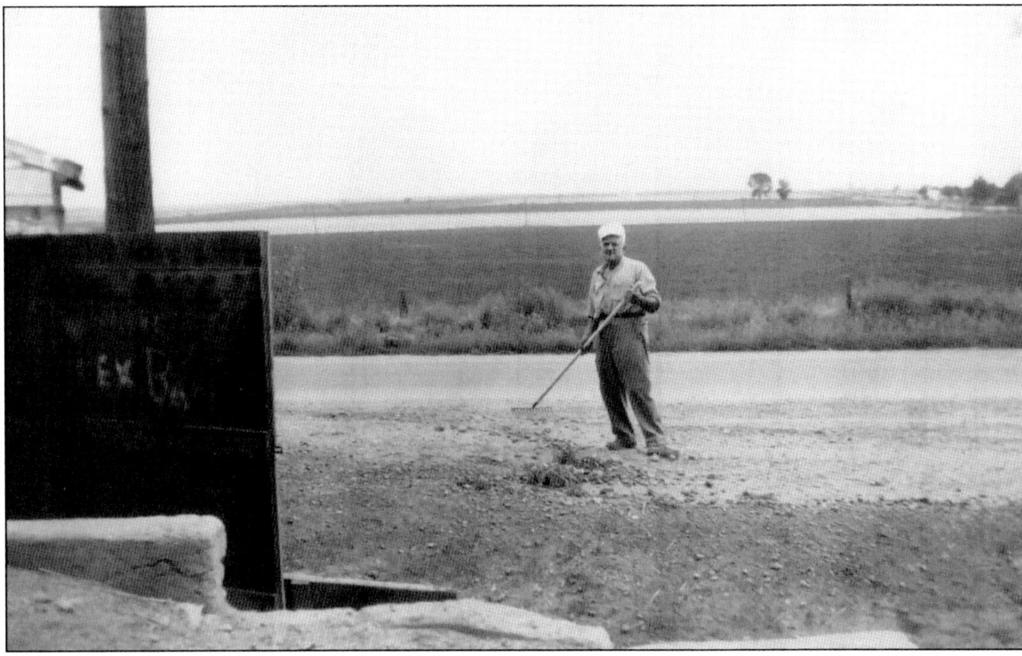

Grain worker Marvin Dixon poses for a photograph at the Denver Elevators in 1946. (Courtesy of CC.)

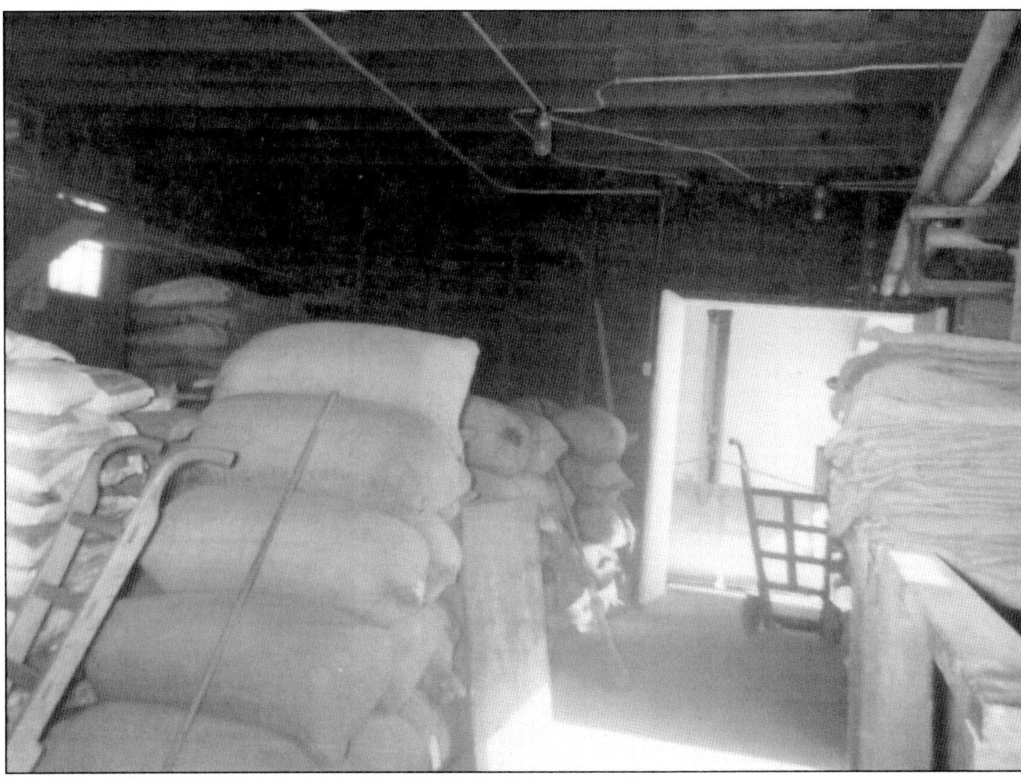

Grain storage bags are seen here at the Denver Elevators. Wheat farming was a profitable venture in 1955, when this photograph was taken. (Courtesy of CC.)

This is a storage bin at the Denver Elevators. The elevators located were south of Frederick on Highway 52. They were a prominent landmark and were often used in giving directions. (Courtesy of the Town of Frederick.)

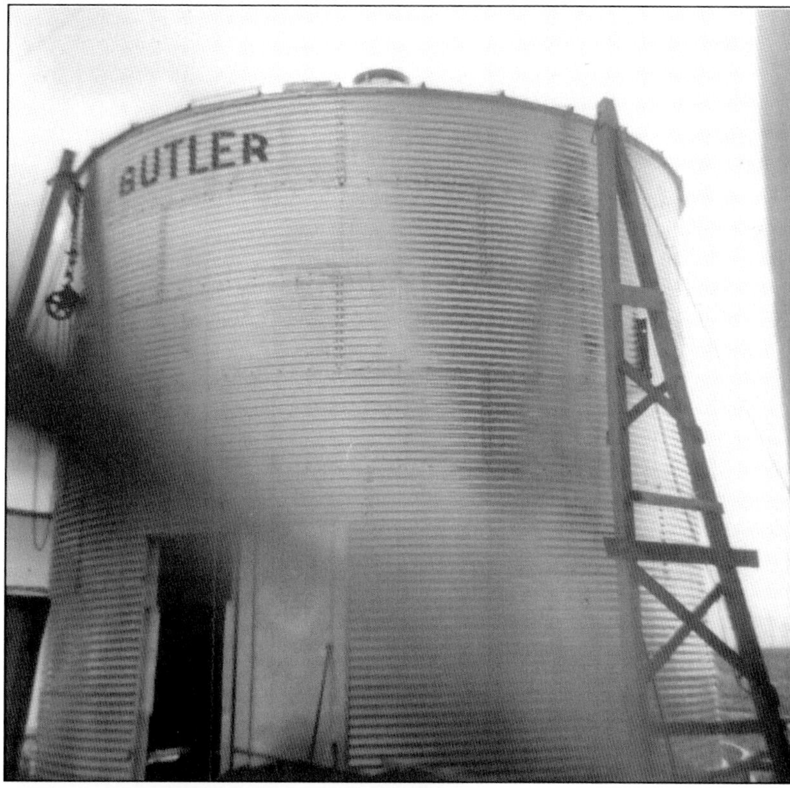

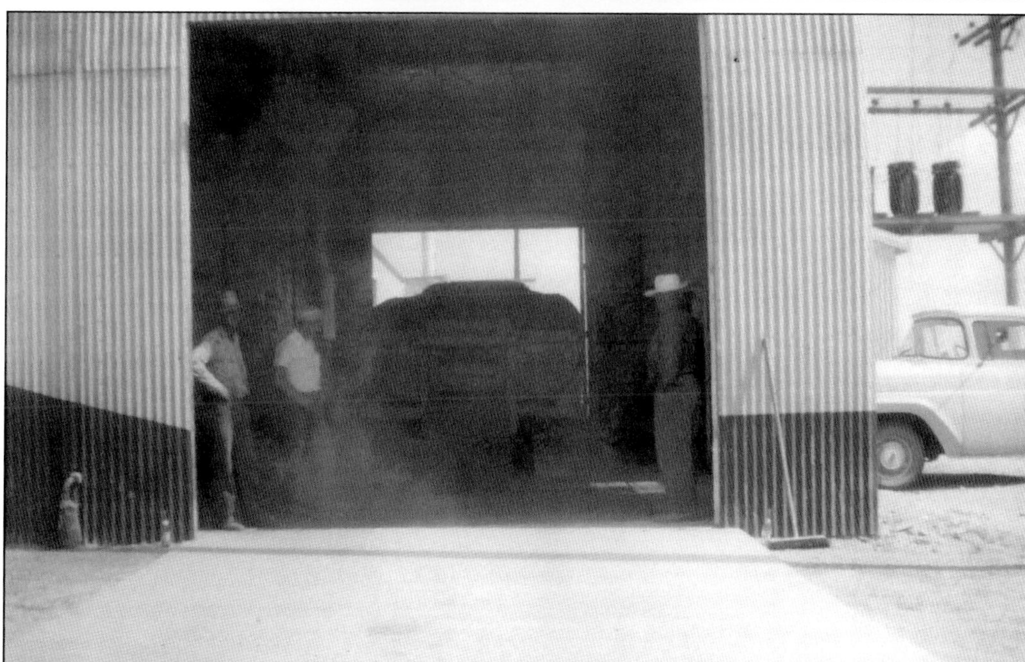

This photograph shows the operations at Dixon Feed & Grain, as a truck dumps its load of grain at the elevator during the harvest of 1958. (Courtesy of CC.)

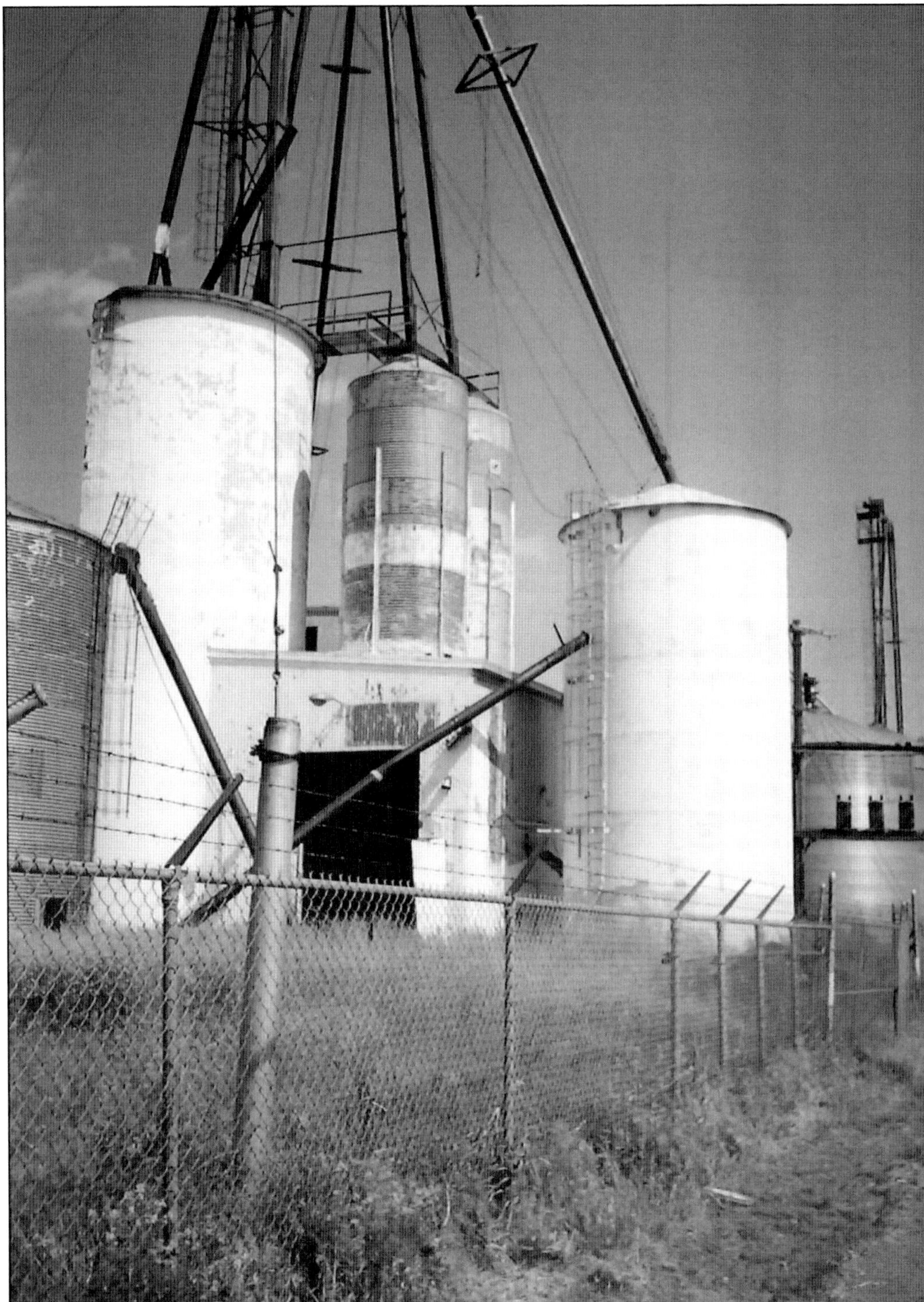

The old Denver Elevators are seen here. Through the years, it was known as the Denver Elevators, and then Dixon Feed & Grain, after Marvin and Leona Dixon purchased the elevators in 1961. (Courtesy of CC.)

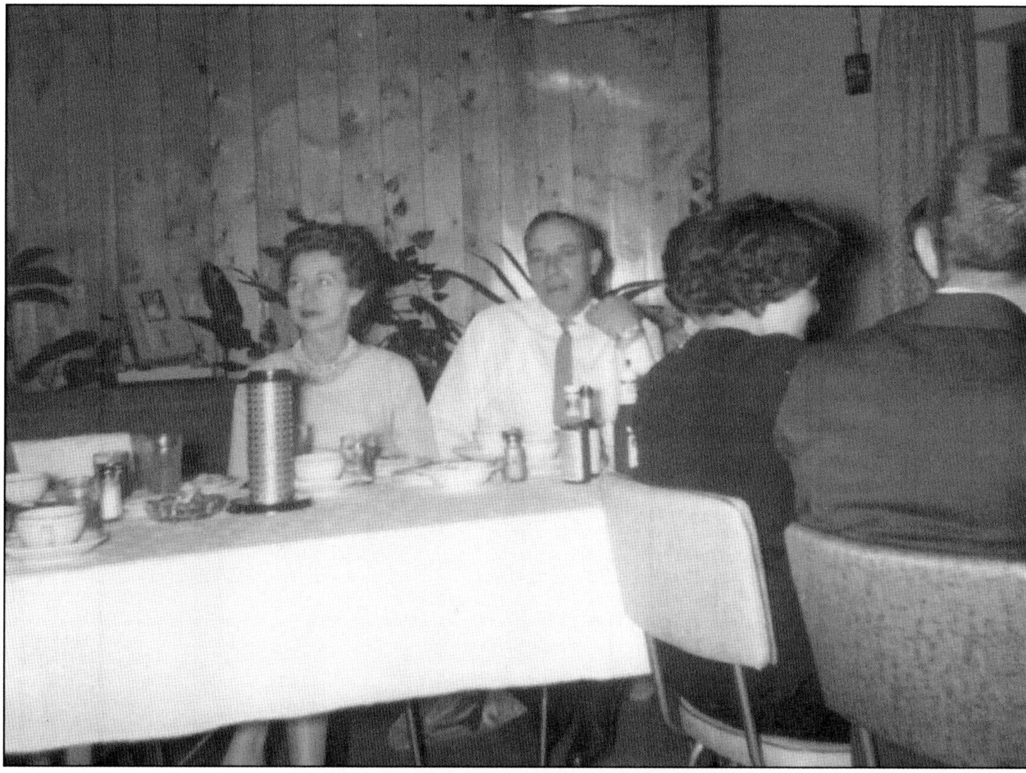

Alice and Adam Lepore are seen here at Lepore's Restaurant in 1962. (Courtesy of CC.)

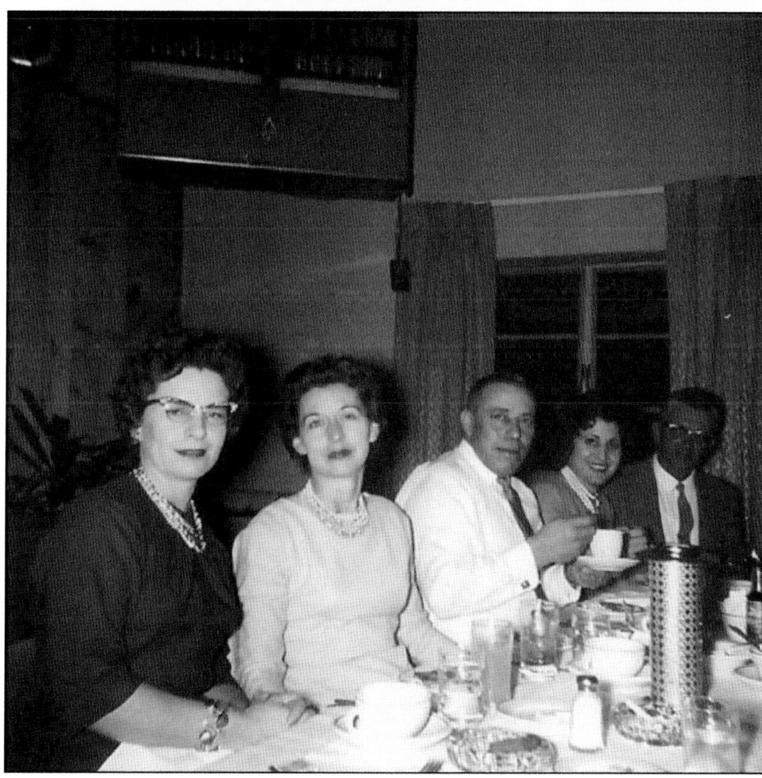

From left to right, Leona Dixon, Alice Lepore, Adam Lepore, Lily Hattel, and Alex Hattel are seen here at Lepore's Restaurant in 1962. (Courtesy of CC.)

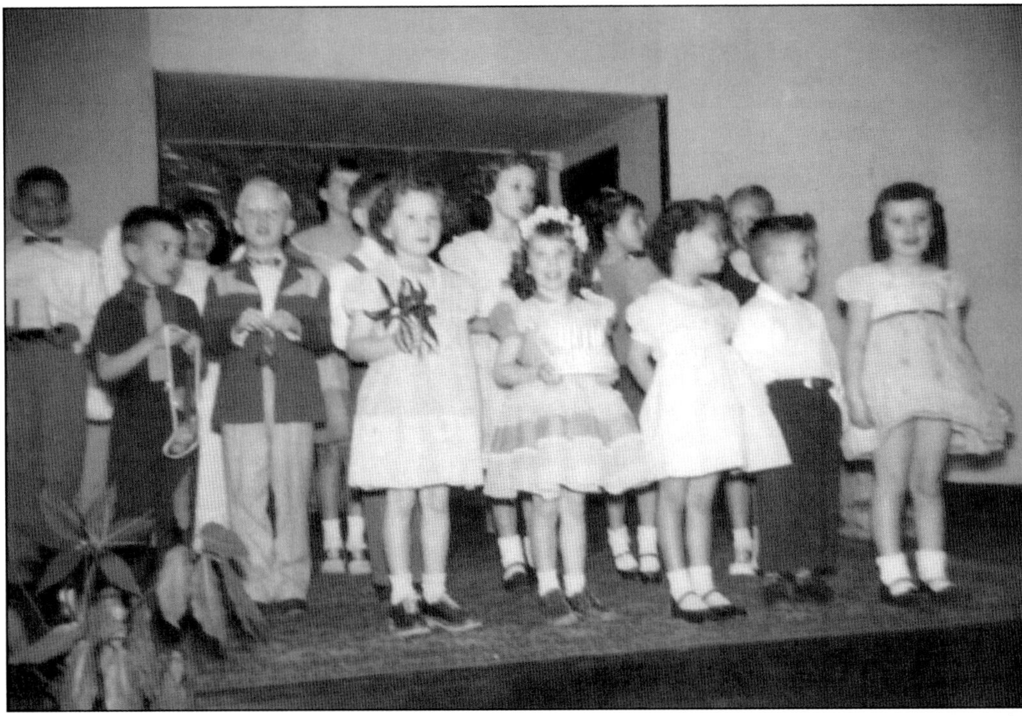

This is the Easter program at Frederick Christian Church. Standing second from the left in the first row is Barb Baker, and standing in the first row on the far right is Cathy Dixon. This picture was taken in 1959. (Courtesy of CC.)

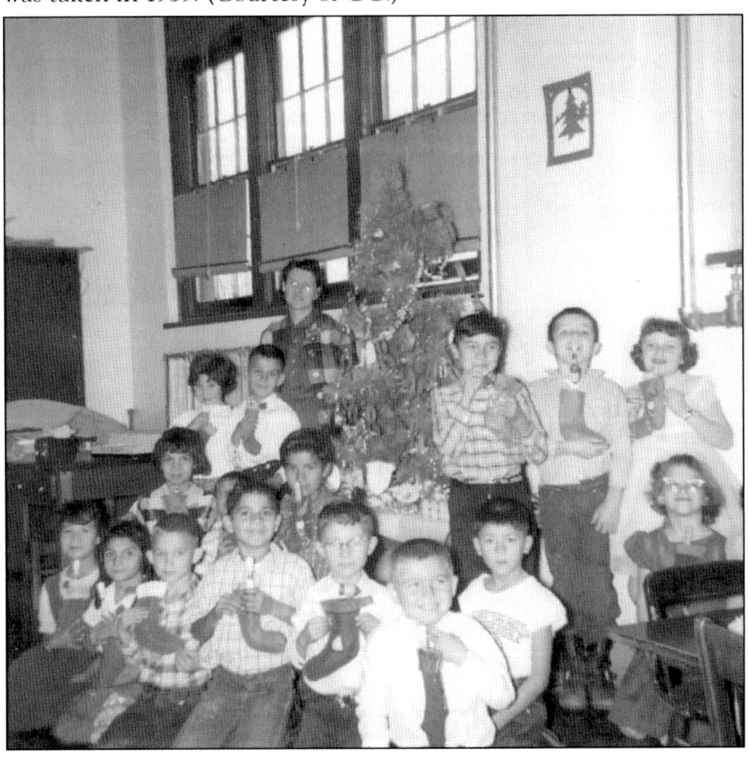

Mabel Zimmerman's second-grade class is seen here at their Christmas party at Frederick Elementary School in 1959. (Courtesy of CC.)

This is a photograph of a school dance in the Frederick gymnasium in 1967. Seen from left to right are Rita Morrow, Gerald Petrus, Henry Rivera, Bob Alvarez, and Mary Hamilton. (Courtesy of CC.)

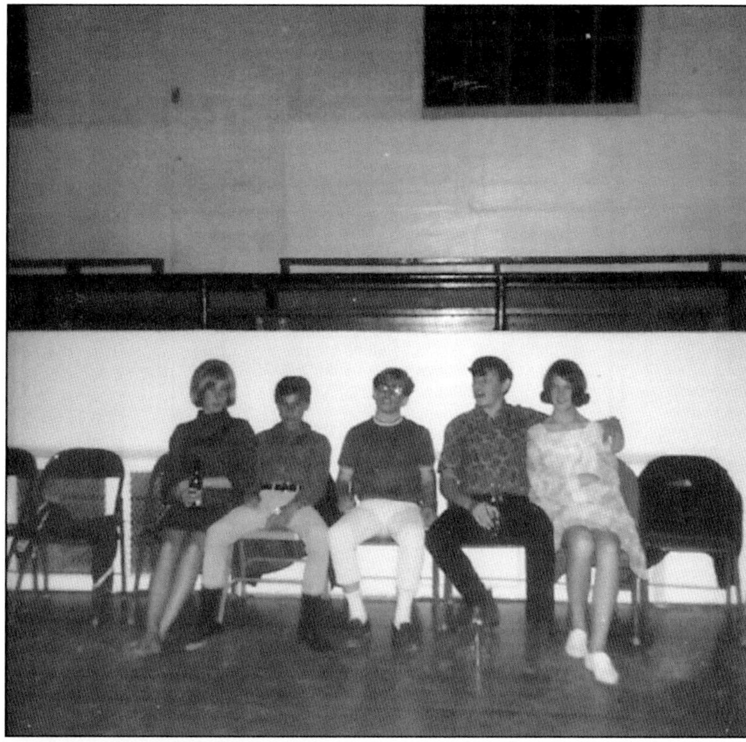

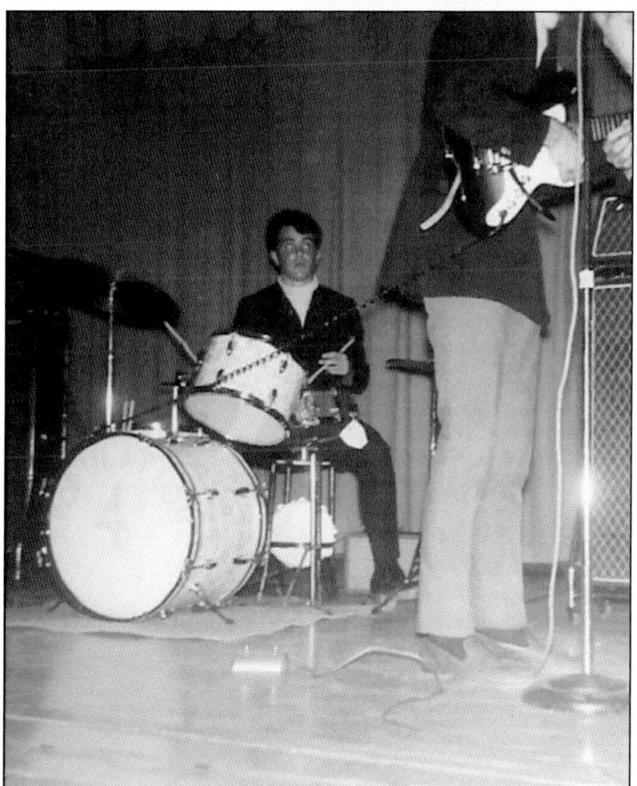

Tim DiGregorio, the drummer for the Population 4 Band, is seen here in 1967. (Courtesy of CC.)

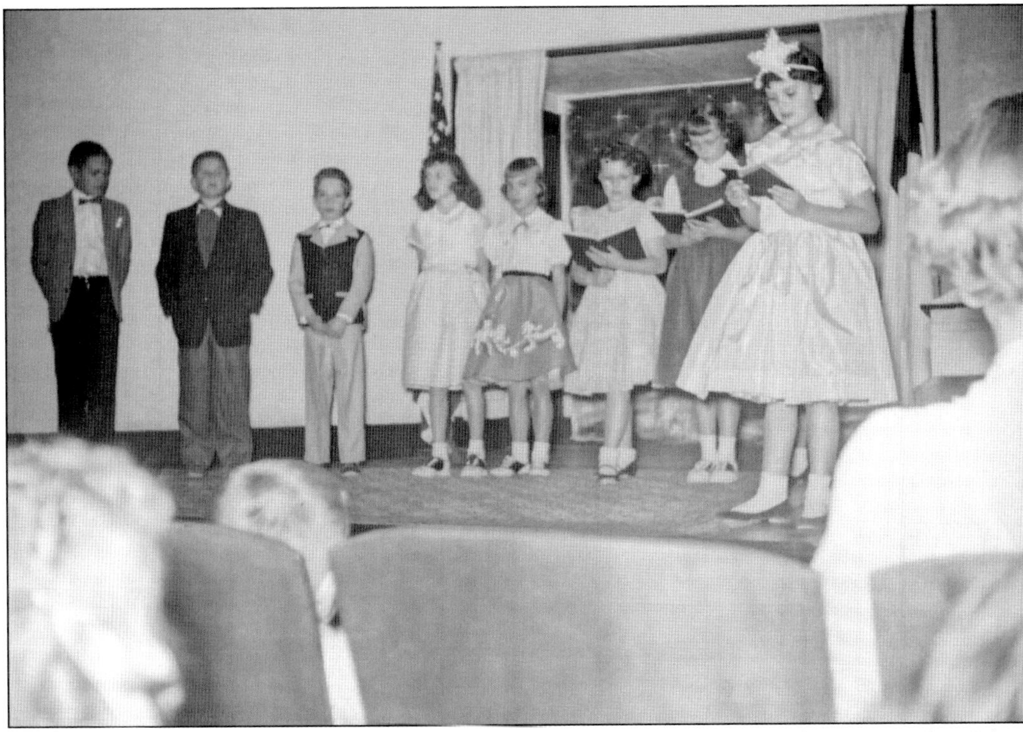

This Easter pageant was held at the Frederick Christian Church in 1957. (Courtesy of BTB.)

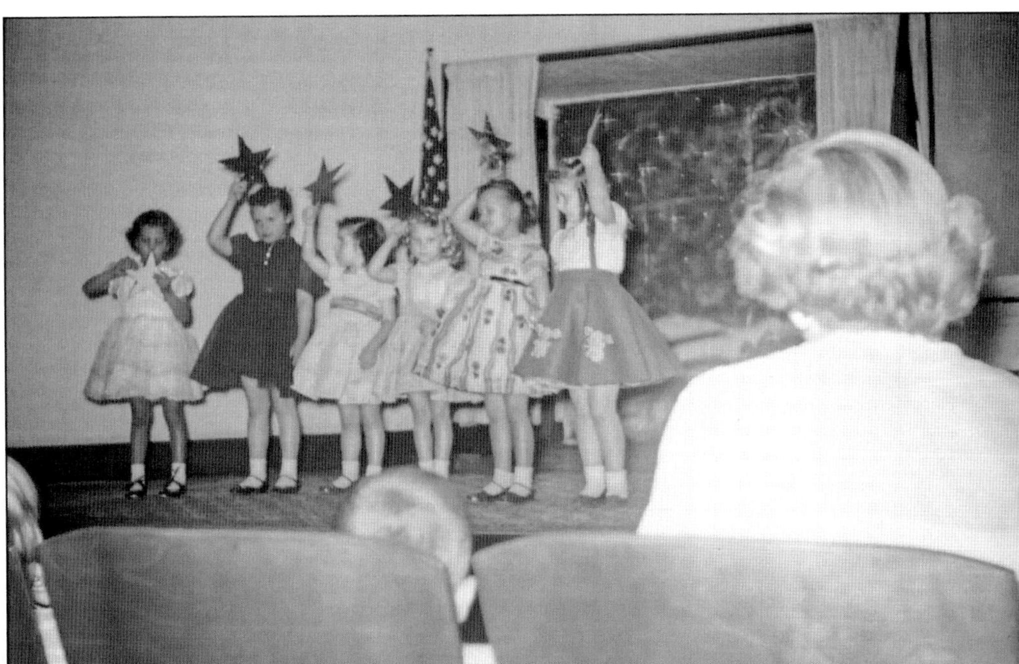

This is another view of the 1957 Easter pageant at Frederick Christian Church. Note the girl standing on the right with the little elephants on her skirt, Cathy Dixon. (Courtesy of BTB.)

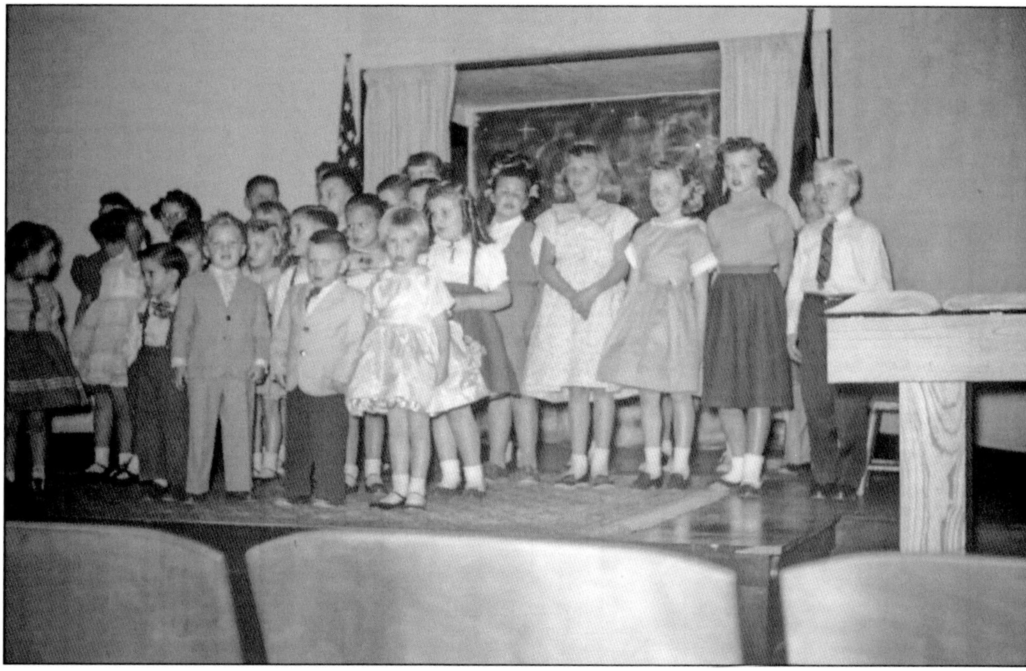

This is another photograph of the 1957 Frederick Christian Church Easter pageant. (Courtesy of BTB.)

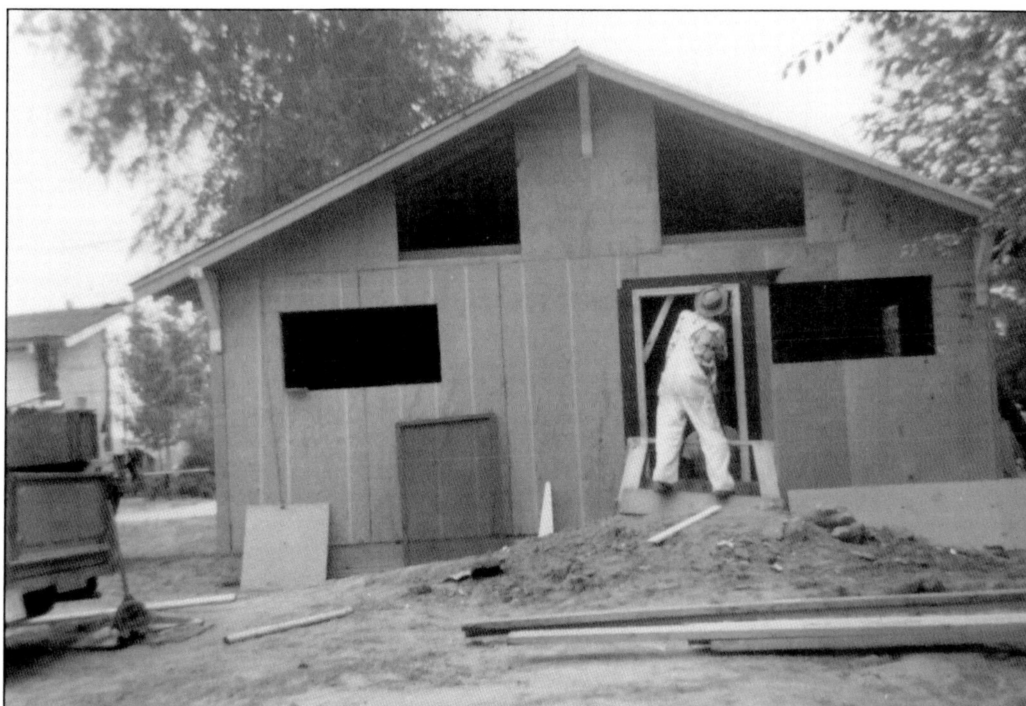

Max McNeil works on remodeling the Dixon home at 250 Buchanan Avenue in Firestone in 1958. While it looks like a complete rebuilding, it was actually just an extensive remodeling. (Courtesy of CC.)

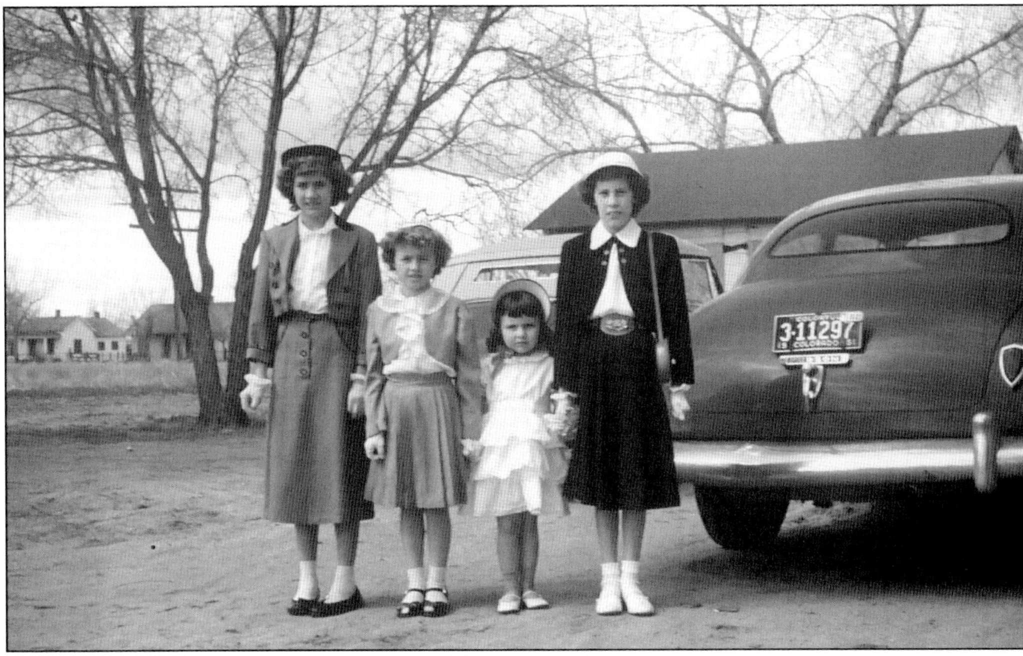

This photograph was taken in front of the Baker home in Evanston in 1952. Standing from left to right are Myrna Ciocchetti, Claudia Jo Ciocchetti, Linda Baker, and Donna Shaw. (Courtesy of BTB.)

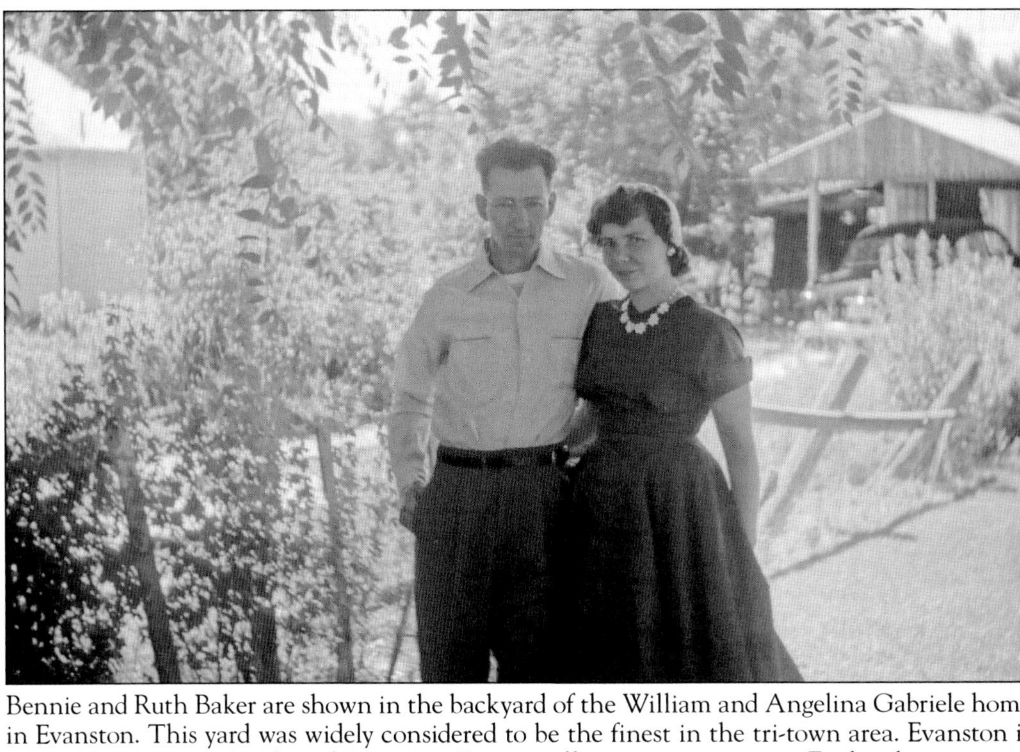

Bennie and Ruth Baker are shown in the backyard of the William and Angelina Gabriele home in Evanston. This yard was widely considered to be the finest in the tri-town area. Evanston is located between Frederick and Firestone. Despite efforts to annex it into Frederick, it remains part of unincorporated Weld County. (Courtesy of BTB.)

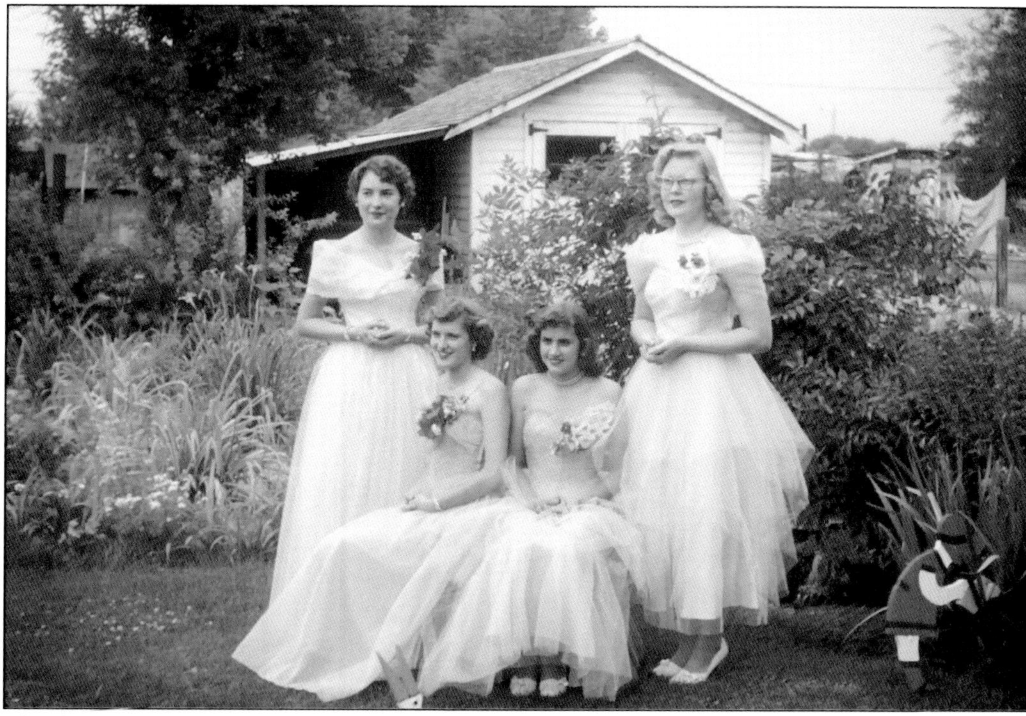

This homecoming dance photograph was taken in the Gabriele backyard. From left to right are Phyllis Fiori, Wilamae Graham, Myrna Ciocchetti, and Joan Patterson. (Courtesy of BTB.)

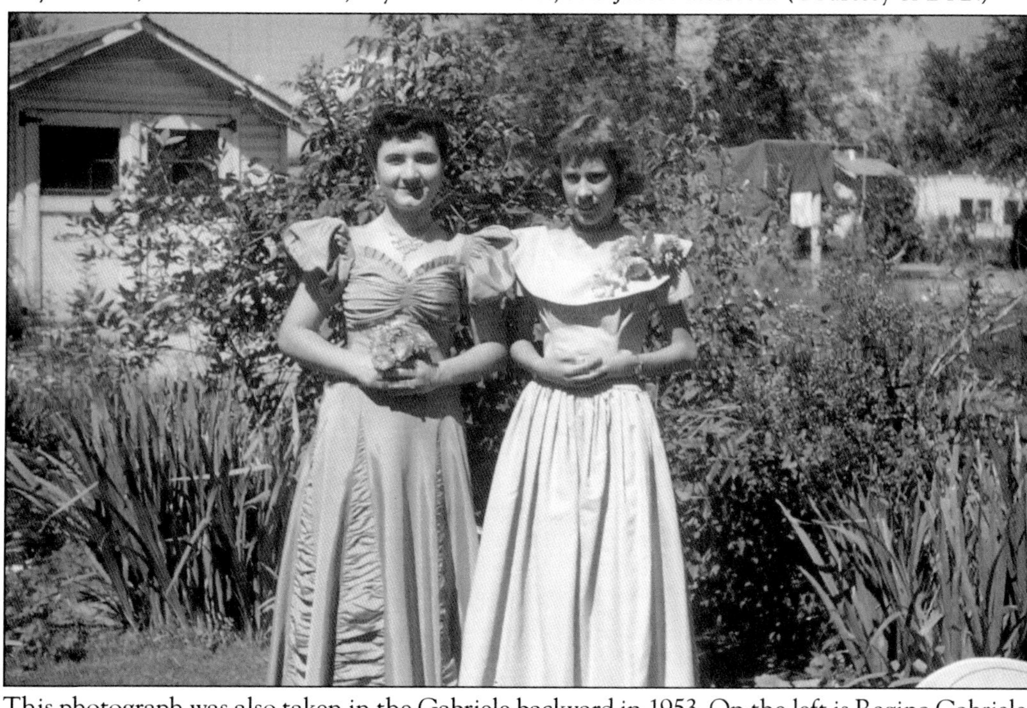

This photograph was also taken in the Gabriele backyard in 1953. On the left is Regina Gabriele, and on the right is Donna Shaw. Shortly after this photograph was taken, Shaw passed away from leukemia. (Courtesy of BTB.)

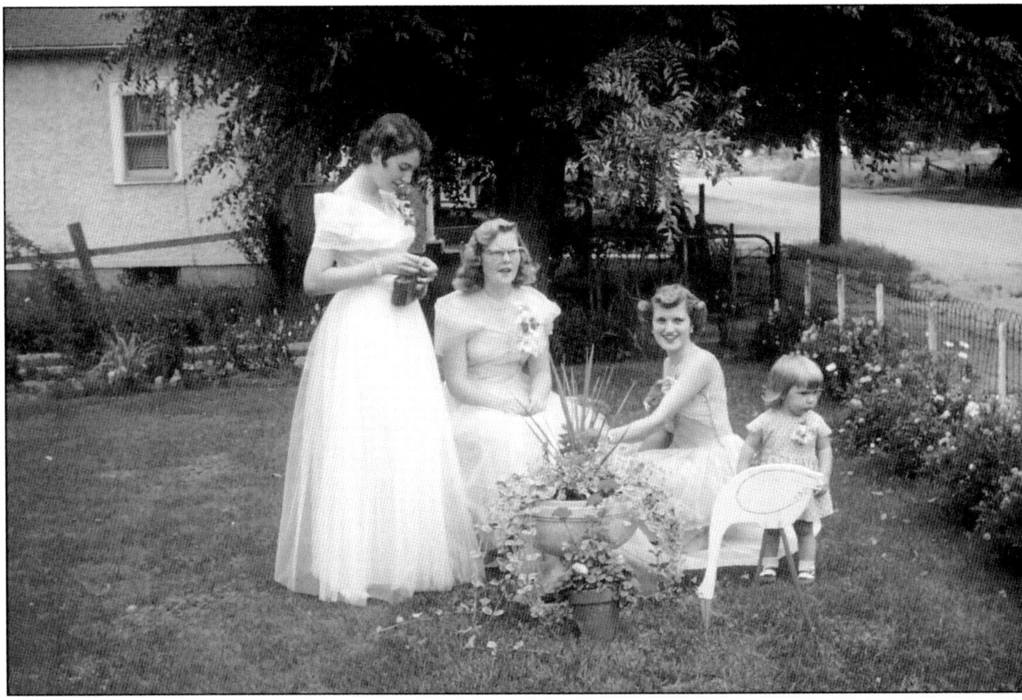

This photograph was taken in the Gabriele yard in 1958. These ladies, except for young Trudy Baker on the right, are preparing for the homecoming dance. From left to right, the older girls are Phyllis Fiori, Joan Patterson, and Wilma Graham. (Courtesy of BTB.)

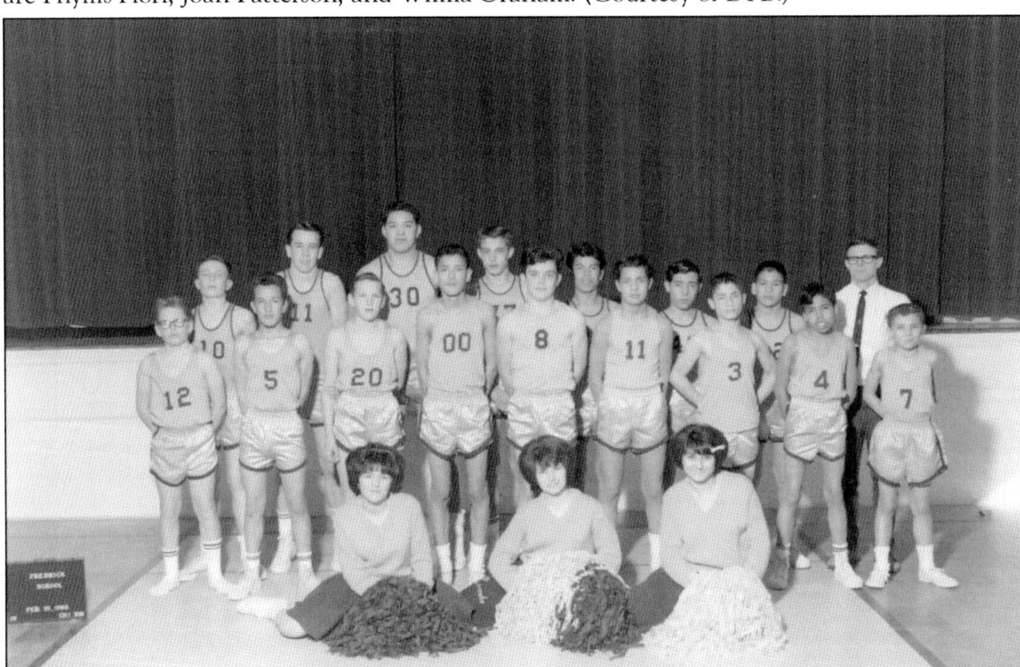

The 1965 Frederick High School basketball team is seen here with coach Jim Harrison. (Courtesy of BTB.)

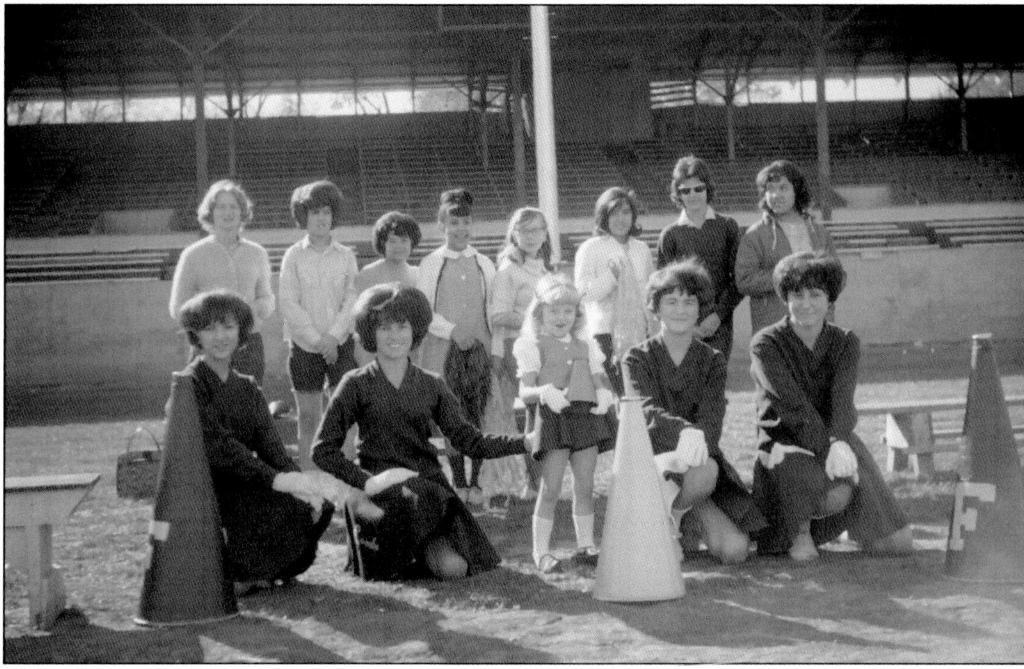

The Frederick High School football team pep club is seen here in 1962. They are, from left to right, (kneeling) Ida Marquez, Linda Villani, Jamie Fern, Marla Waremberg, and Emily DeGelaranido; (standing) Sharon Evans, Kathy Klippenger, Caroline DiLullo, Linda Garcia, Barb Baker, Dorothy Hurtado, Micki Christ, and Mary Garcia. (Courtesy of BTB.)

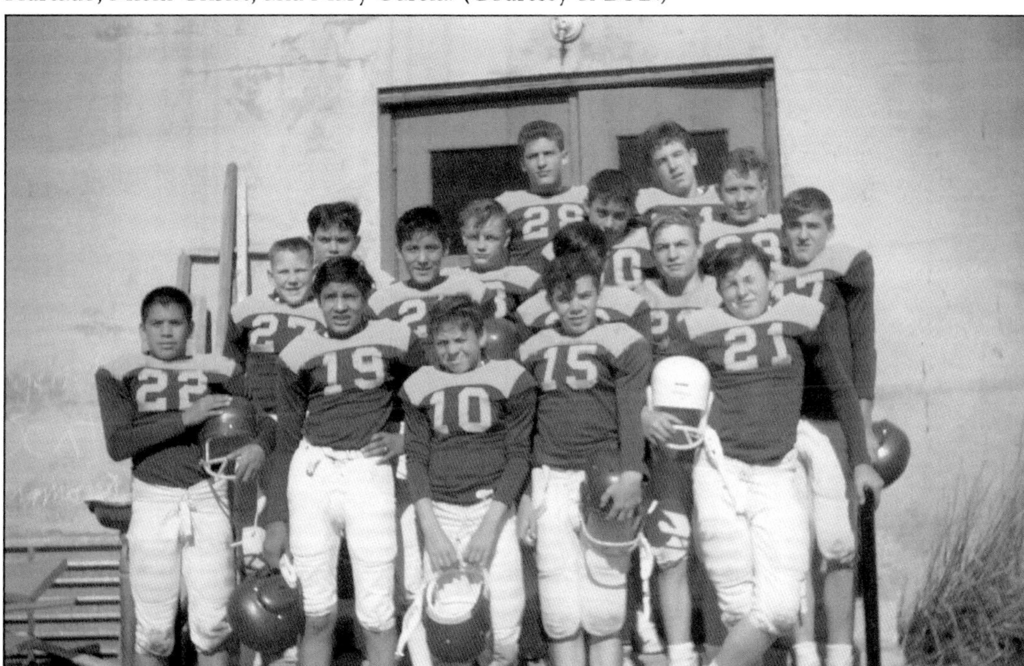

The 1965 Frederick High School football team is seen here. In 2012, the football team had its best finish, falling just one game short of the state championship game. (Courtesy of BTB.)

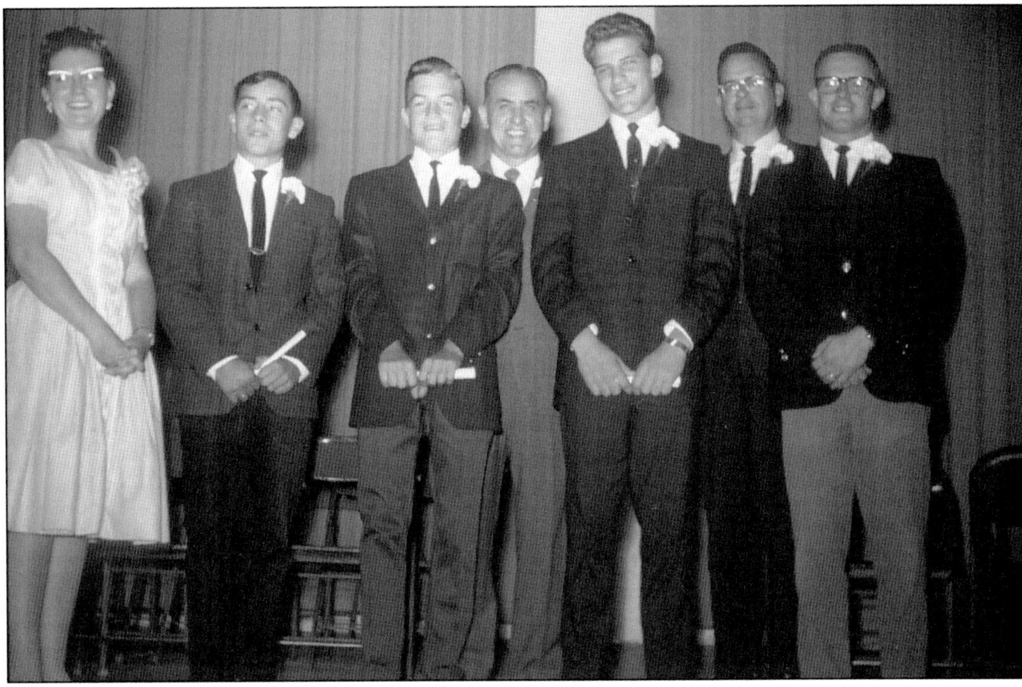

The 1968 Frederick High School graduating class is seen here at the continuation ceremony. From left to right, they are Nadine Warren, Dan Sedillo (voted best musician), Joe Irwin (best scholastic), Mr. Tesone, Rick Bauer (best athlete), Mr. Kier, and Jim Harrison. (Courtesy of BTB.)

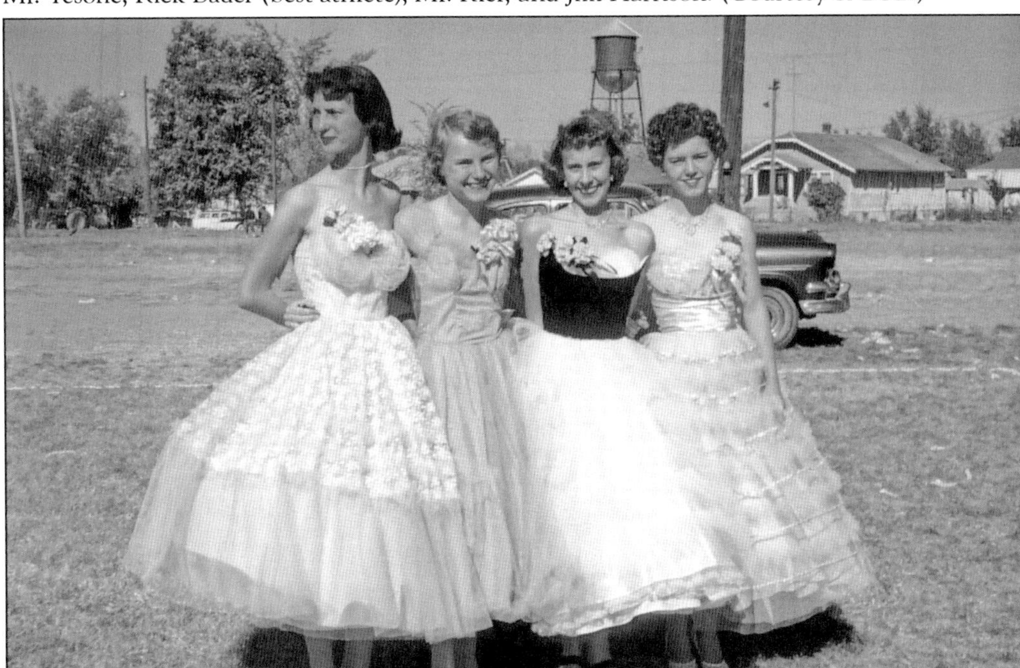

The 1957 homecoming court included, from left to right, Mary Rasetti, Shirley Balen, Donna Shaw, and Beverly Melick. (Courtesy of BTB.)

This photograph shows the laying of sewer lines and the paving of streets in Evanston. (Courtesy of BTB.)

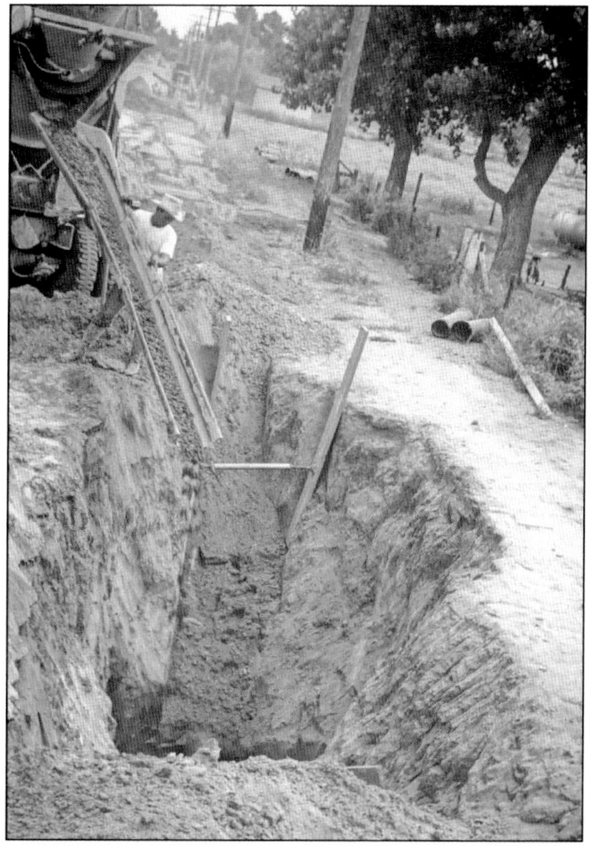

This photograph shows Chuck Baker's birthday party in 1959 at Thompson Hall, a very small dance location serving the town of Frederick. (Courtesy of BTB.)

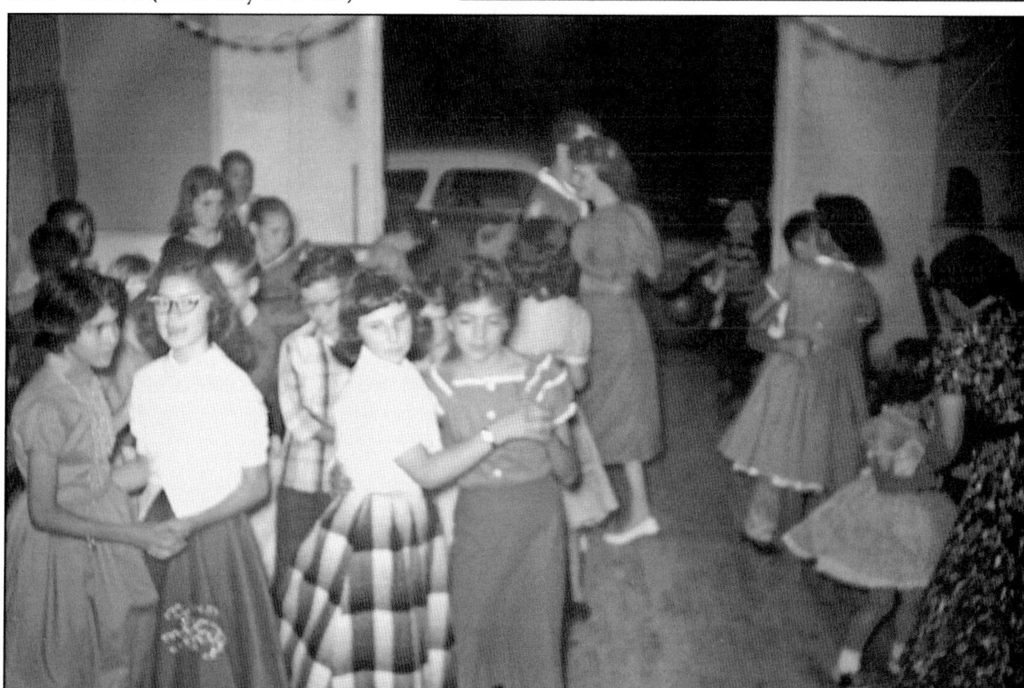

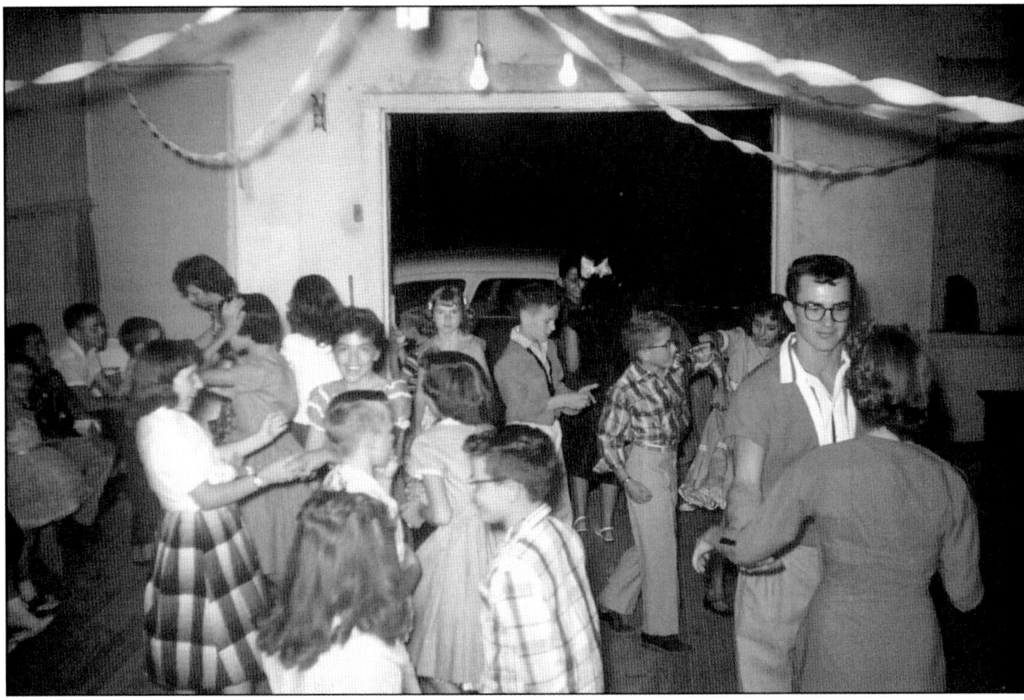

This is another photograph from Chuck Baker's birthday celebration dance at Thompson Hall in September 1959. (Courtesy of BTB.)

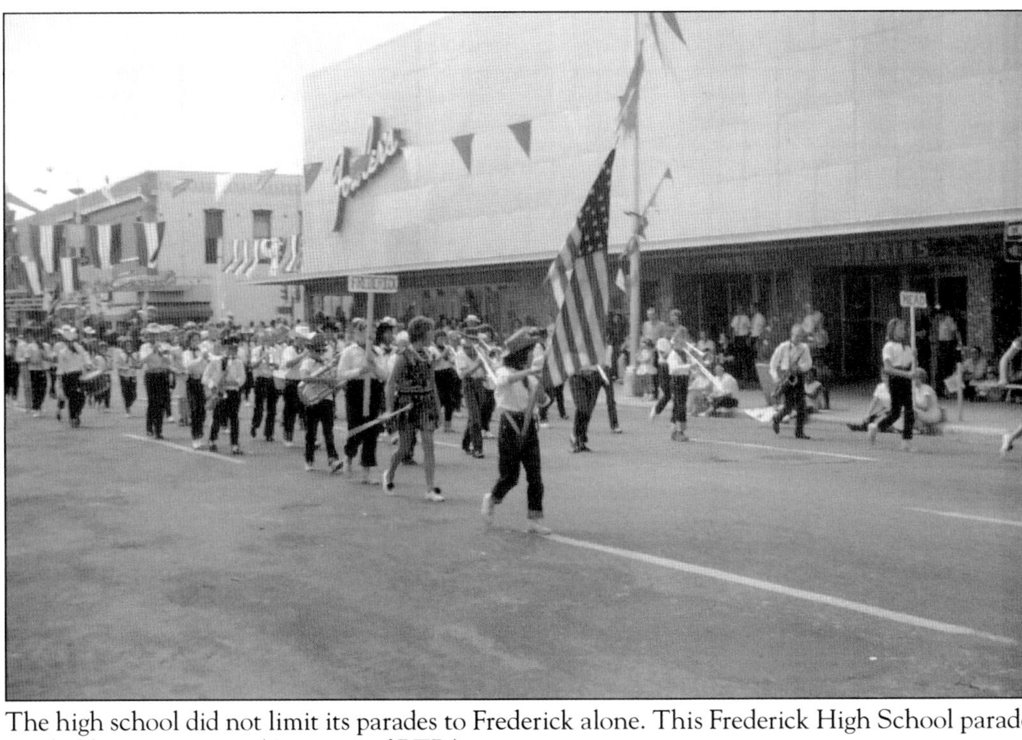

The high school did not limit its parades to Frederick alone. This Frederick High School parade was held in Longmont. (Courtesy of BTB.)

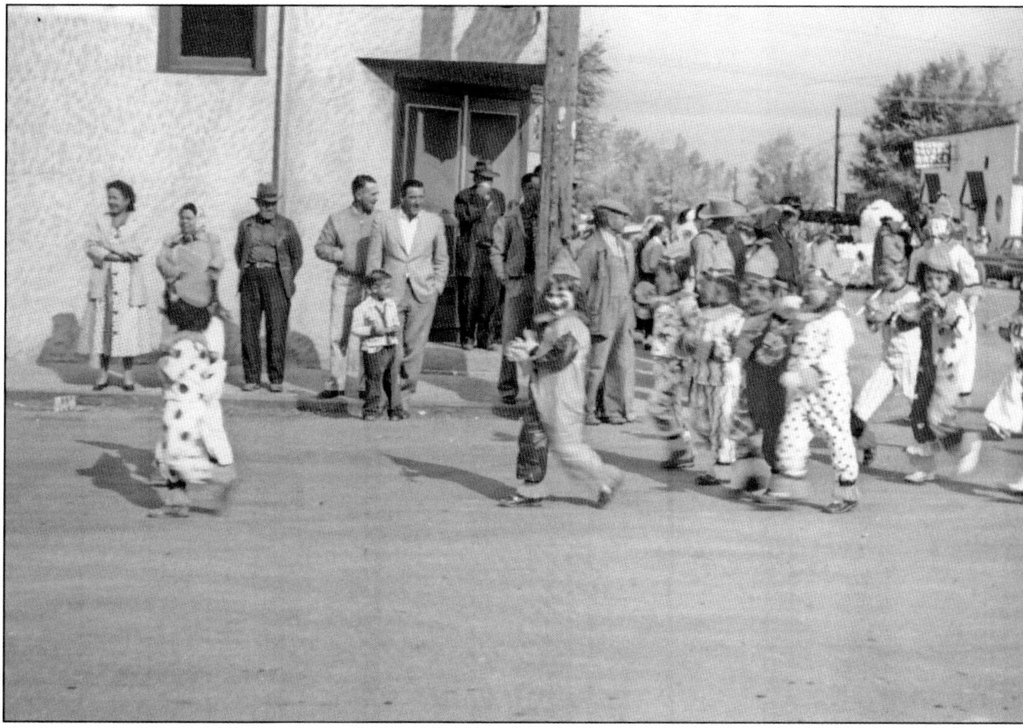

Frederick students parade down Fifth Street. The building in the back right is the Friendly Tavern. (Courtesy of BTB.)

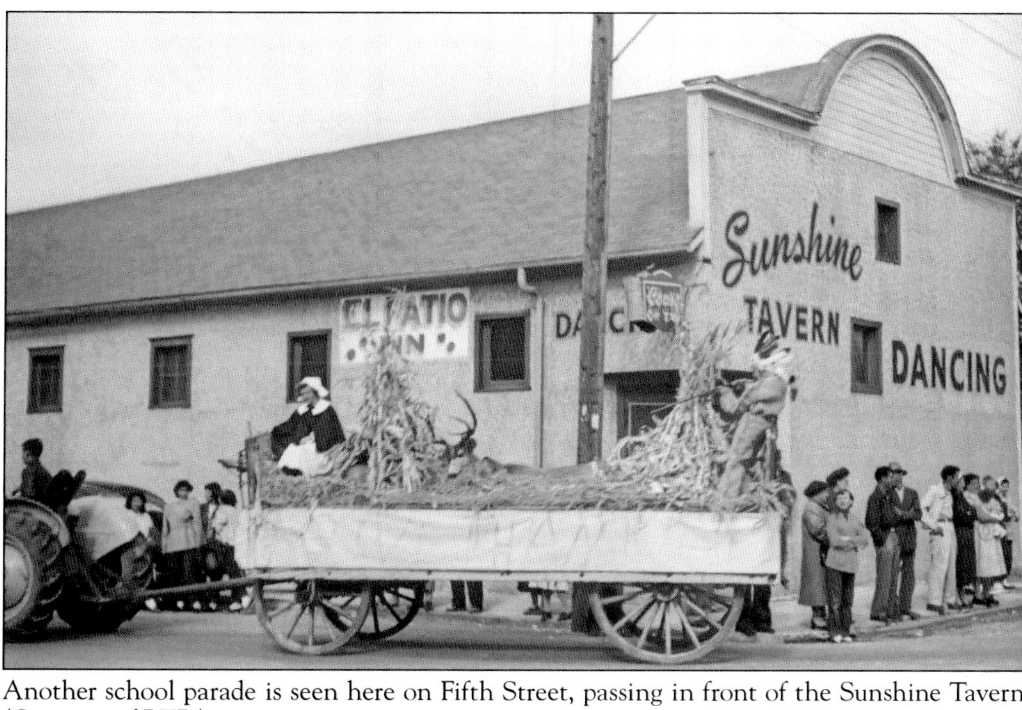

Another school parade is seen here on Fifth Street, passing in front of the Sunshine Tavern. (Courtesy of BTB.)

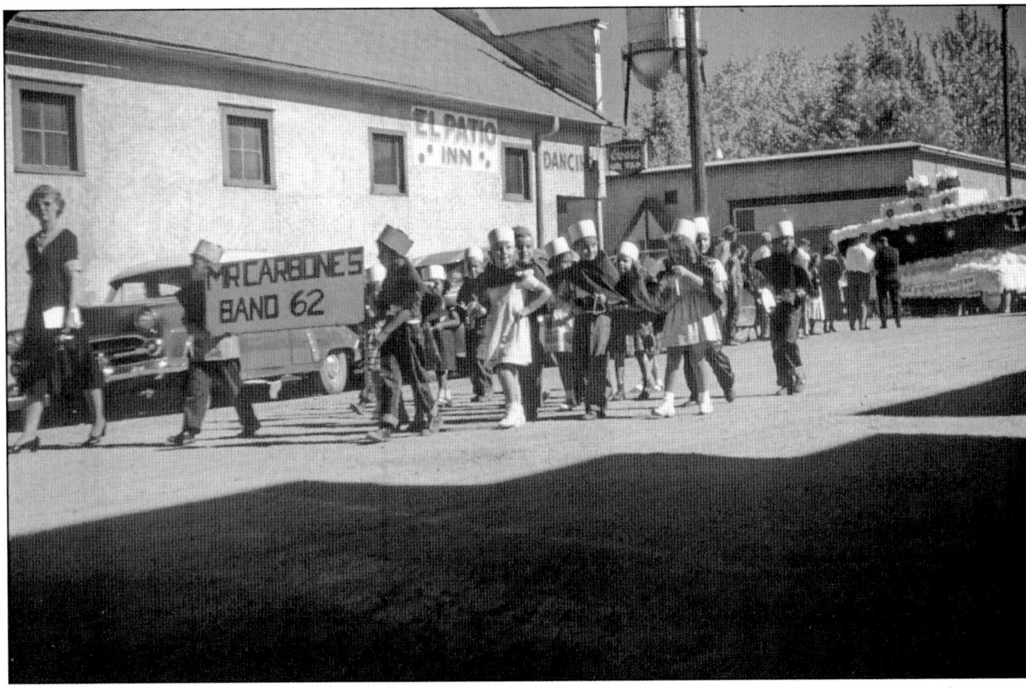

This homecoming parade passes in front of the Sunshine Tavern. The building in the background is the church rectory for St. Theresa's Catholic Church. In the far background is the Frederick water tower. Since the water tower is still standing, this photograph was taken before 1963. (Courtesy of BTB.)

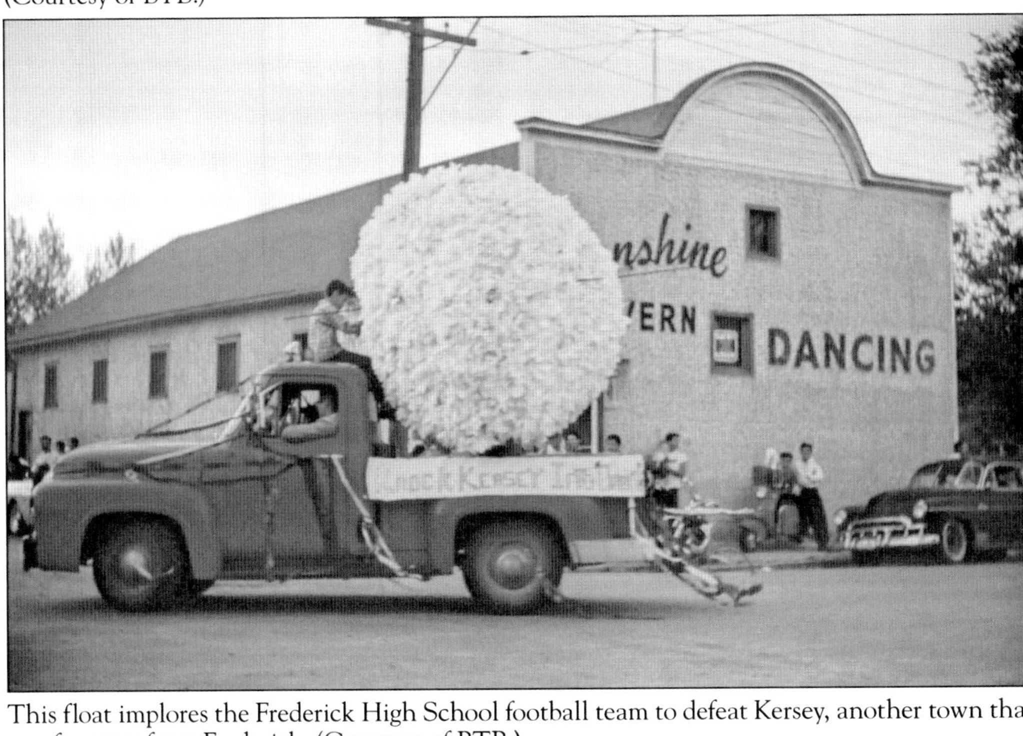

This float implores the Frederick High School football team to defeat Kersey, another town that was far away from Frederick. (Courtesy of BTB.)

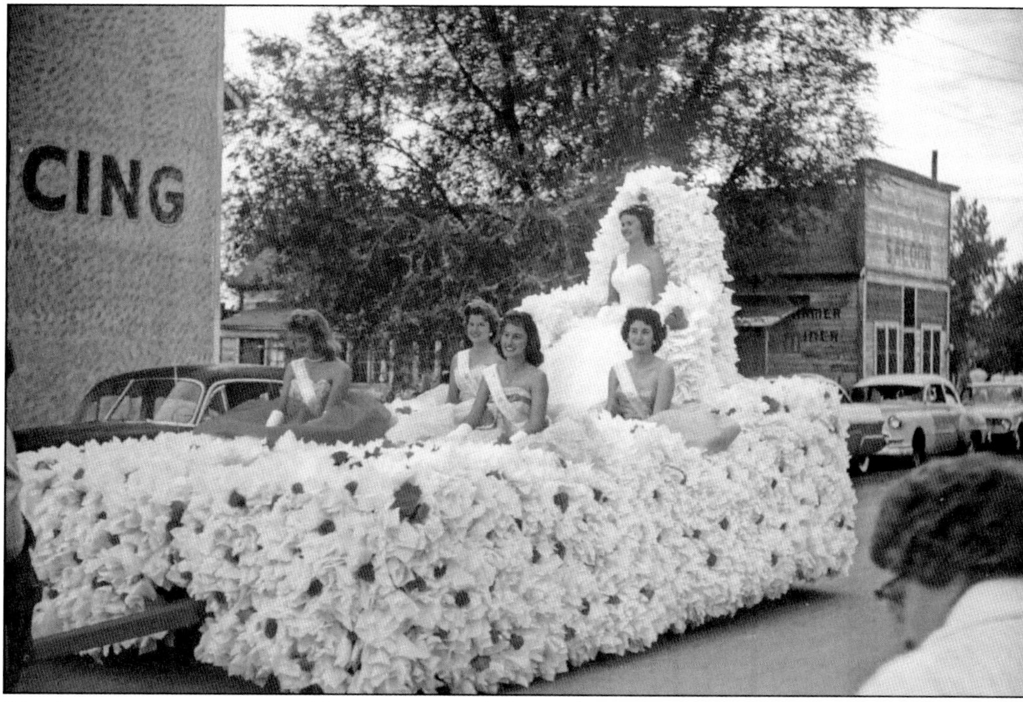

The homecoming queen and her court travel down the street on their float. Sitting from left to right are Beverly Spellings, Janice Evezich, Emilia Guadanoli, Judy Trott, and Janet Zadel. On the extreme left is the Sunshine Tavern. In the background is the former home of the *Farmer and Miner* newspaper and one of the many taverns that populated Fifth Street. This photograph was taken in 1961. (Courtesy of BTB.)

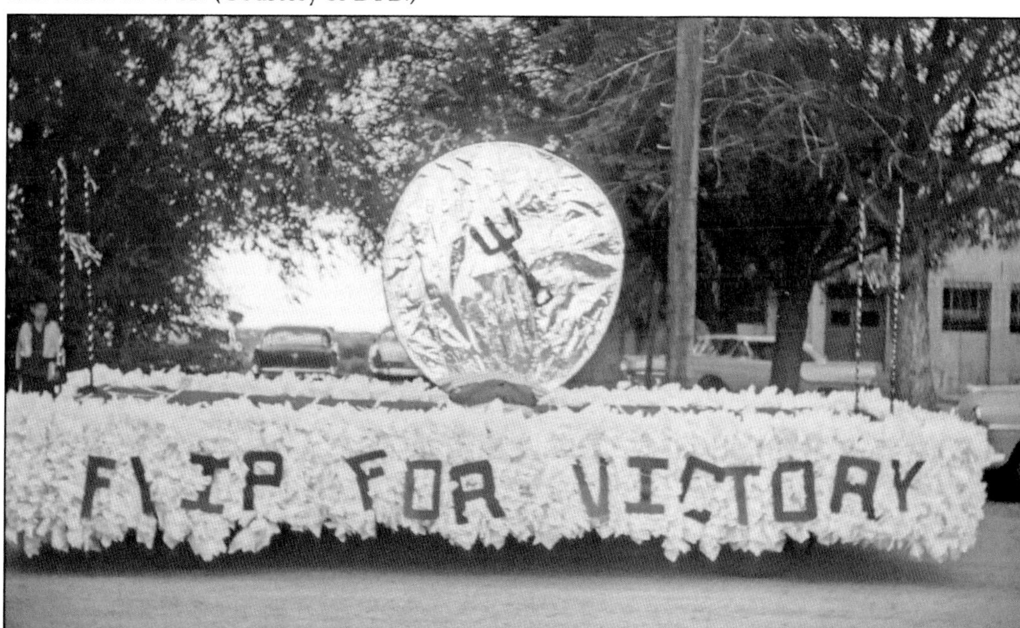

Another homecoming float takes its place, with the gymnasium in the background. This float was part of the homecoming celebration of 1961. (Courtesy of BTB.)

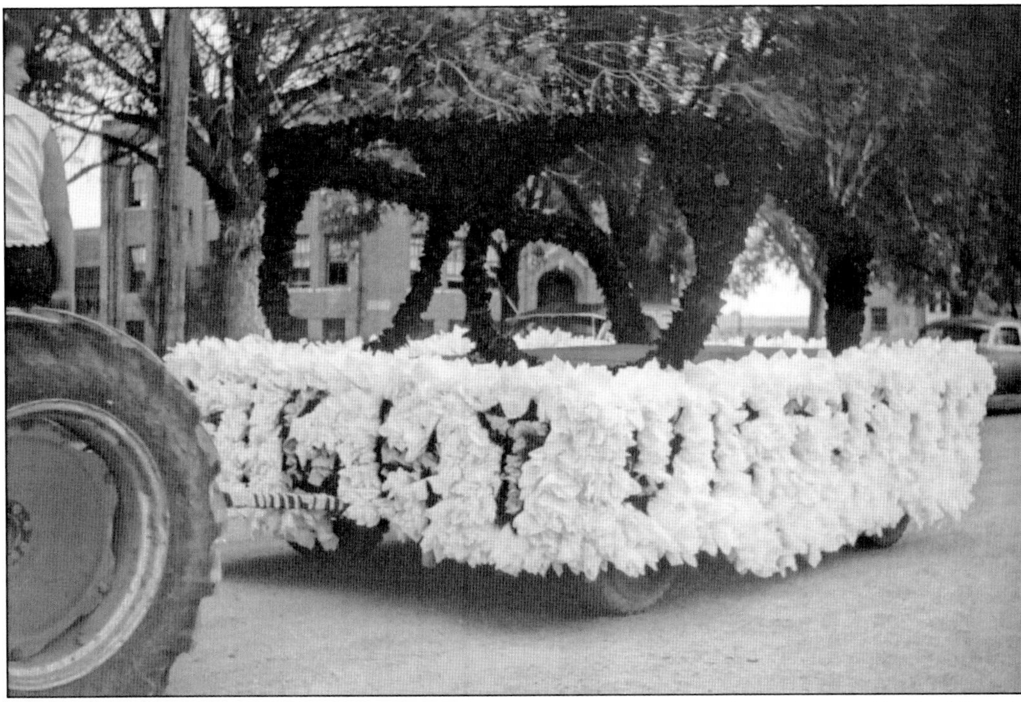

It is unclear what this float represents, other than a gigantic pair of eyeglasses. The building in the background is Frederick High School. (Courtesy of BTB.)

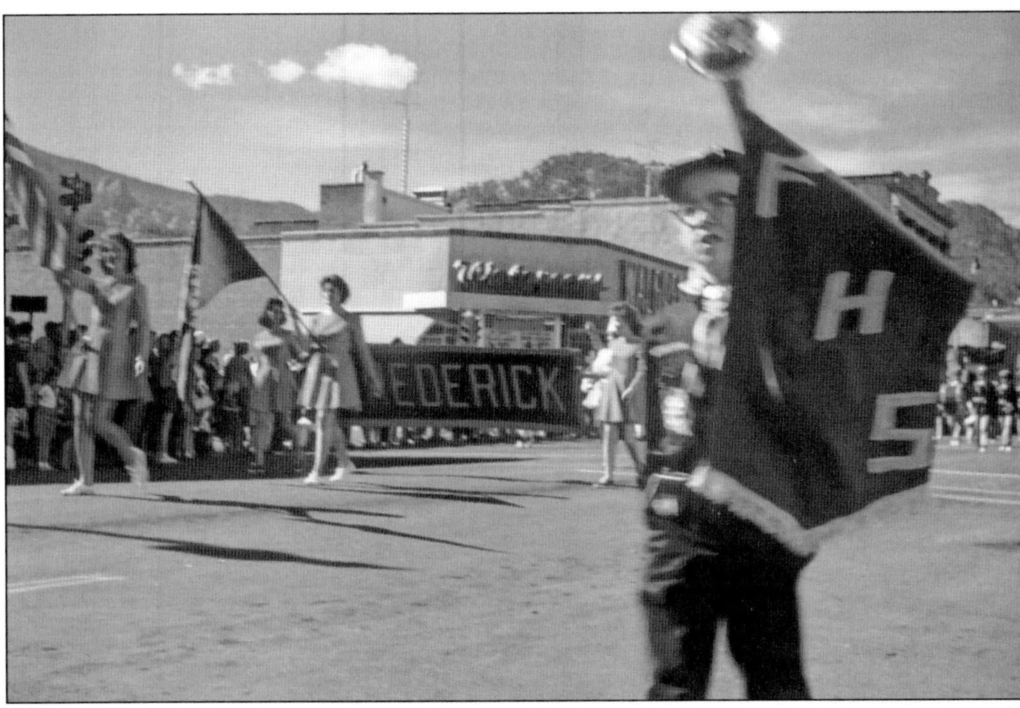

Frederick High School students are seen here marching in Boulder. The mountains in the background make it clear that the photograph was not taken in Frederick. (Courtesy of BTB.)

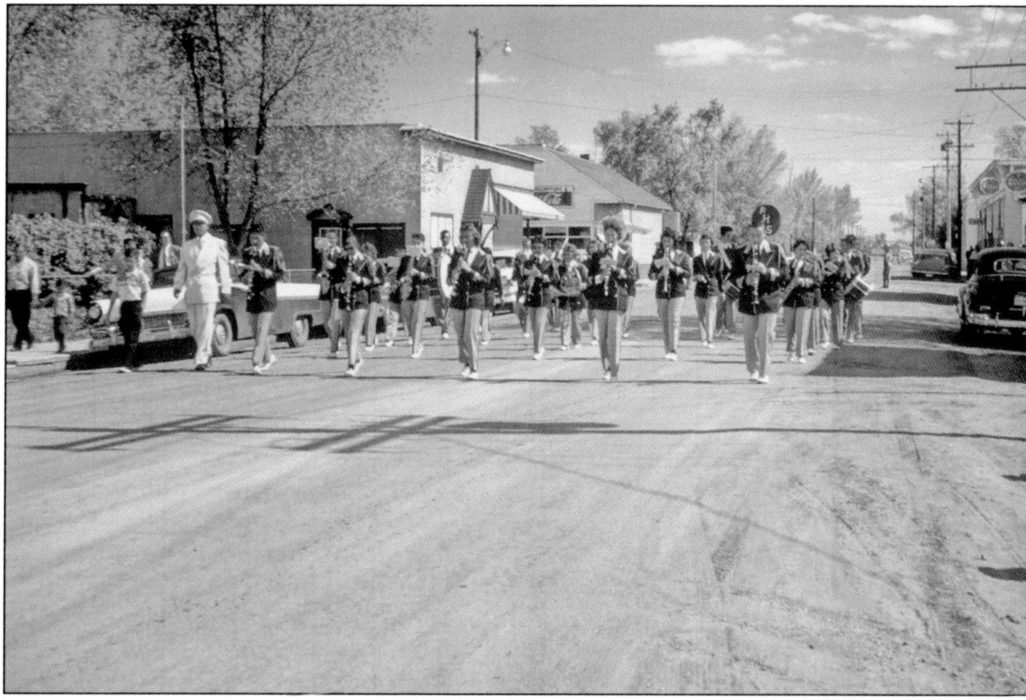

The Frederick High School marching band participates in the homecoming parade. (Courtesy of BTB.)

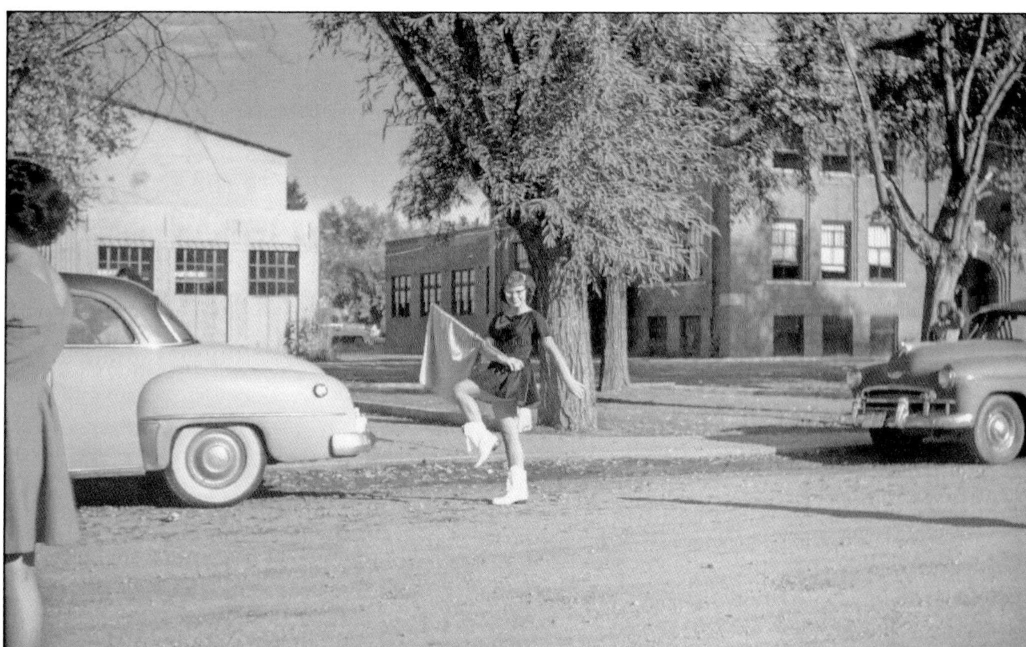

Drum major Linda Baker is seen here before the start of a parade. Frederick High School is on the right and the gymnasium is on the left. (Courtesy of BTB.)

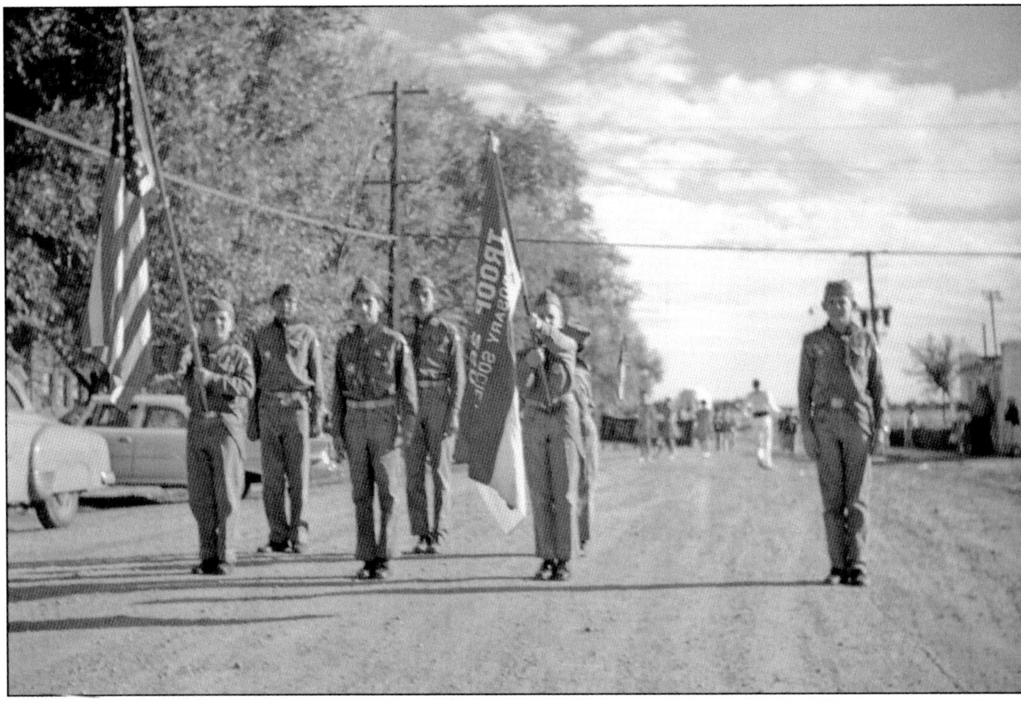

This group of Boy Scouts marches through town in a homecoming parade. This photograph was taken near the start of the parade. (Courtesy of BTB.)

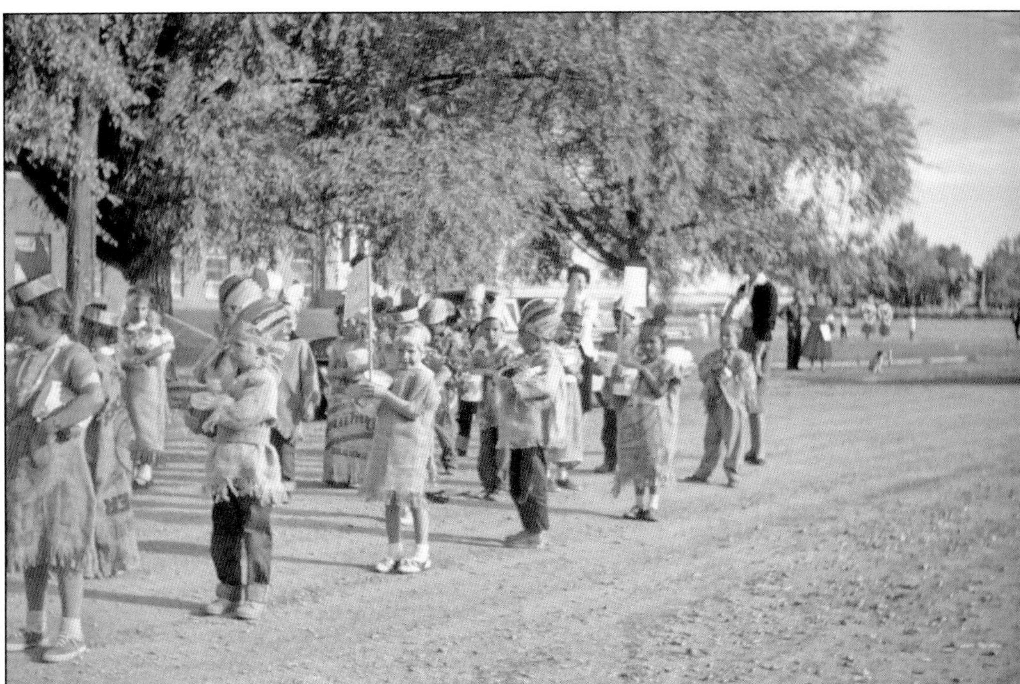

Frederick Elementary School students are dressed up as Indians for this homecoming parade. This photograph was taken in 1961. (Courtesy of BTB.)

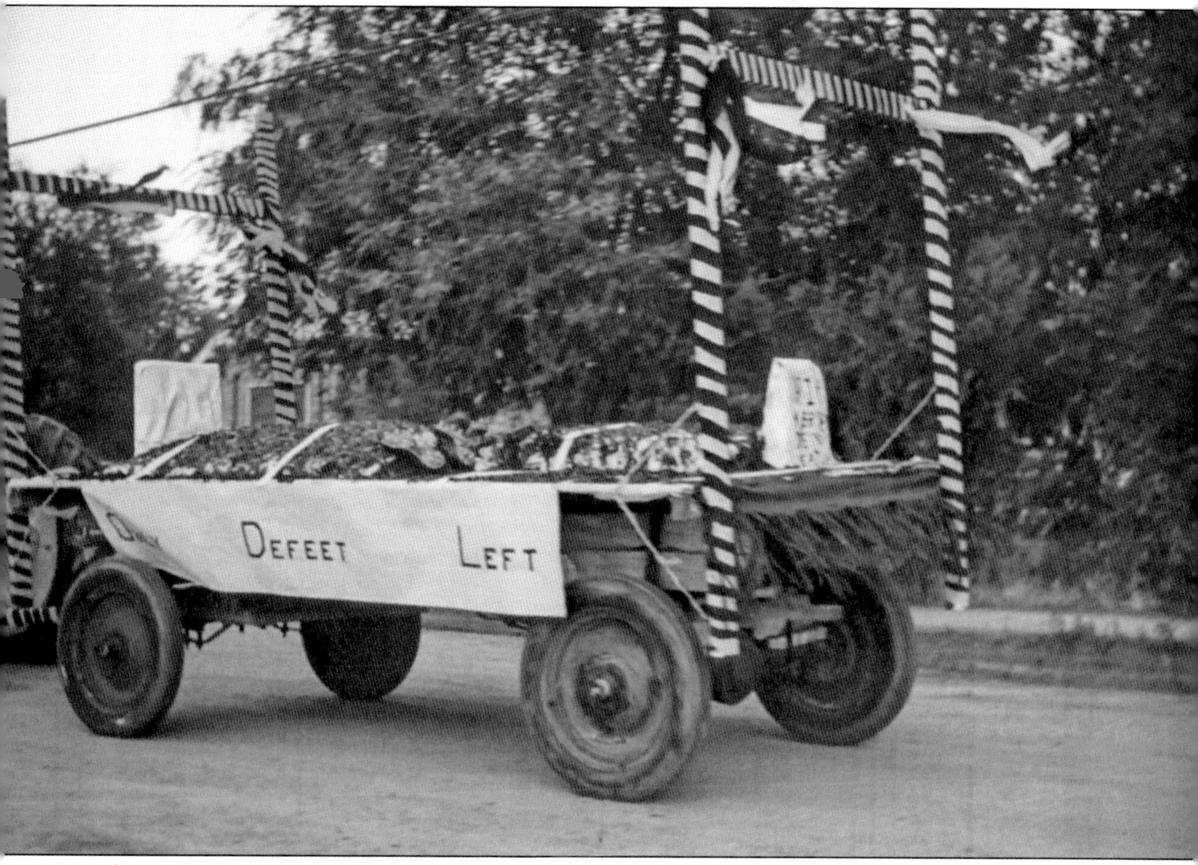

It is clear that a lot of thought went into the making of these floats. Before the parade, the floats were gathered in a field on the outskirts of Frederick for judging. This photograph shows an inventive homecoming float being pulled through the outskirts of Frederick. (Courtesy of BTB.)

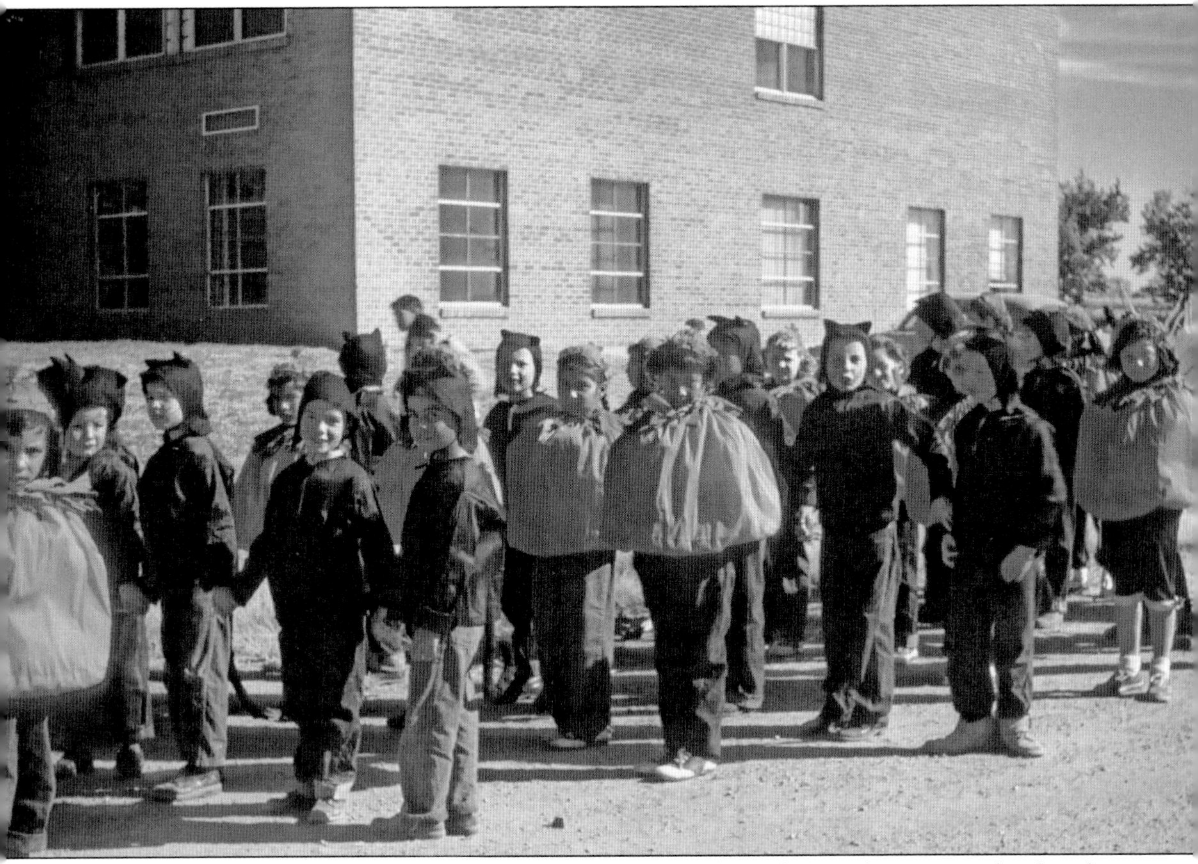

All ages of students participated in the homecoming parade, including elementary school students, as seen here. The building in the background is Frederick High School. (Courtesy of BTB.)

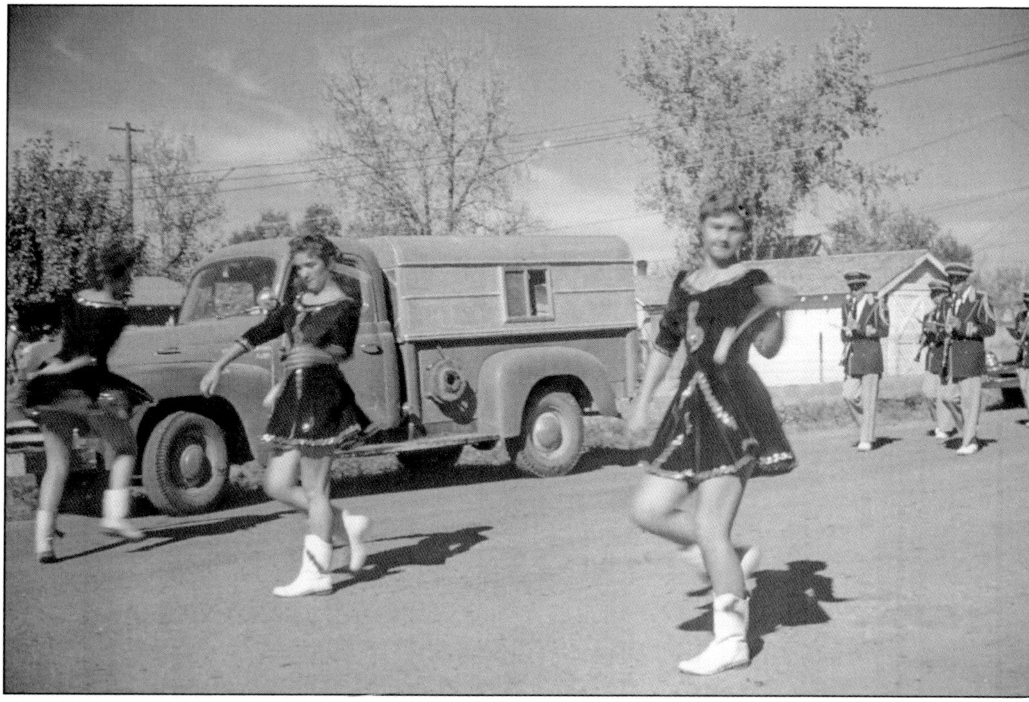

Cheerleaders participate in the homecoming parade on the outskirts of Frederick. (Courtesy of BTB.)

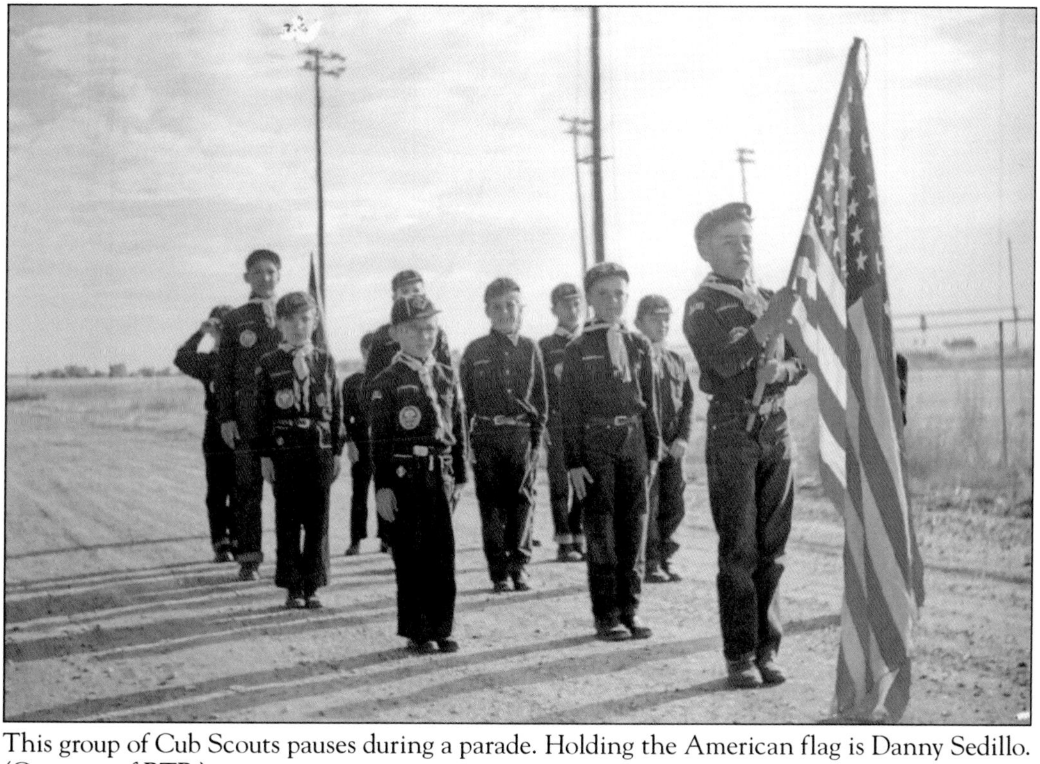

This group of Cub Scouts pauses during a parade. Holding the American flag is Danny Sedillo. (Courtesy of BTB.)

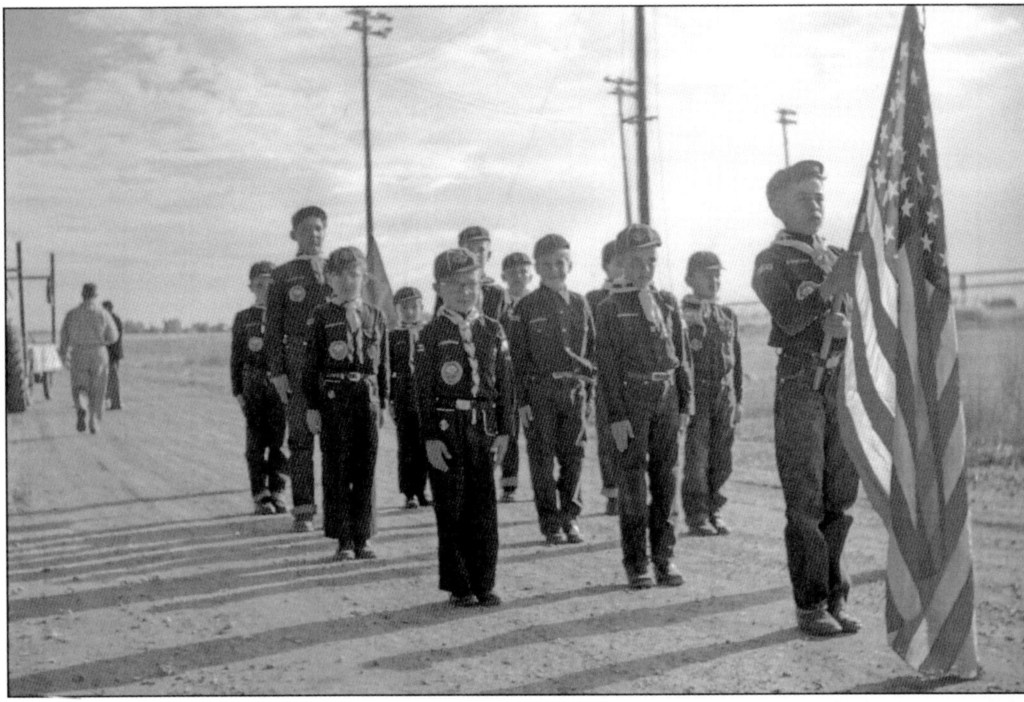

Every community organization participated in homecoming. This photograph shows one of the local Cub Scout troops. (Courtesy of BTB.)

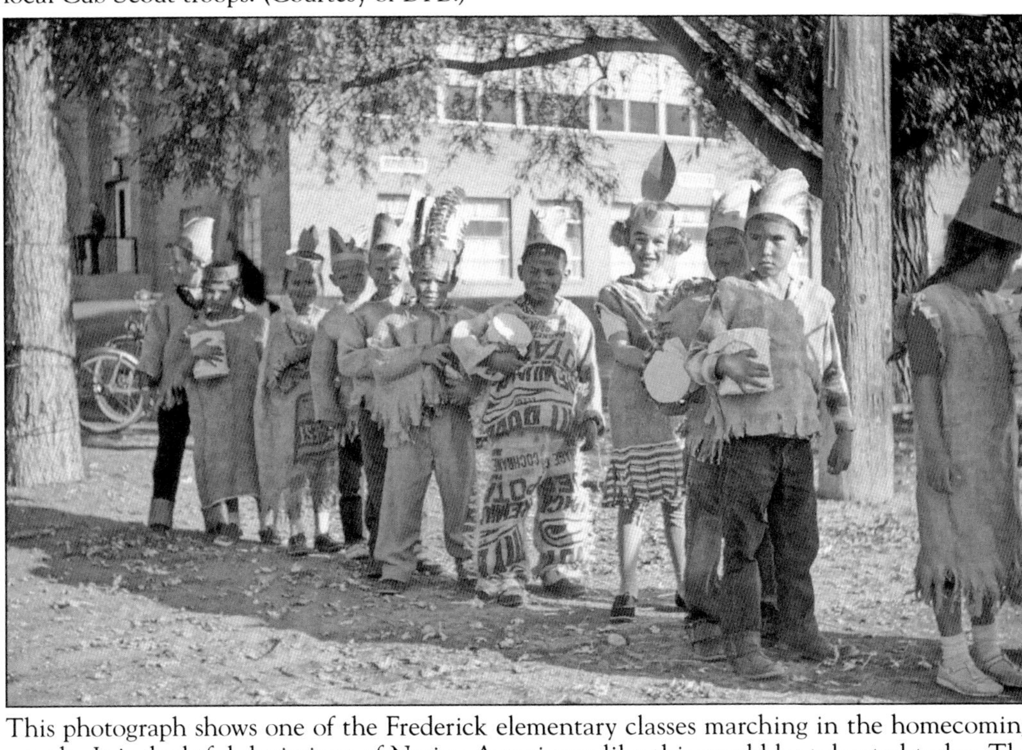

This photograph shows one of the Frederick elementary classes marching in the homecoming parade. It is doubtful depictions of Native Americans like this would be tolerated today. The building in the background is the high school. (Courtesy of BTB.)

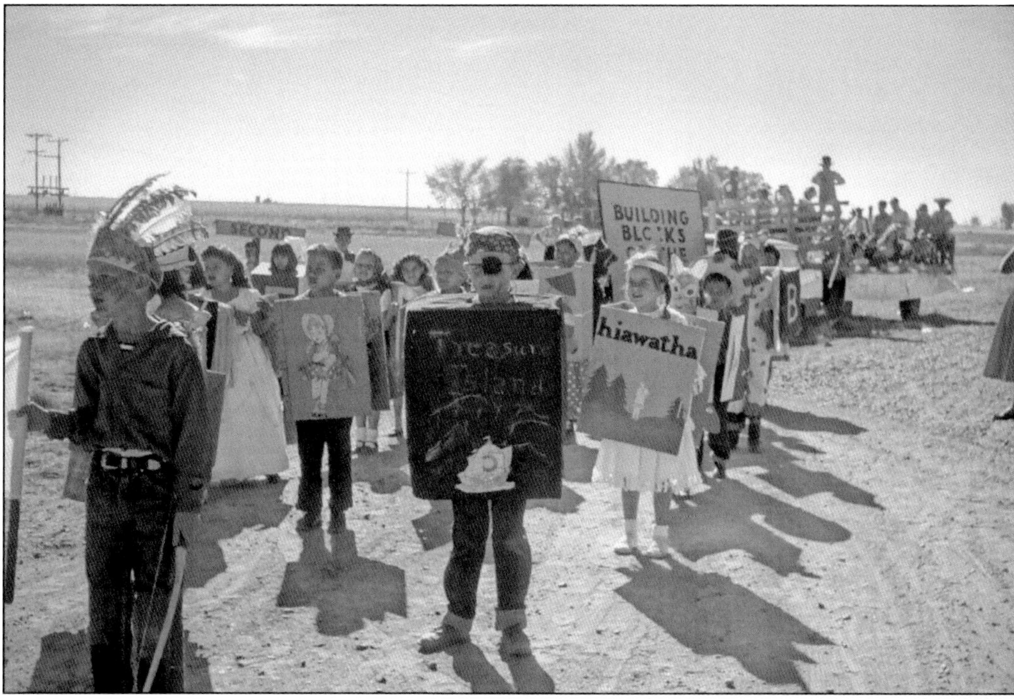

Elementary students are all dressed up for one of the homecoming events. This photograph represents one elementary school grade. (Courtesy of BTB.)

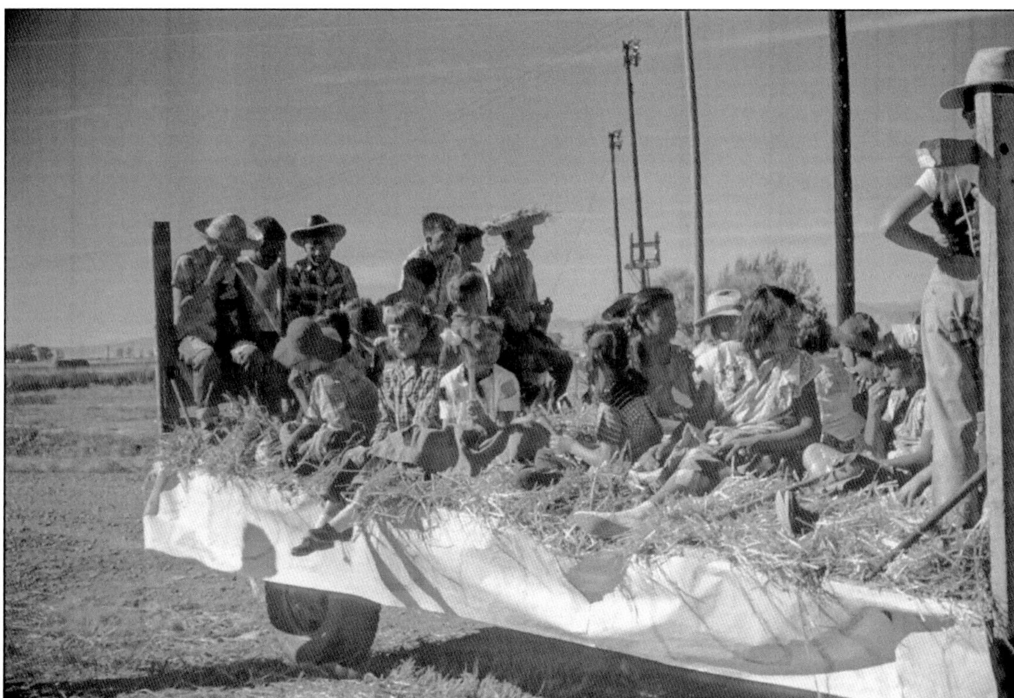

More young, dressed-up students are seen on this float. Each elementary class dressed according to a theme and tried to out do the other classes. (Courtesy of BTB.)

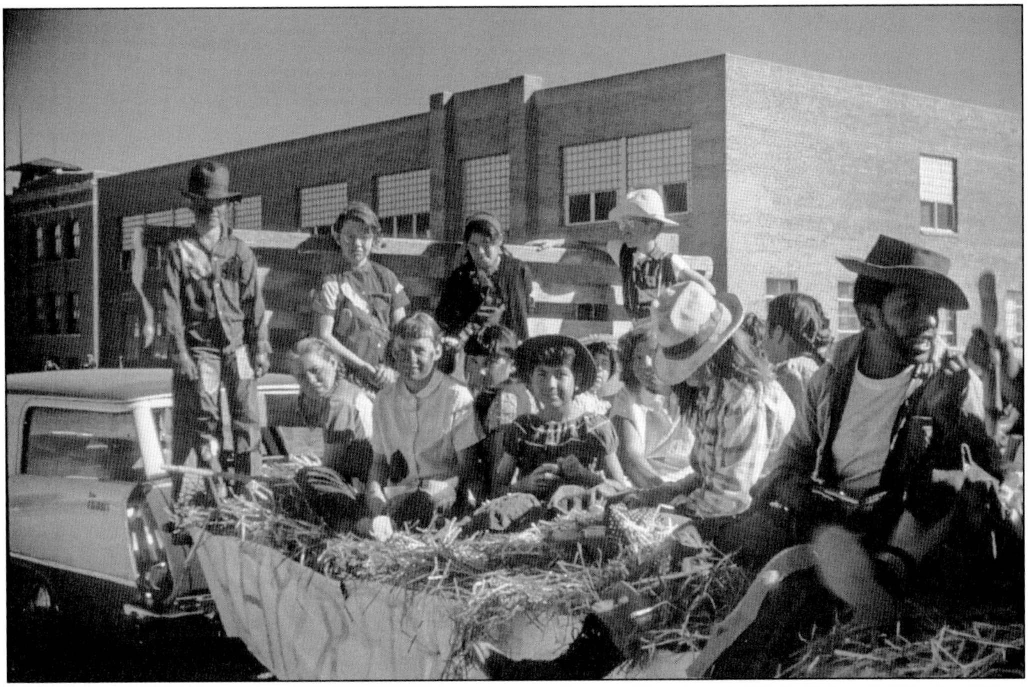

This photograph of a homecoming float was taken in front of Frederick High School. The building in the background replaced the original high school. (Courtesy of BTB.)

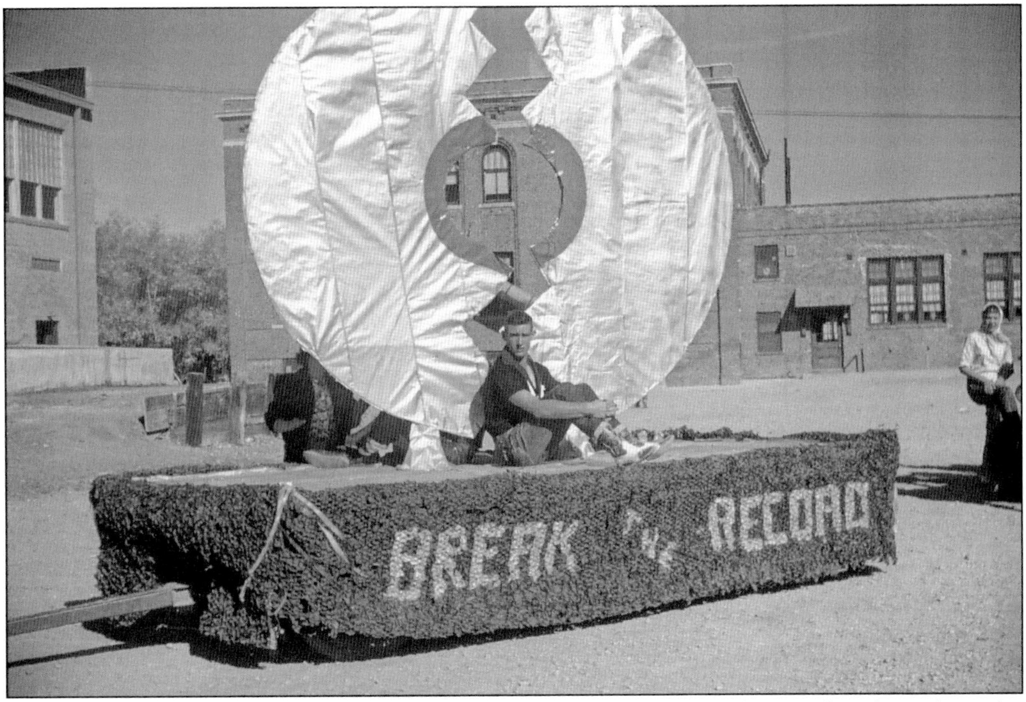

This is another inventive homecoming float. The building in the background to the right is the original high school. (Courtesy of BTB.)

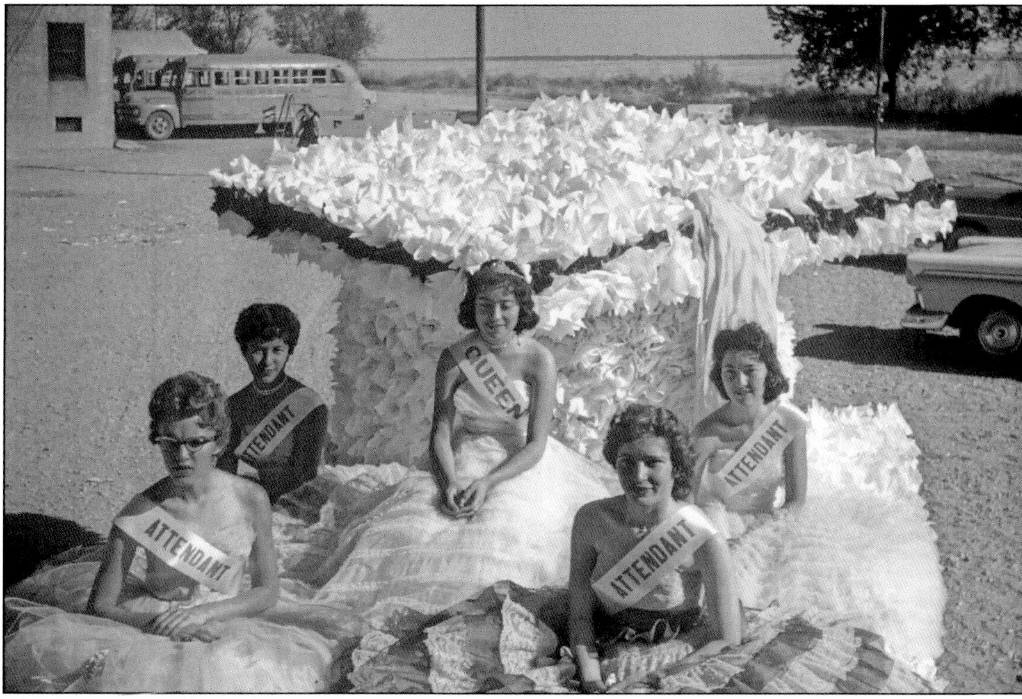

This photograph shows the homecoming queen and her attendants. From left to right are (first row) Josephine Luque and Kathy Stanstie; (second row) Lucille Marquez, Gloria Salazabar, and Laberta DiSalle. This photography was taken in 1958. (Courtesy of BTB.)

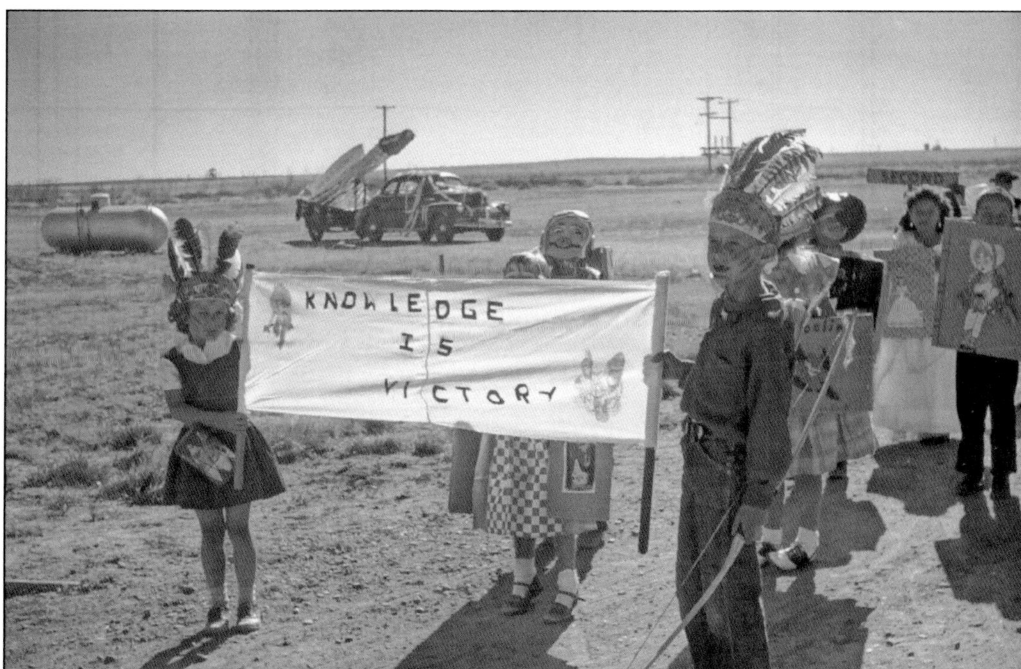

These students are dressed up as Indians for the homecoming parade. They hold up a sign that says, "Knowledge is Victory." (Courtesy of BTB.)

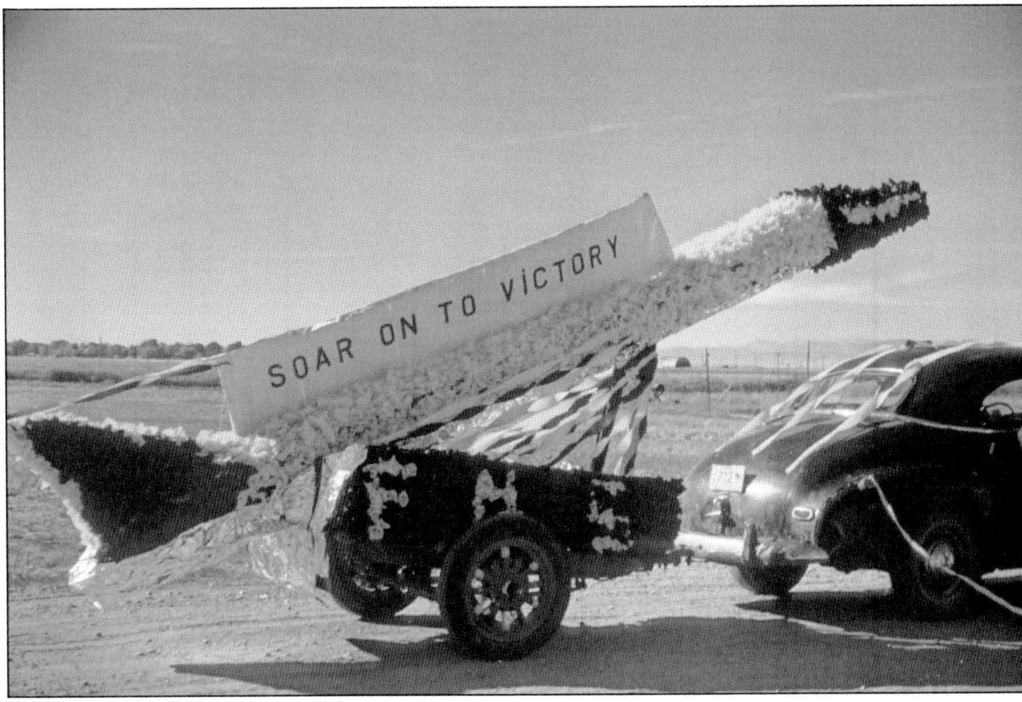

Due to the rocket theme, it is likely that this photograph was taken in the 1960s. (Courtesy of BTB.)

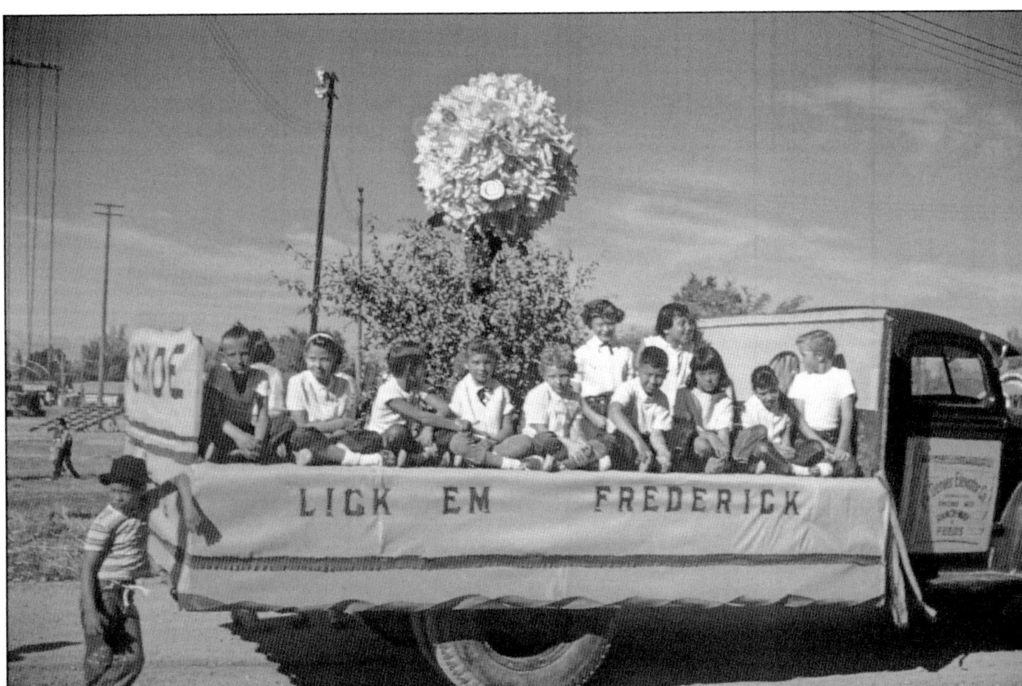

This is another one of the many homecoming floats made by Frederick elementary students. (Courtesy of BTB.)

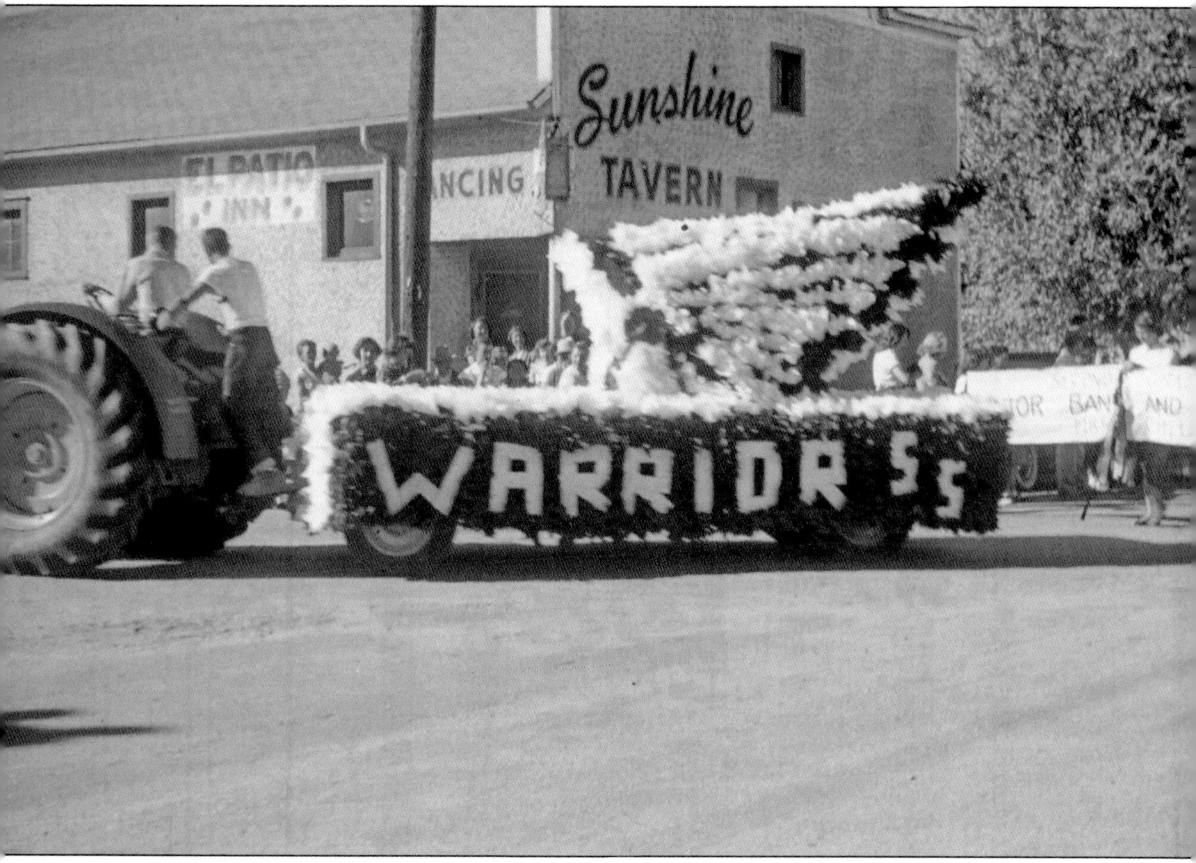

This float spurred on the Frederick High School Warriors in 1955. The building in the background was known both as the Sunshine Tavern and the El Patio Inn. (Courtesy of BTB.)

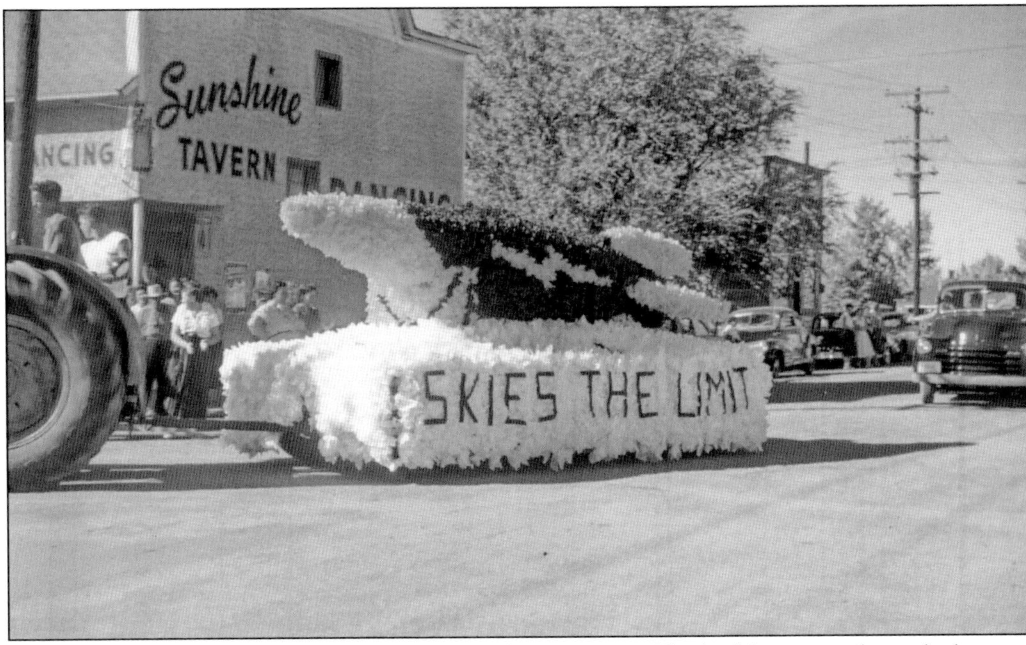

Another elaborate float turns around the Sunshine Tavern. The building seen through the trees to the far right is the old *Farmer and Miner* newspaper building. The *Farmer and Miner* is still being published and serves the tri-town region. (Courtesy of BTB.)

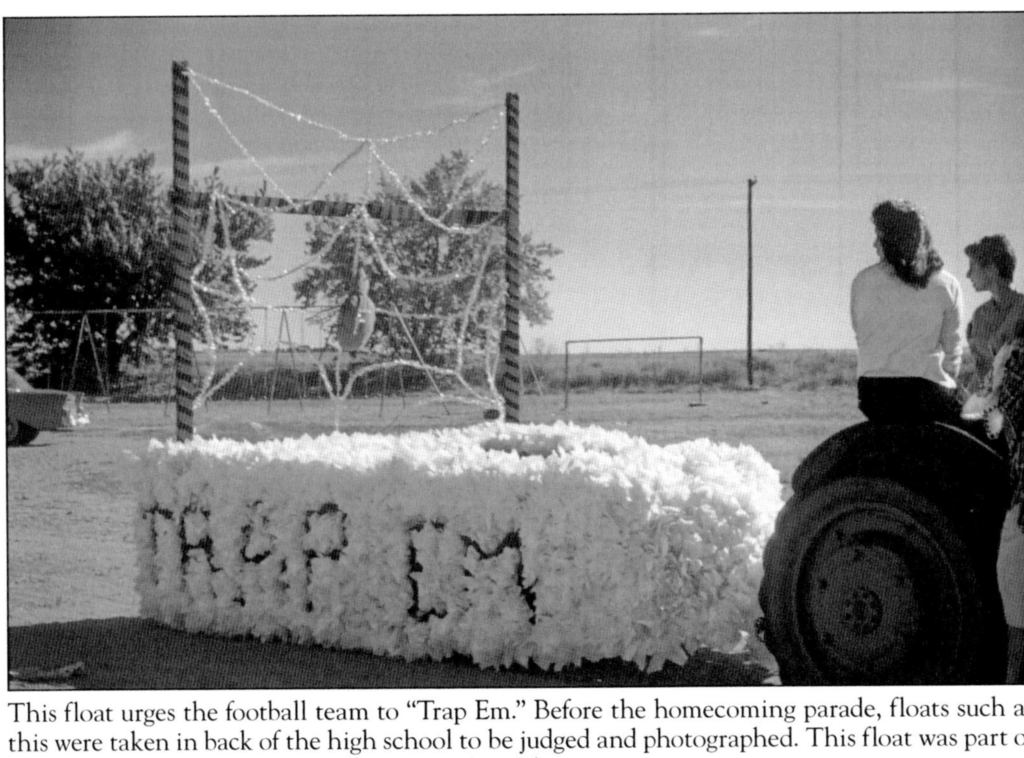

This float urges the football team to "Trap Em." Before the homecoming parade, floats such as this were taken in back of the high school to be judged and photographed. This float was part of the 1955 homecoming parade. (Courtesy of BTB.)

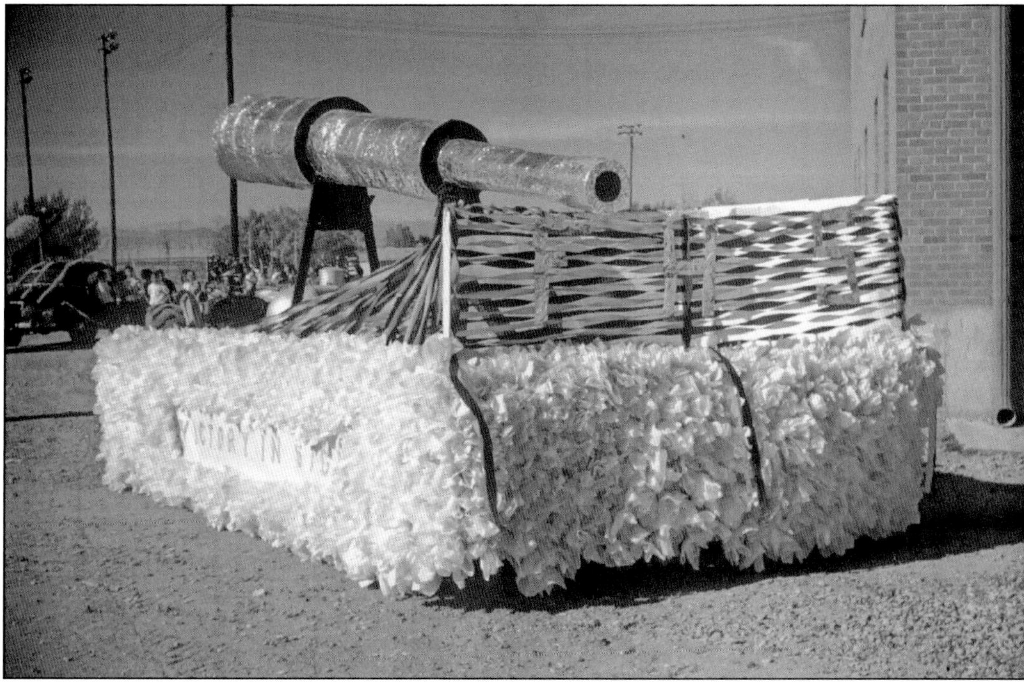

This is another one of the many elaborate homecoming floats Frederick was known for. This float was judged as part of the 1955 homecoming parade. (Courtesy of BTB.)

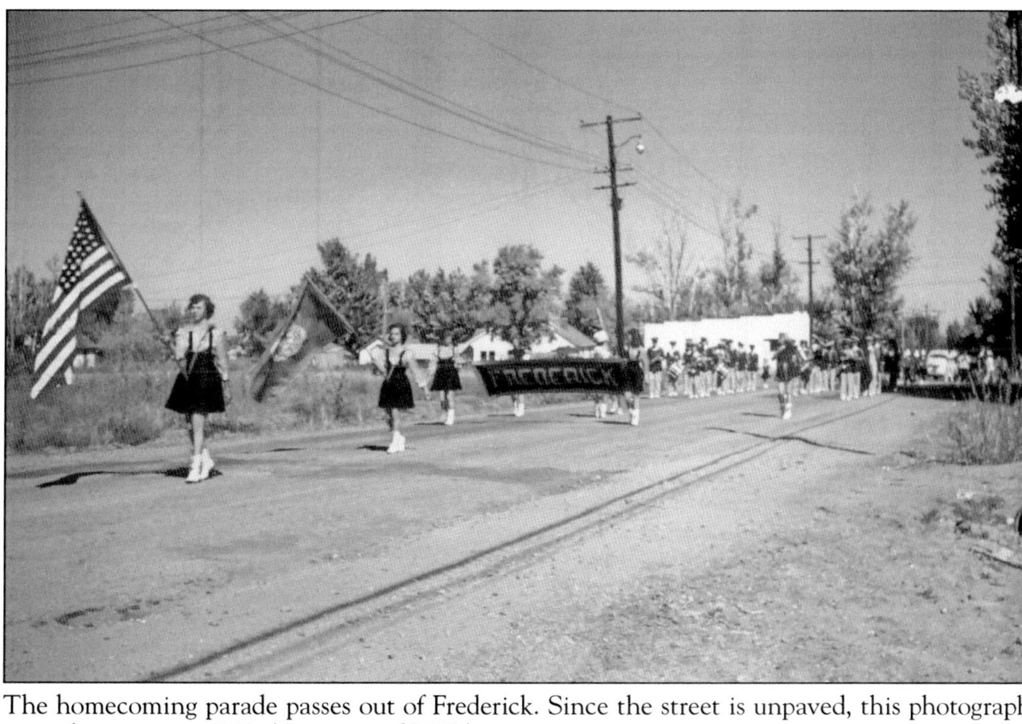

The homecoming parade passes out of Frederick. Since the street is unpaved, this photograph was taken prior to 1963. (Courtesy of BTB.)

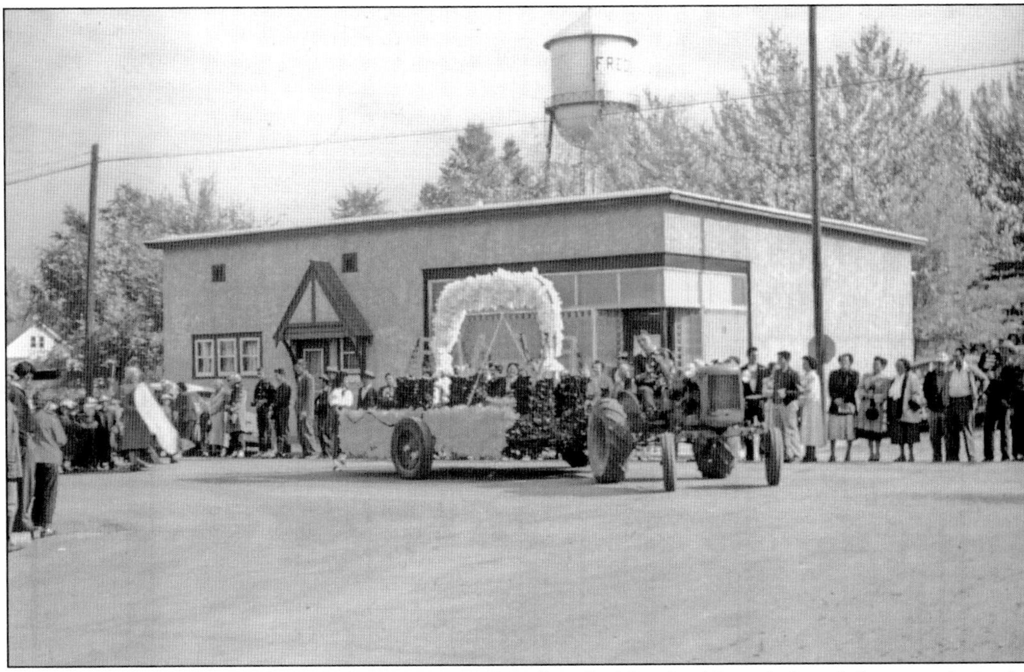

This homecoming parade travels west out of Frederick. The building behind the parade is the church rectory, and the water tower is behind that in the distance. (Courtesy of BTB.)

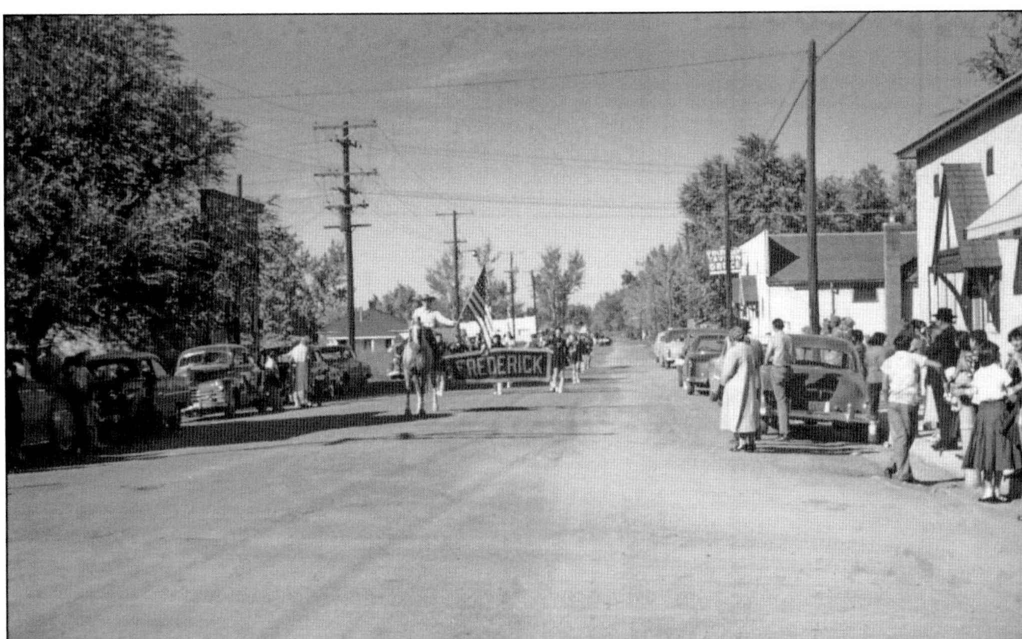

Fifth Street was a popular vantage point from which to watch the parade. This photograph shows the homecoming parade passing down Fifth Street. (Courtesy of BTB.)

Six

A Bright Future

Throughout its history, Frederick has been forced to confront changing economic and social conditions. Rather than become stagnate, the Frederick community has met each challenge with enthusiasm and innovation. Frederick started as a community founded on coal mining. As mining began to decline, farming grew to take its place. Oil and gas also became a major economic benefit to Frederick, as well as in other northern Colorado communities.

Today, Frederick faces a major challenge incorporating itself into the larger community of northern Colorado. Open spaces no longer dominate the area between Denver and the Wyoming border. The greater northern Front Range has grown and filled in, and Frederick must now decide how it will take its place in this larger community.

An important aspect of this process is managing growth. At the same time, growth must be placed in the larger framework of surrounding communities. Frederick, Firestone, and Dacono all strive to expand, and expansion is best achieved through annexation. However, uncontrolled or poorly planned annexation will produce conflict with neighboring communities. Frederick, as well as the other tri-town communities, wants to expand its business base. Whether this expansion takes place through flagpole annexations outside of old town boundaries or whether Frederick's downtown expands remains to be decided. Whichever direction is chosen, it is clear that the town's planning commission will become more central to town government.

Frederick's government structure will also be forced to change. As Frederick grows through residential expansion, pressures on services such as schools, fire and police, and road maintenance will grow. Frederick's government will have to change from a purely volunteer structure to one more dedicated to full-time governance. All of these issues will have to be addressed by the board of trustees.

Frederick has come a long way since the time when its only residents were Indians, coyotes, snakes, and seams of coal. Frederick has become an integral part of the northern Colorado region and will soon have to address big-city issues. However, it has not, and will not, forget its small-town roots.

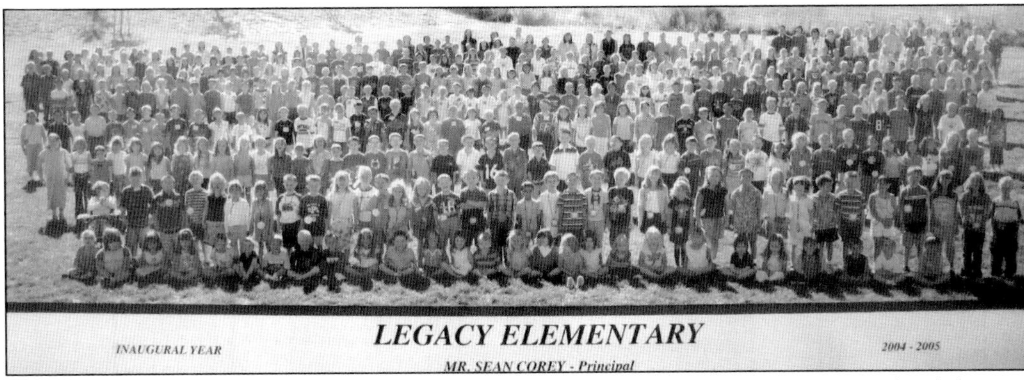

This photograph shows the students, teachers, and staff at Legacy Elementary School, located just west of Frederick. Legacy is one of several schools that had to be built to accommodate the increasing population. (Courtesy of the Town of Frederick.)

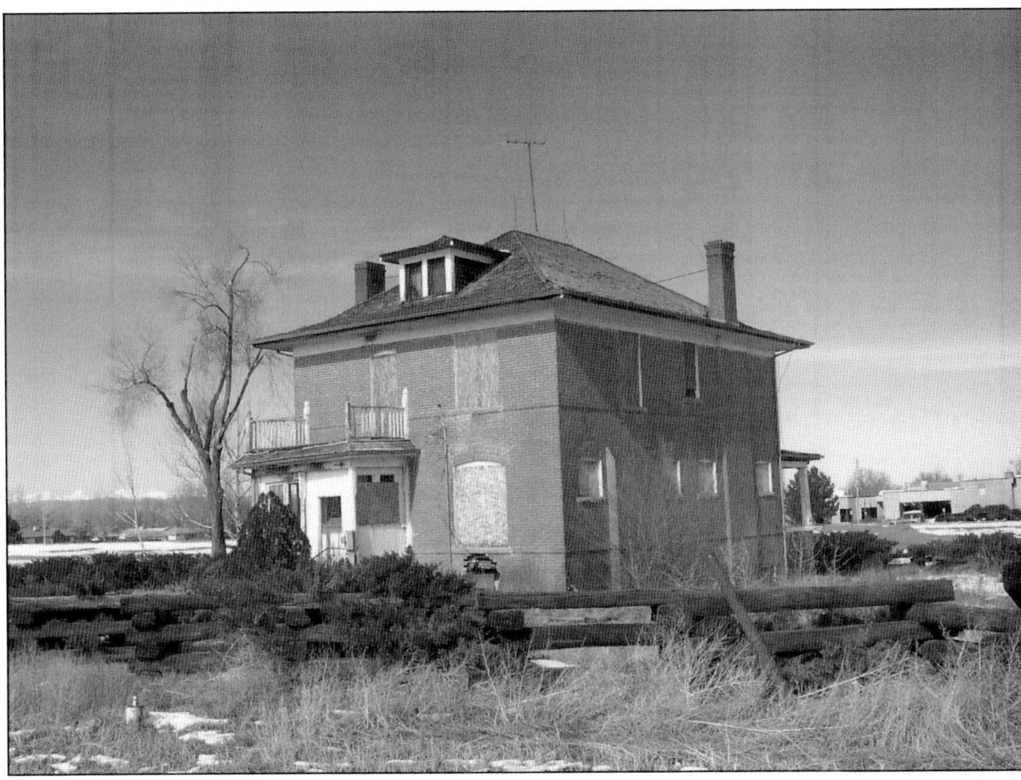

This was the farmhouse on the old Johnson farm. Frederick purchased the building with the hope of refurbishing it and moving it to a new location. Unfortunately, five months after this photograph was taken, the farm burned to the ground. Arson was suspected. (Courtesy of the Town of Frederick.)

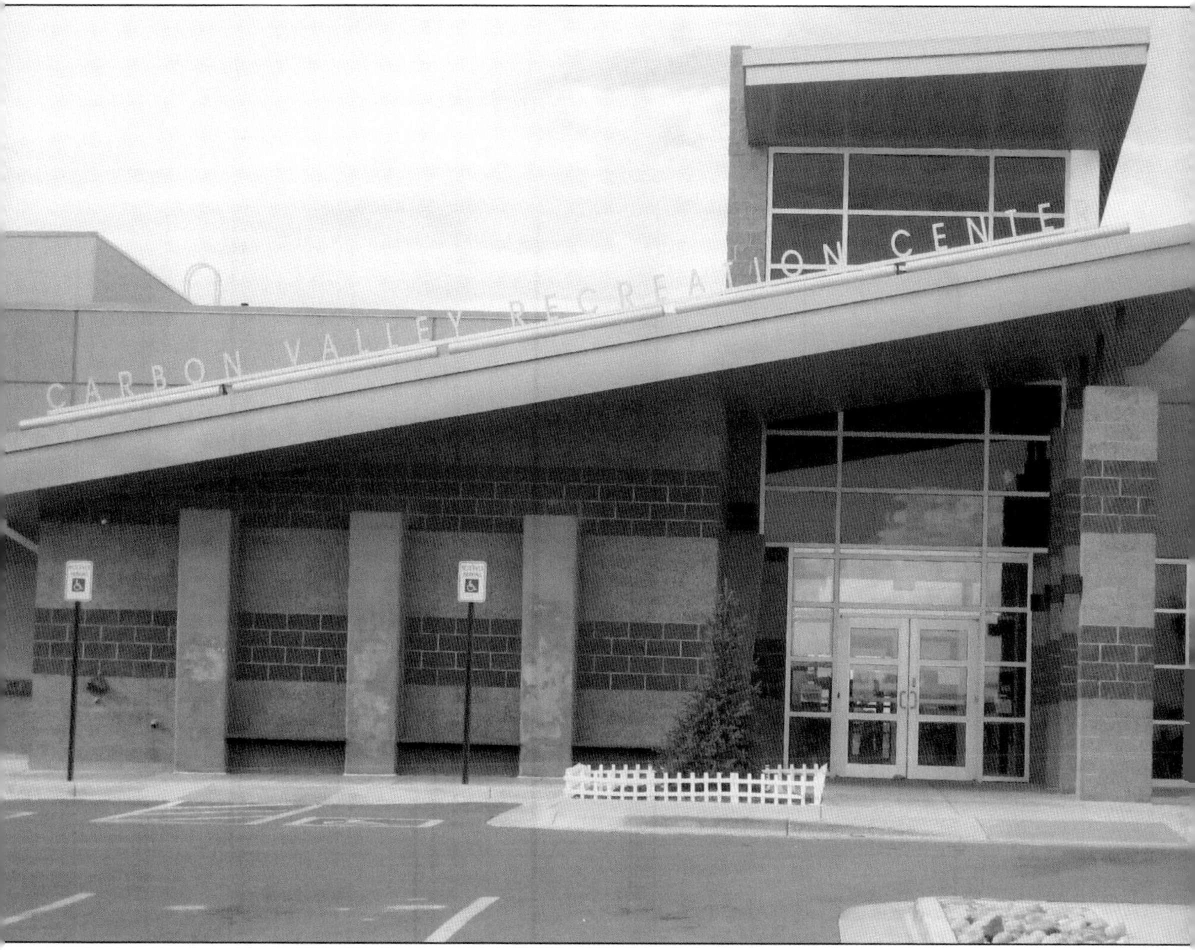

Carbon Valley Recreation Center features a weight room and a full-sized swimming pool, as well as a swimming area for children. Community events are also held at the recreation center. This building is an example of the increased public amenities available to the residents of Frederick and other members of the tri-town communities. (Courtesy of the Town of Frederick.)

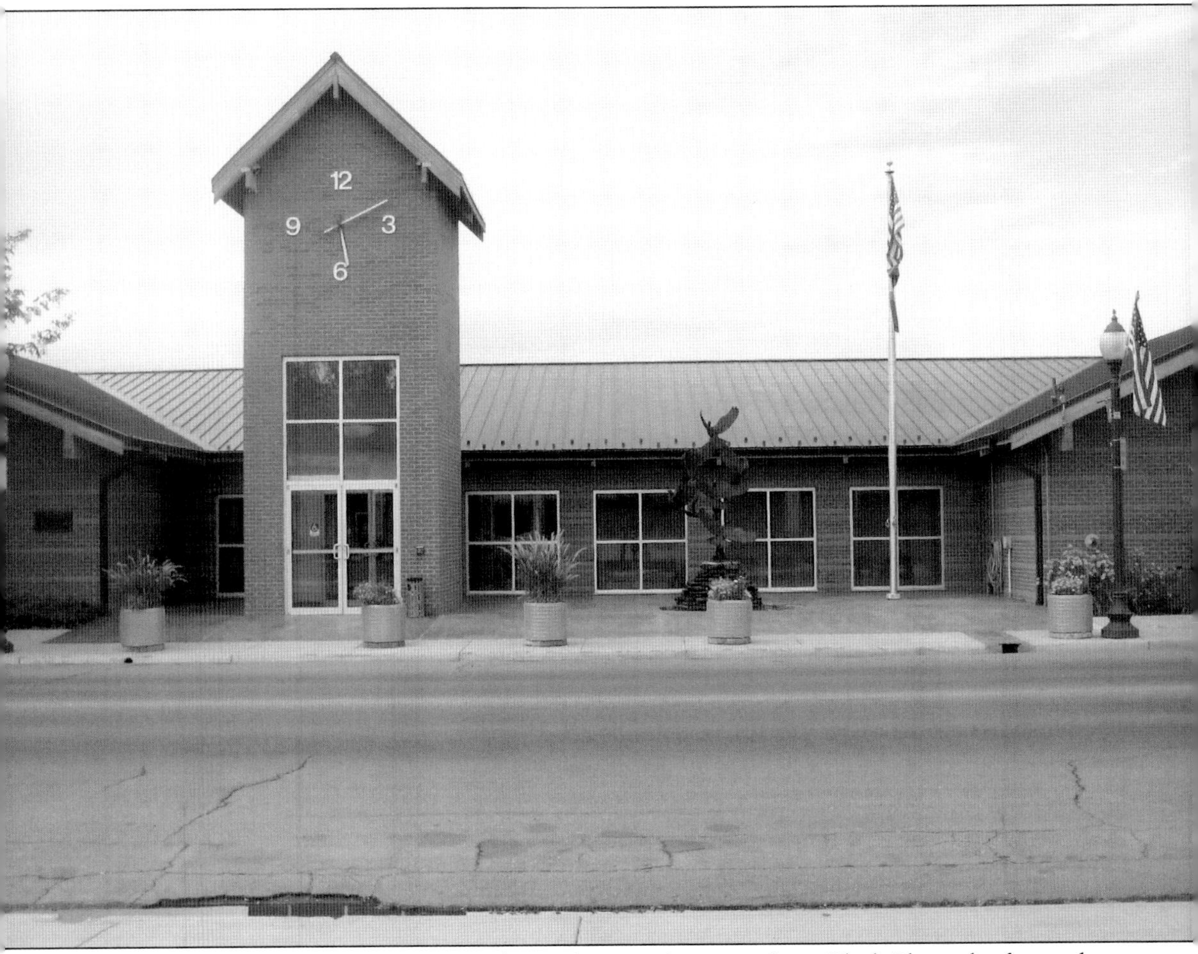

The Frederick Police Department is located across the street from Clark Plaza, the former home of Clark Lumber Company. (Courtesy of the Town of Frederick.)

The Johnson family farmhouse was significant because of its architecture and the beauty of the interior. It represents a second-generation structure because it was constructed of brick, not wood. This photograph shows the staircase in the house. (Courtesy of the Town of Frederick.)

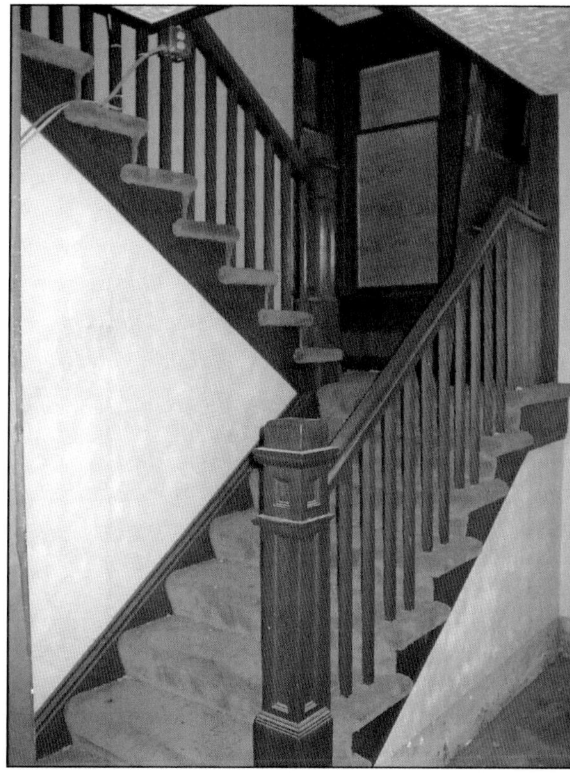

In this photograph of the interior of the Johnson farmhouse, note the stained-glass windows at the top of the boarded-up windows. These stained-glass panels were preserved and moved before the fire. (Courtesy of the Town of Frederick.)

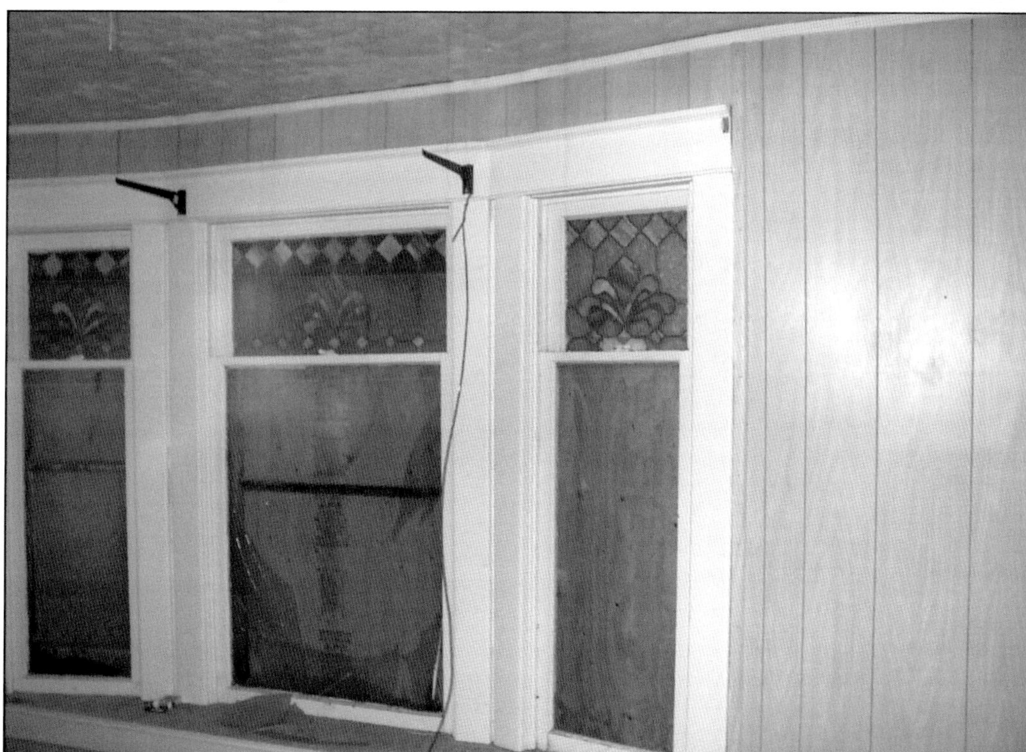

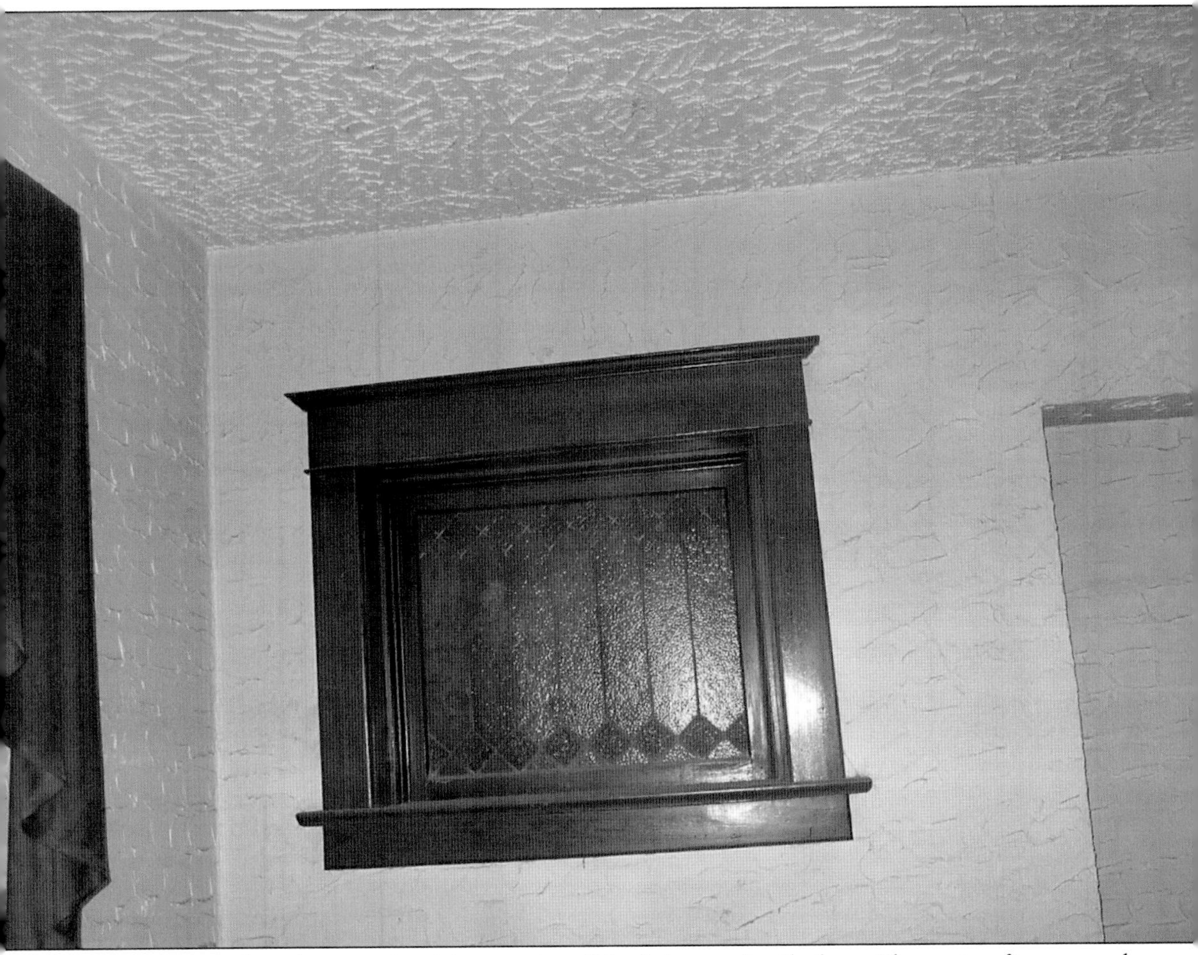

This is another photograph of the interior of the Johnson family farm. Shown is a fine example of stained glass. It is unknown whether this panel survived the fire. (Courtesy of the Town of Frederick.)

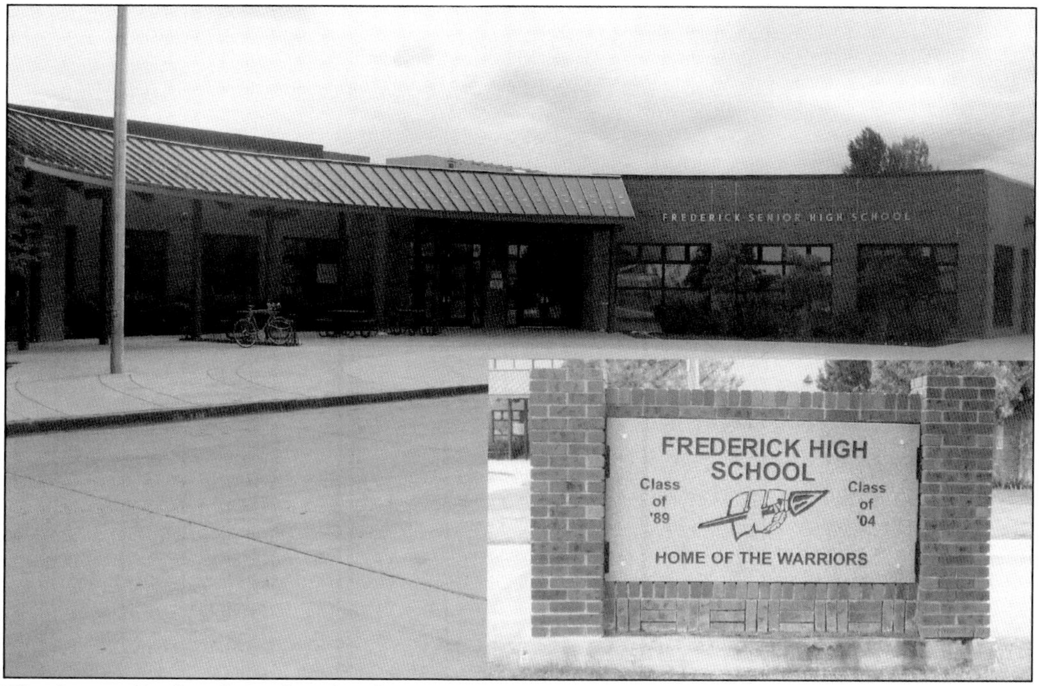

The former Frederick High School is seen here. Due to increasing population, the high school was replaced by a new building across Colorado Boulevard, west of Frederick. This building now serves as the junior high school. (Courtesy of the Town of Frederick.)

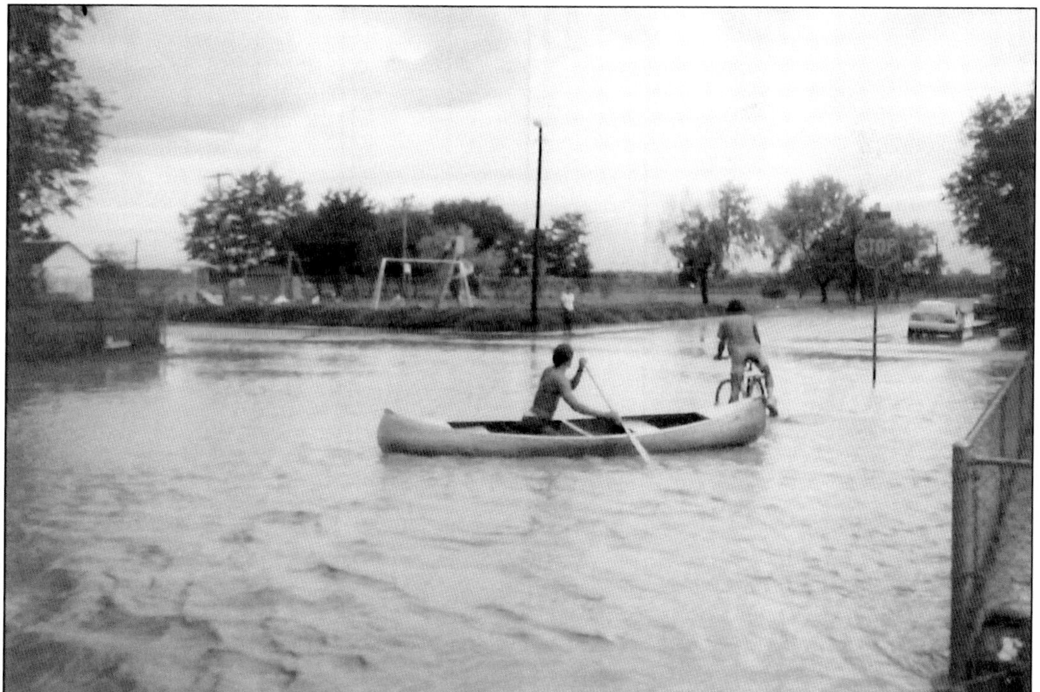

This photograph, taken during the 1998 flood, shows how deep the water can get in the Frederick streets, as a canoe easily maneuvers through the streets. (Courtesy of the Town of Frederick.)

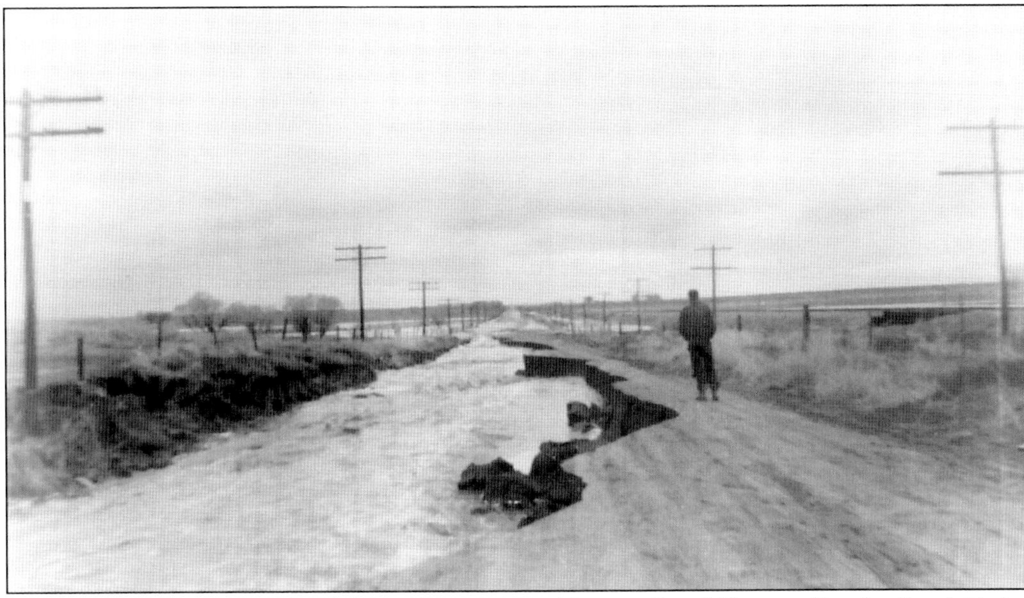

This image from the 1957 flood shows the erosion of County Road 13 caused by the flood. Today, Bella Rosa Golf Course is on the left of the road. To the right and farther south are the Safeway, Adams Bank & Trust, and Ace Hardware. (Courtesy of the Town of Frederick.)

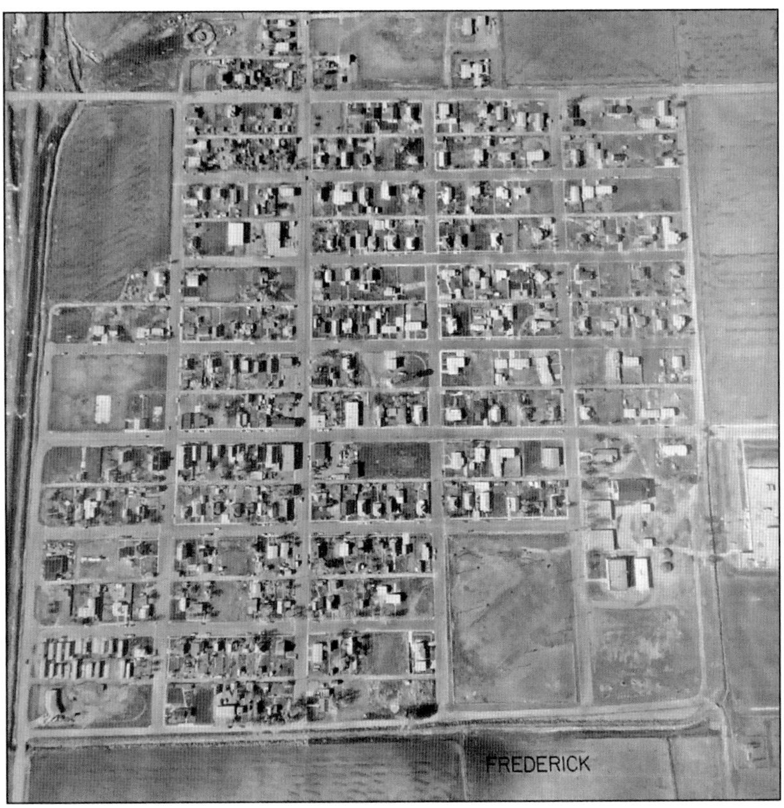

This old photograph of Frederick shows the town prior to the recent annexations. (Courtesy of Town of Frederick.)

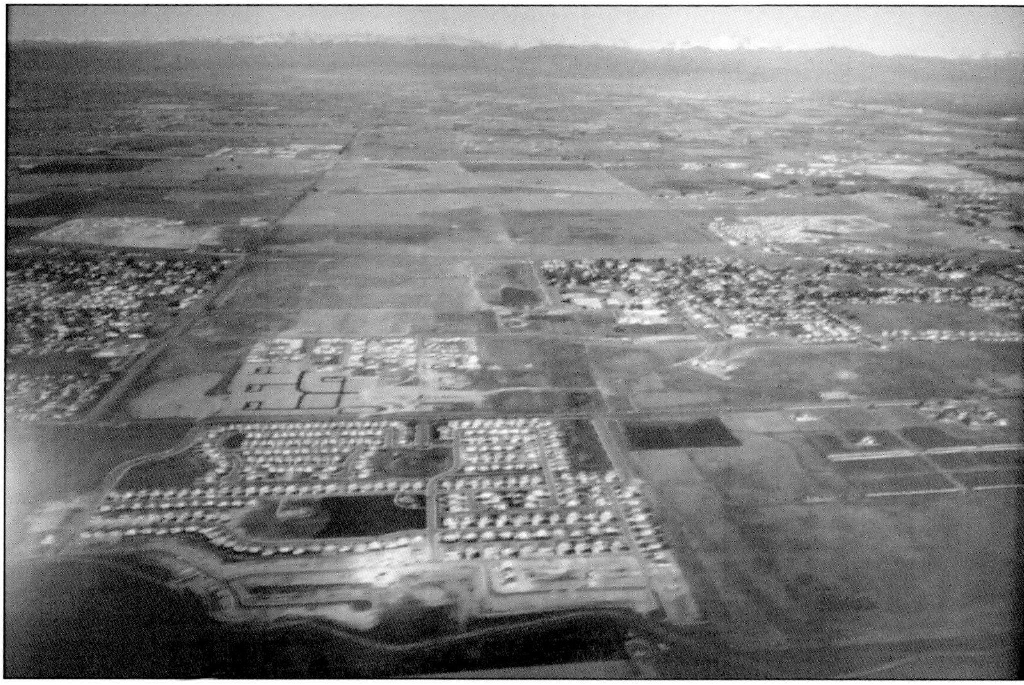

This aerial view of Frederick and the surrounding towns was taken in 2000. Since then, a substantial portion of the empty space in the photograph has been filled in by residences. (Courtesy of the Town of Frederick.)

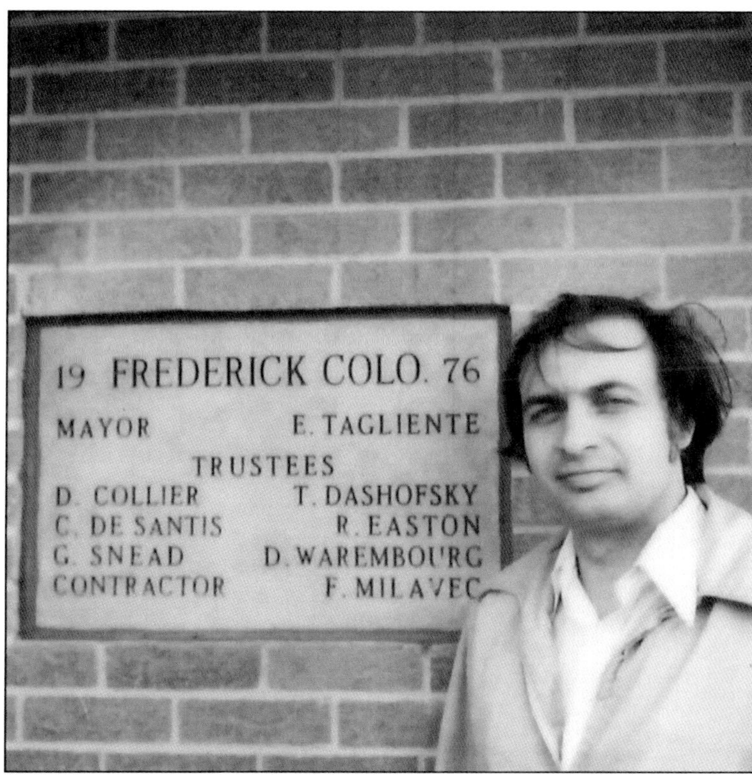

Mayor Ed Tagliente stands in front of the plaque on the Frederick Police Department listing the board of trustees. The police was built on the former site of the old city hall after it was moved to Crist Park. (Courtesy of the Town of Frederick.)

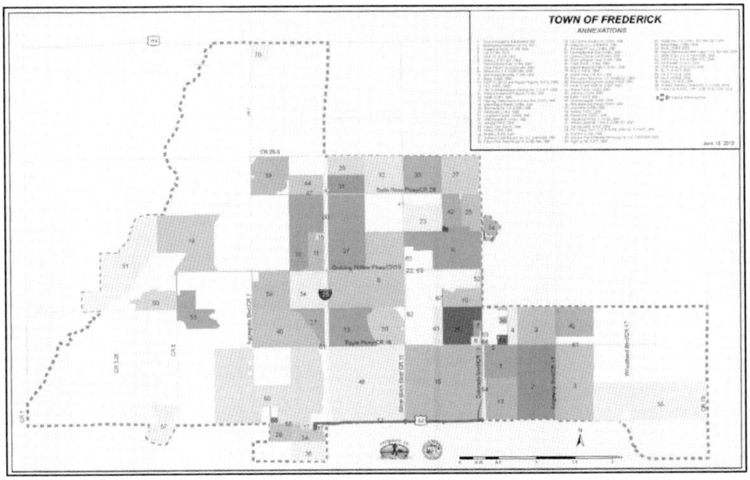

This diagram shows proposed annexations by the Town of Frederick. Annexations are a frequent source of conflict. Evanston, an unincorporated area of Weld County, has resisted annexation both by Firestone and by Frederick. (Courtesy of the Town of Frederick.)

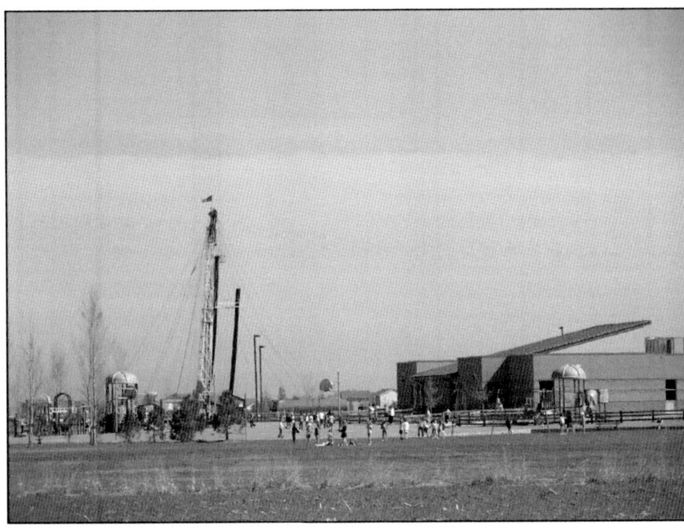

Before, the landscape around Frederick was dominated by mine towers. Now, as the mines have closed, mine towers have been replaced with oil and gas drilling rigs. This photograph shows a rig operating next to Legacy Ridge Elementary School. Frederick residents have always lived close to the land and its natural resources. (Courtesy of Town of Frederick.)

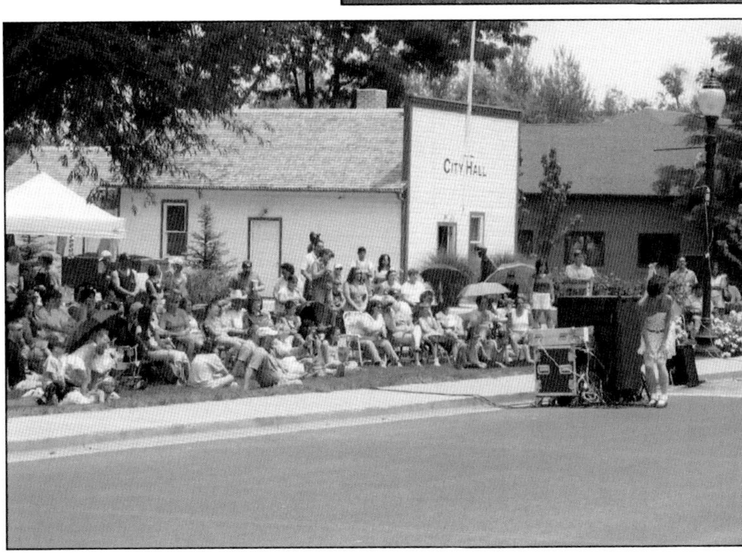

A crowd of onlookers awaits a parade on Fifth Street in 2005. The old city hall is seen in its new location in Crist Park. (Courtesy of the Town of Frederick.)

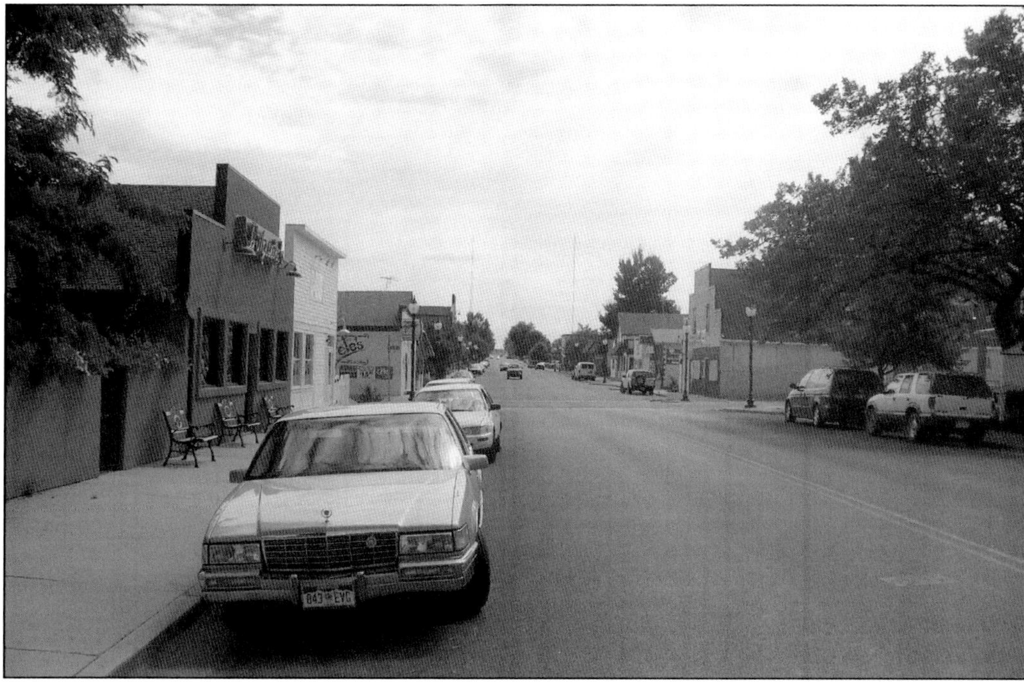

This view looks east along Fifth Street. The downtown architecture still features false fronts, and some of the businesses are still located in buildings that were built in the 1920s. (Courtesy of the Town of Frederick.)

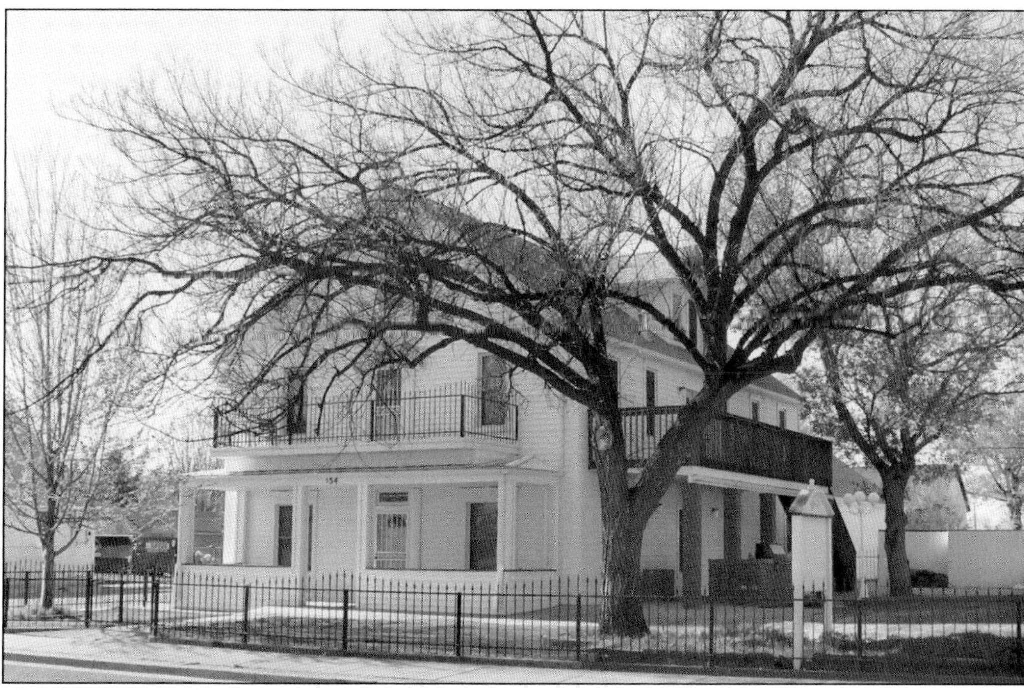

The former McAfee Hotel is now a private residence. Frederick is fortunate to have so many of its old buildings still standing, and the McAfee Hotel is a prime example of that preservation. (Courtesy of the Town of Frederick.)

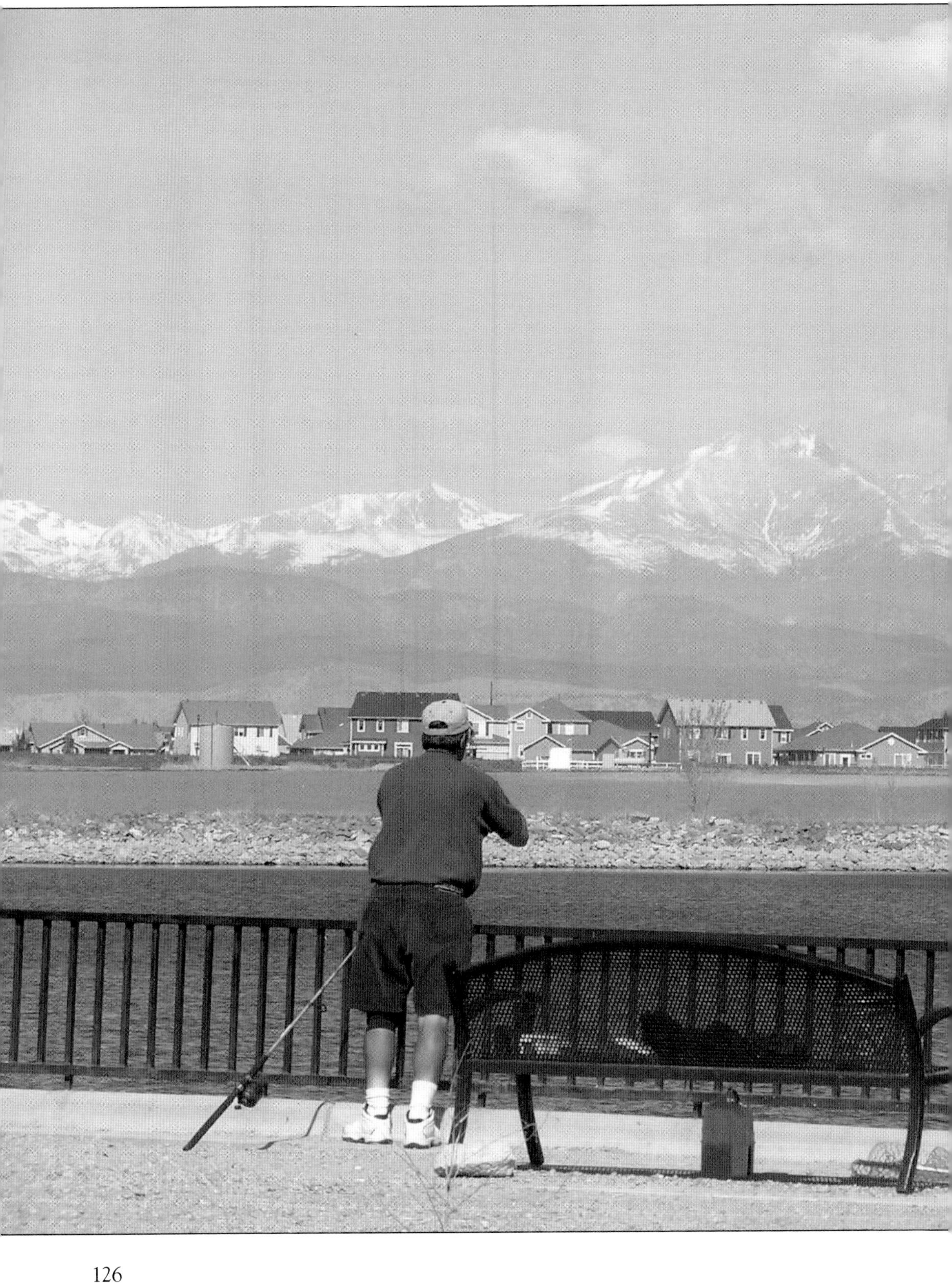

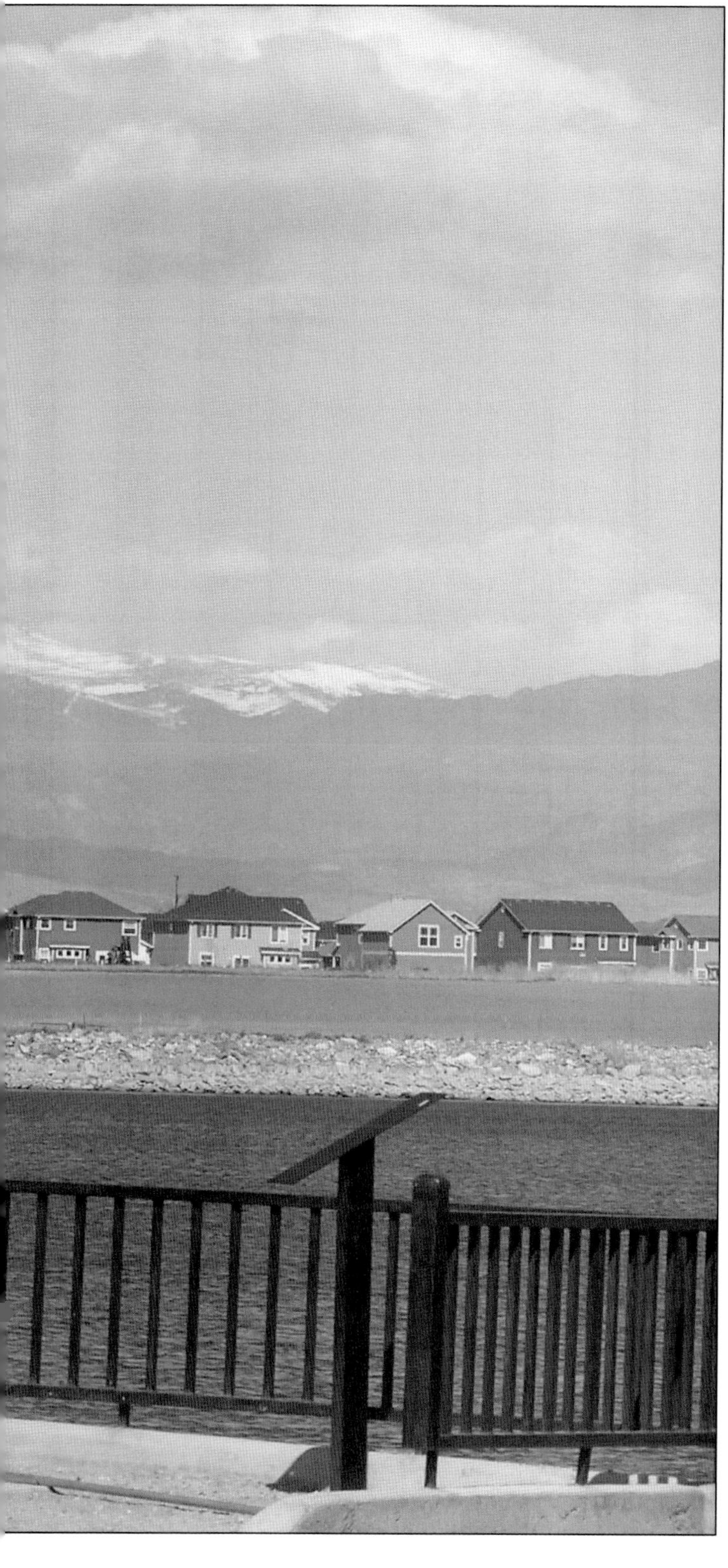

This view looks northeast across Milavec Reservoir. It was taken in 2004 and shows the rapid growth of residential construction Frederick experienced from 2000 to 2008. The mountain in the background is Twin Peaks. Milavec Reservoir is surrounded by picnic areas, a dog park, and a wetlands area. The Bella Rosa Golf Course is north of the reservoir. (Courtesy of the Town of Frederick.)

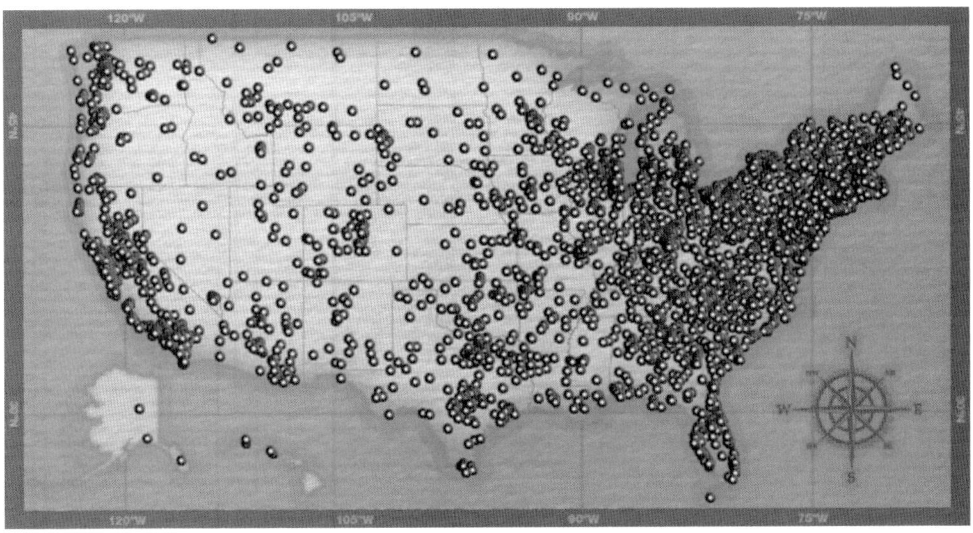

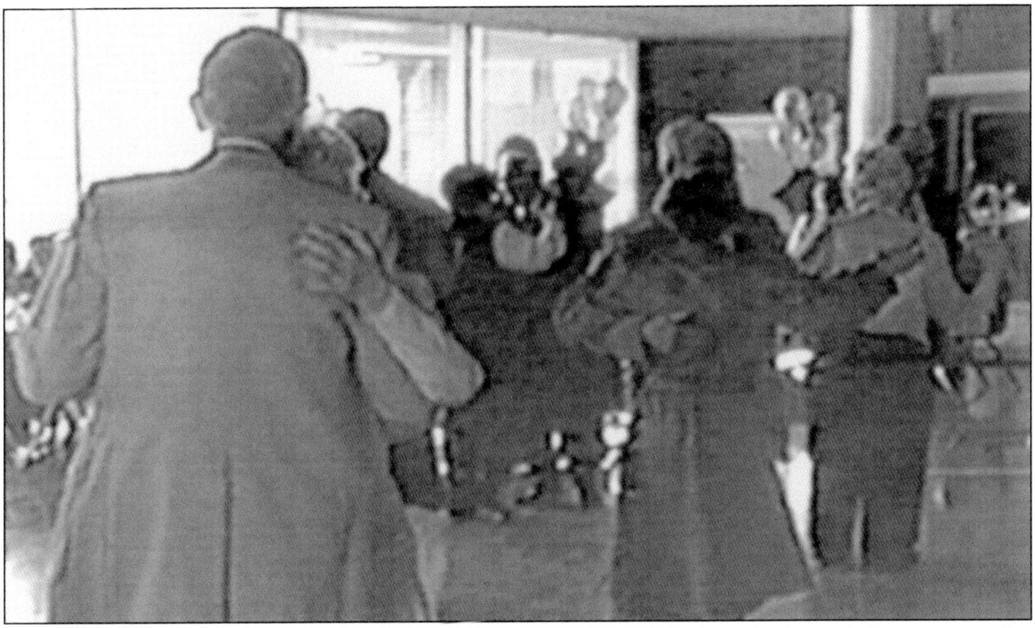

It would make a pleasant evening to watch, in sequence, all the people from different eras who have danced at the pavilion and all the different dances they did. Would the dances be different and reflect the differing tenor of the times in which the celebrants danced, or are the aesthetics and the mood and the aura of old Sylvan Beach so powerful that the viewer would just see one long, slow, graceful Texas waltz, unbroken but for changing fashions?

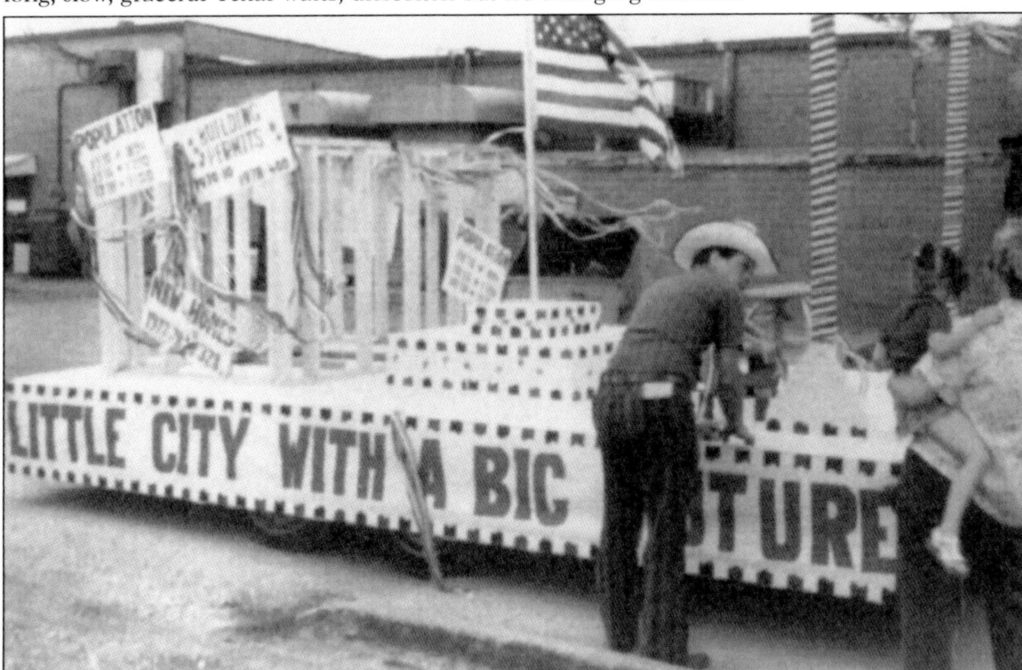

This image shows yet another Sylvan Beach Festival parade being readied. The float shown here was entered by Lomax. Lomax was, for a time, an independent community; in fact, La Porte mayor Norman Malone served as mayor of both Lomax and La Porte at various times.

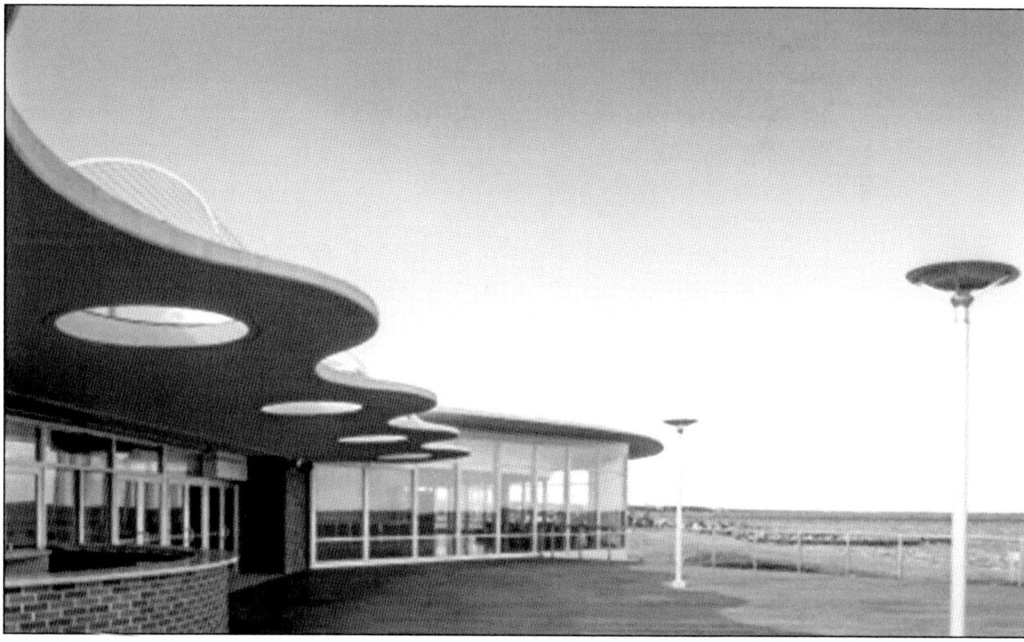

The following description comes from the application to list the pavilion in the National Register of Historic Places. The newly restored pavilion sits on concrete columns 10 feet above grade. There are three elements of the structure: the octagonal ballroom pavilion (previously described as round) with a hardwood floor; the foyer (primarily for the food service or concession area); and the triangular outdoor terrace deck. The glass enclosure and the street and bay sides of the dance area provide a dramatic vista both within and outside. The concrete piers on which the structure rests go 35 feet deep into the ground. There is also a wood-surface promenade deck around the perimeter of the terrace deck and the bay side of the dance area. The band stage now sits at the north end of the dance floor, in front of the dancers. After Hurricane Alicia, a 13-foot levee was built around the bay side of the pavilion.

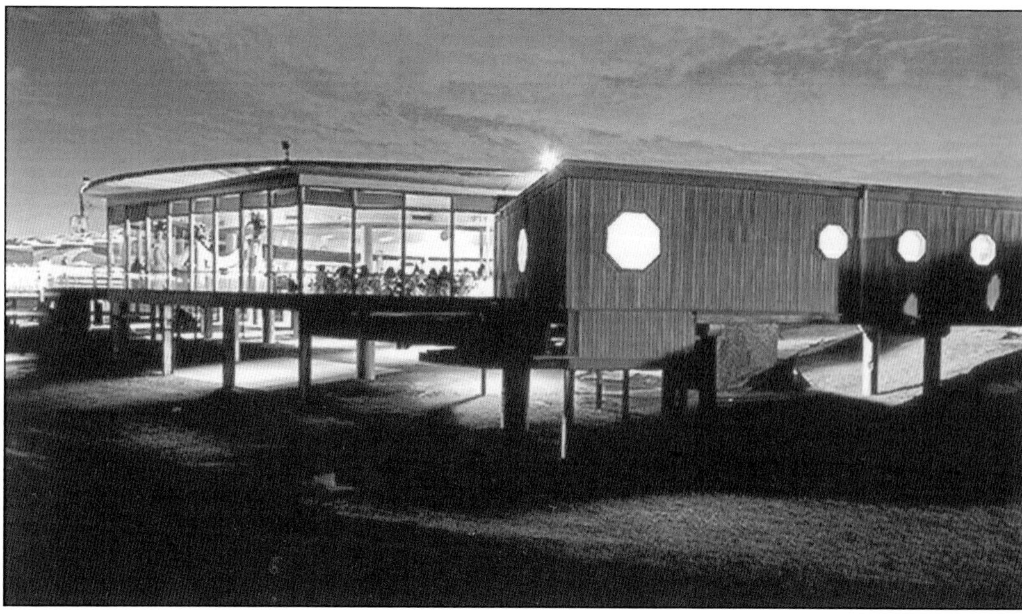

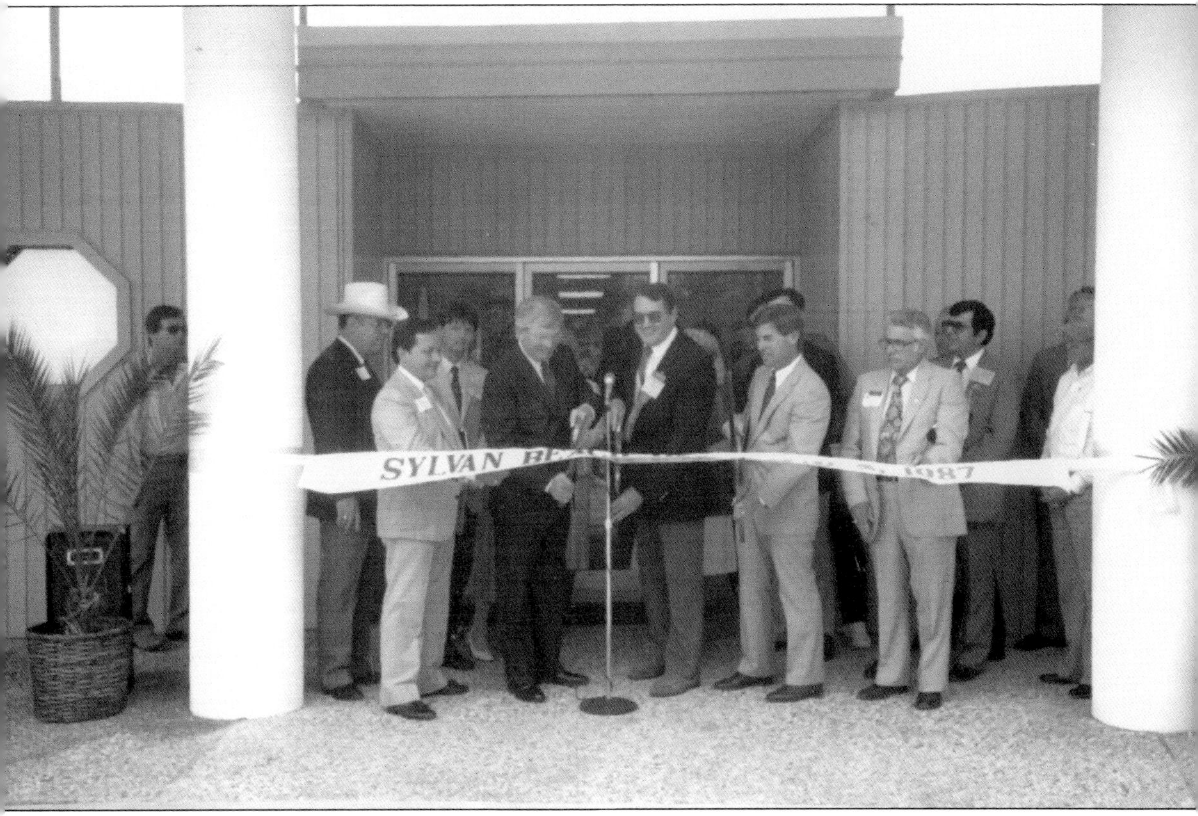

At the 1987 opening of the restored Sylvan Beach Pavilion, La Porte mayor Norman Malone and Gov. Mark White cut the ribbon while City of La Porte and Harris County dignitaries observed.

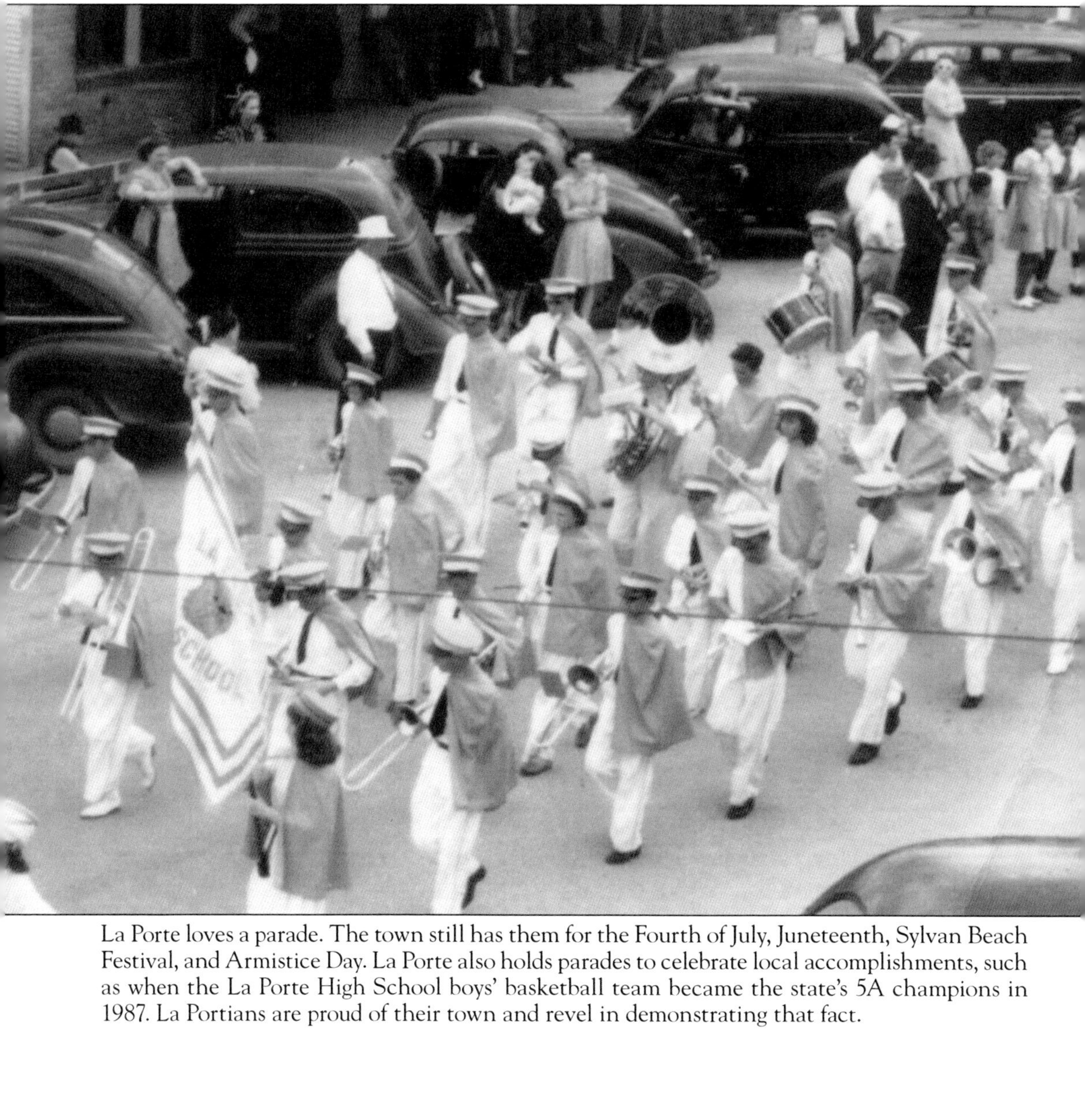

La Porte loves a parade. The town still has them for the Fourth of July, Juneteenth, Sylvan Beach Festival, and Armistice Day. La Porte also holds parades to celebrate local accomplishments, such as when the La Porte High School boys' basketball team became the state's 5A champions in 1987. La Portians are proud of their town and revel in demonstrating that fact.

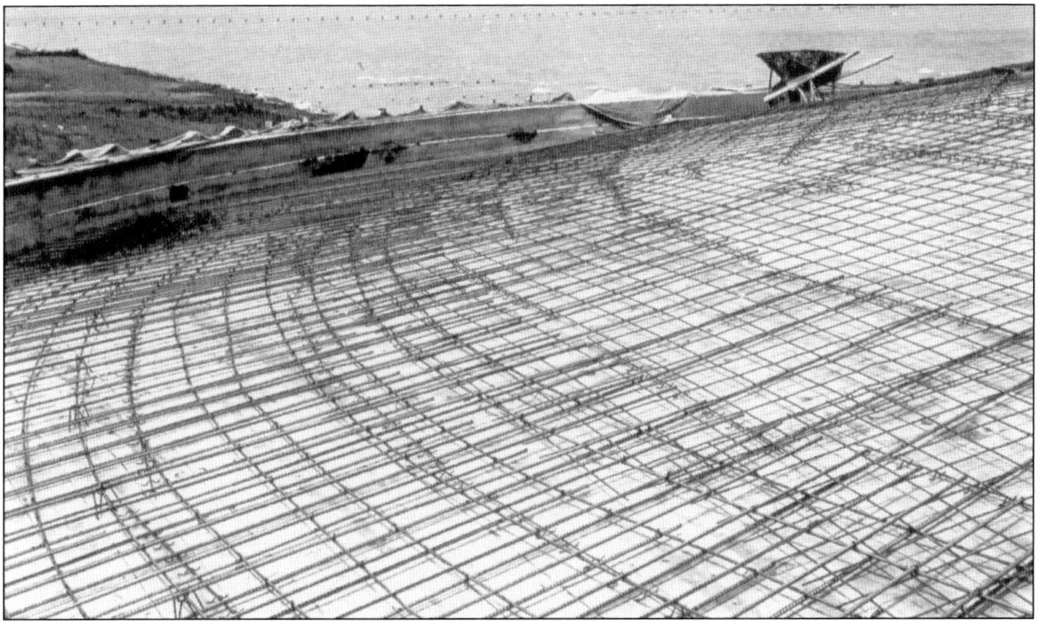

The ballroom pavilion is "roofed with a thin shelled, steel-reinforced concrete dome that is 135 feet in diameter," according to the application for listing the pavilion in the National Register of Historic Places. This photograph shows the 1956 construction of the dome.

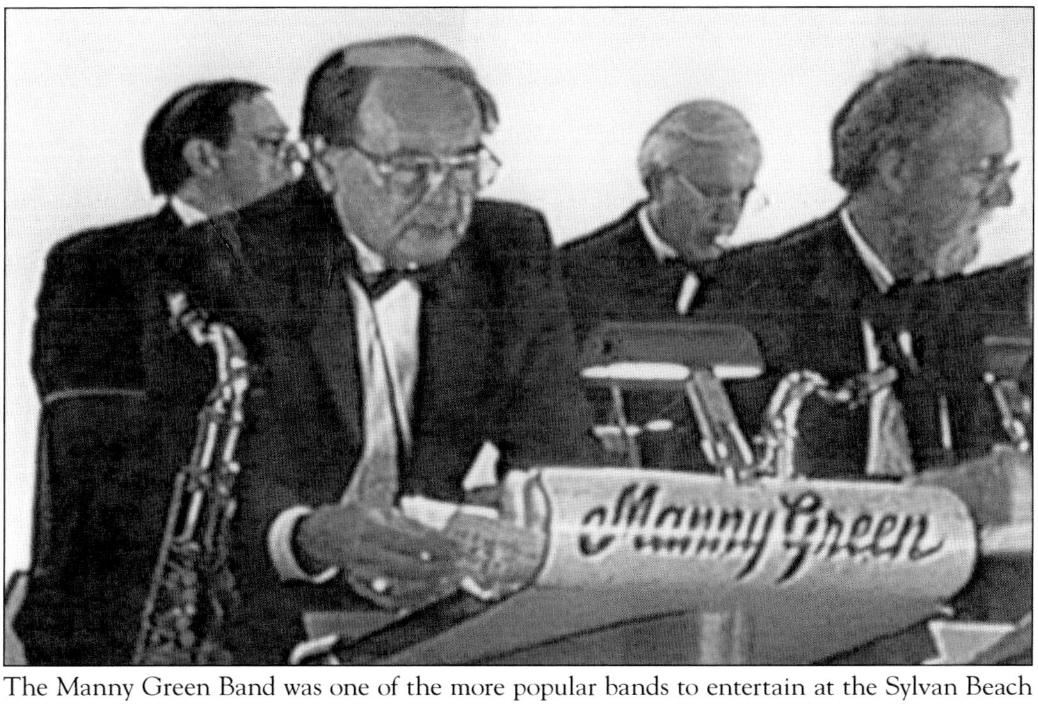

The Manny Green Band was one of the more popular bands to entertain at the Sylvan Beach Pavilion over the last 30 years. Manny Green is pictured here during one of his performances at the pavilion.

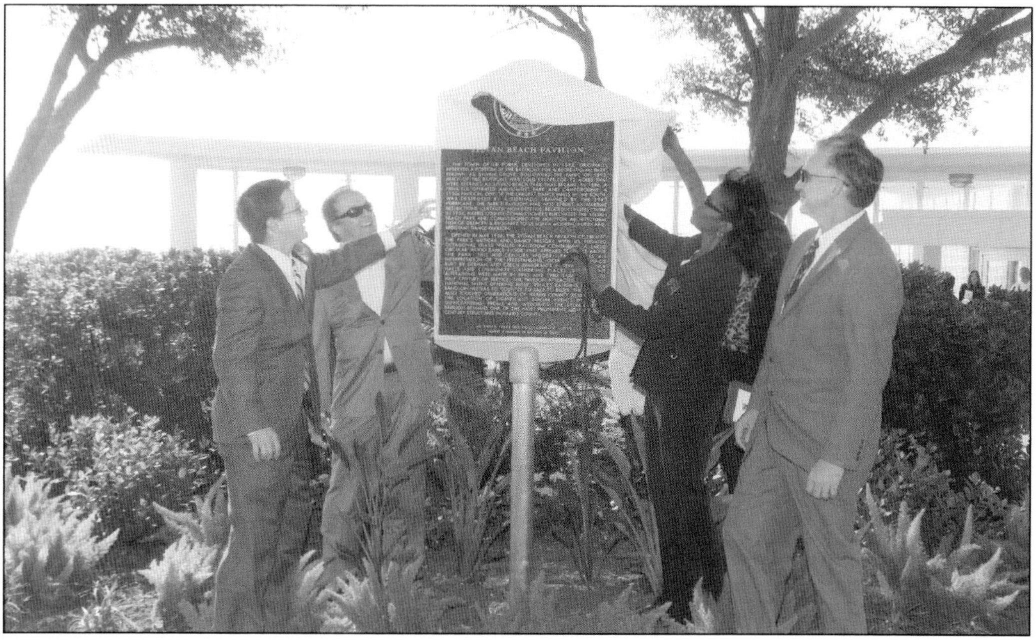

La Porte resident Ted Powell worked tirelessly to preserve the Sylvan Beach Pavilion. Through his efforts and his group, the Friends of the Sylvan Beach Park & Pavilion, the pavilion is now a State Archeological Landmark, a Texas Historical Landmark, and is listed in the National Register of Historic Places. After Hurricane Ike, Powell and his group worked to help obtain almost $5 million in funds to restore and preserve the pavilion. The image above shows, from left to right, Harris County Commissioner Jack Morman, La Porte mayor Louis Rigby, Harris County Historical Commission member Deborah Blacklock-Sloan, and Powell unveiling the plaque from the Texas Historical Commission. The efforts and collaboration of Powell, Mayor Rigby, Harris County Historical Commission chairman Janet K. Wagner, Commissioner Morman, and countless others came to fruition and were celebrated with the unveiling of the plaque and the reopening of the pavilion at a ceremony held on October 25, 2013. The restoration by Kirksey Architects remains faithful to the pavilion's original design. In the image below, Mayor Rigby (left) and Commissioner Morman shake hands.

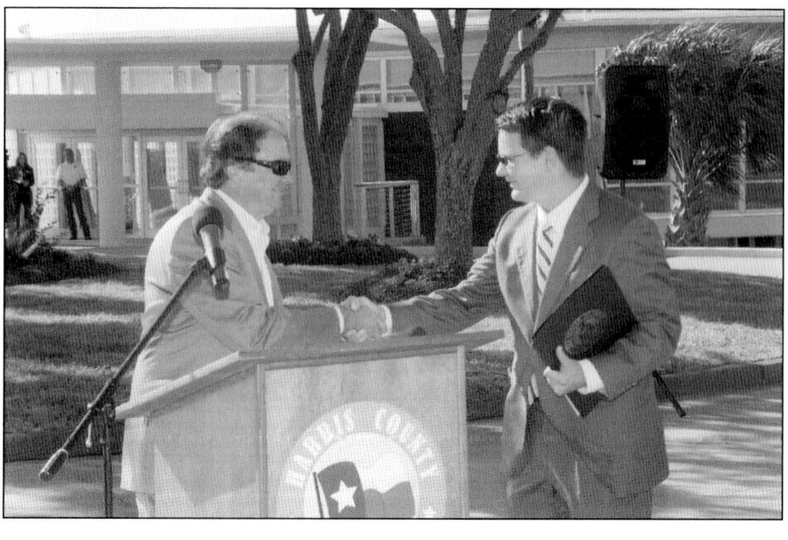

BIBLIOGRAPHY

Bayshore Sun (La Porte, TX)

Black, Gordon, "Allien Interested Early Builders in La Porte," Heritage Society Presents La Porte, *Bayshore Sun*, December 21, 1973.

———, The Way It Was, *Bayshore Sun*, December 30, 1990.

———, "La Porte in 1906," The Way It Was, *Bayshore Sun*, 1991.

———. The Way It Was, *Bayshore Sun*, 1983.

Canada, J.W. *Life at Eighty: Memories and Comments by a Tarheel in Texas*. La Porte, TX: self-published, 1952.

Foxworth, Erna B. *The Romance of Old Sylvan Beach: A Hundred Years of Amusement and Nostalgia*. Austin, TX: Waterway Press, 1986.

La Porte Bay Area Heritage Society. *Summer Folks 'n Year-Round Neighbors*. La Porte, TX: Texas Marquee Publishing, 1992.

Nolan, Ray [president of the La Porte Bay Area Heritage Society]. Interview by Ann Malone. December 5, 2010.

The Eyes of Texas Travel Guide. Houston, TX: KPRC-TV News Department, 1977.

www.ci.la-porte.tx.us

www.tshaonline.org